CORNERSTONE

Opening Doors to Career Success

Second Edition

Robert M. Sherfield
COLLEGE OF SOUTHERN NEVADA

Patricia G. Moody
UNIVERSITY OF SOUTH CAROLINA

D1404678

Prentice Hall
Upper Saddle River, New Jersey
Columbus, Ohio

Library of Congress Cataloging-in-Publication Data

Sherfield, Robert M.
  Cornerstone : opening doors to career success / Robert M. Sherfield,
Patricia G. Moody. — 2nd ed.
    p. cm.
  Includes bibliographical references and index.
  ISBN-13: 978-0-13-503003-5 (pbk.)
  ISBN-10: 0-13-503003-X (pbk.)
  1. Success—Psychological aspects.   2. Self-actualization (Psychology)   3. Academic achievement.
I. Moody, Patricia G.   II. Title.
BF637.S8M597 2010
158—dc22

2008043488

Vice President and Editor in Chief: Jeffery W. Johnston
Executive Editor: Sande Johnson
Development Editor: Jennifer Gessner
Permissions Coordinator: Rebecca Savage
Editorial Assistant: Lynda Cramer
Senior Managing Editor: Pamela D. Bennett
Project Manager: Kerry J. Rubadue
Production Coordination: Thistle Hill Publishing
  Services, LLC
Art Director: Candace Rowley

Text Design and Illustrations: Kristina Holmes
Cover Images: I-Stock/Shutterstock
Cover Design: Kristina Holmes
Media Producer: Autumn Benson
Media Project Manager: Rebecca Norsic
Senior Operations Supervisor: Matthew Ottenweller
Operations Specialist: Susan W. Hannahs
Vice President, Director of Sales and Marketing:
  Quinn Perkson
Marketing Coordinator: Brian Mounts

This book was set in Bembo by Integra Software Services. It was printed and bound by Quebecor World Color/Versailles. The cover was printed by Phoenix Color Corp./Hagerstown.

Photo Credits: David Mager/Pearson Learning Photo Studio, p. 2; Getty Images–Stockbyte, p. 7; © Stockdisc, pp. 8, 110, 225; © Photodisc, pp. 13, 160, 182, 186, 271 (top), 273, 289; © BananaStock Ltd., pp. 15, 47, 49, 184, 189, 209, 219; Patrick White/Merrill, pp. 16 (top), 55, 65, 75 (bottom), 115, 163, 235, 259; Laima Druskis/PH College, pp. 16 (bottom), 270; © Corbis RF, pp. 24, 34, 63, 208, 223, 230; © Chris Pizzello/Reuters/Corbis, p. 27; Eimantas Buzas/Shutterstock, p. 30; Scott Cunningham/Merrill, pp. 37, 44; Frank LaBua/PH College, p. 39; © STR/epa/Corbis, p. 51; © ThinkStock/SuperStock, p. 58; © Image 100 Ltd., pp. 75 (top), 246, 292; Michael Nagel/Stringer/Getty Images, Inc.–Getty News, p. 78; J. Nourok/ PhotoEdit, p. 80; Jupiter Images–Comstock Images, p. 86; © Bob Daemmrich, p. 90; Keld Navntoft/AFP/Getty Images, p. 98; Courtesy of www.istockphoto.com, pp. xvi, 106, 156, 240; © Katy Winn/Corbis, p. 122; Index Open, p. 128; © Neal Preston/Corbis, p. 139; Richard Haynes/Prentice Hall School Division, p. 140; George Stroud/Getty Images Inc.–Hulton Archive Photos, 164; Anthony Magnacca/Merrill, p. 172; Andersen Ross/Jupiter Images–PictureArts Corporation/Brand X Pictures Royalty Free, p. 178; © Hulton-Deutsch Collection/Corbis, p. 188; Jupiter Images–PictureArts Corporation/Brand X Pictures Royalty Free, p. 204; David Cannon/Getty Images, p. 213; © Sonya Etchison–Fotolia, p. 214; © Image Source Limited, pp. 244, 255; Time Life Pictures/DMI/Getty Images, p. 247; © Ramin Talaie/Corbis, p. 251 (top); © Paul Mounce/ Corbis, p. 251 (center); © Kurt Krieger/Corbis, p. 251 (bottom); Jupiter Images–Liquidlibrary, p. 266; © Najlah Feanny/ Corbis, p. 271 (bottom). All photos in the features The Big Why and From Ordinary to Extraordinary were provided by the photo subjects.

Pearson Education Ltd., London
Pearson Education Singapore Pte. Ltd.
Pearson Education Canada, Inc.
Pearson Education–Japan
Pearson Education Australia PTY, Limited

Pearson Education North Asia, Ltd., Hong Kong
Pearson Educatión de Mexico, S.A. de C.V.
Pearson Education Malaysia Pte. Ltd.
Pearson Education Upper Saddle River,
  New Jersey

Prentice Hall
is an imprint of

www.pearsonhighered.com

10 9 8 7 6 5 4 3 2 1
ISBN-13: 978-0-13-503003-5
ISBN-10:   0-13-503003-X

brief contents

contents

one thrive   3
Discovering Your Potential, Nurturing Change, and Thriving Through Goal Setting

two engage   31
Cultivating Your Personal Motivation and Academic Passion

communicate   59

three

Enhancing Your *Interpersonal Communication Skills*, Developing Your *Emotional Intelligence*, and Celebrating *Cultures*

prioritize   87

four

Planning Your *Time* and *Reducing Stress*

prosper   107

five

Protecting Your Future Through Managing Your Money and Debts Wisely

six
read   129
Building Your *Reading and Comprehension Skills*

seven
learn   157
Using Your *Dominant Intelligence,* Learning Style, and Personality Type to *Become an Active Learner*

eight

record   179

Cultivating Your *Listening Skills* and Developing a *Note-Taking System* That Works for You

nine

understand   205

Empowering Your *Memory*, Creating Your *Study Plan*, and *Taking Tests* Successfully

ten think   241

Expanding Your Aptitude for *Critical Thinking* and *Problem Solving*

eleven plan   267

Preparing for Success in the *World of Work . . .* and Beyond

mystudentsuccesslab

"Teaching an online course, offering a hybrid class, or simply introducing your students to technology, just got a whole lot easier and EXCITING!"

To help students build college success and career development skills, students must *apply* what they learn. MyStudentSuccessLab (www. mystudentsuccesslab.com) offers students a self-paced, interactive, virtual lab designed to offer *application* and *practice* of their skills. By developing strategies that work best for them, students experience greater relevance, motivating them to achieve success.

Working with a number of our authors and faculty members, we created a lab experience that provides interactive critical-thinking cases, a goal setting and journaling tool, reflection exercises, video with applications, interactive simulations, and more. MyStudentSuccessLab is a unique, valuable learning tool that offers:

GENERAL Student Success TOPICS, including:

- Welcome to College/College Culture, Academic Skills, Life Skills, and Career Skills

Within EACH TOPIC:

- Objectives, Pre-Assessment, E-book (with Multimedia features), Interactive Case Study, Interactive Activity, Goal Setting and Journaling tool, and Comprehension Test

Posted to the COURSE RESOURCES Section:

- Understanding Plagiarism guide, Prentice Hall Planner, Student Reflection Journal, *10 Ways to Fight Hate,* Student Success Supersite, and Dictionary of Contemporary English Online

Chapter features to support your course objectives:

- **Pre-Assessment**—Students have the opportunity to take a pre-test before reading each chapter. Their test results identify chapter topics they must master. The assessment feedback identifies students' strengths and weaknesses so they can learn more effectively.
- **E-book with multimedia**—*Cornerstone: Opening Doors to Career Success,* Second Edition, is available on this site with MSSL links embedded throughout for ease of use. Gain access to content, including interactive chapter features, video, weblinks, journal prompts, self-assessments, chapter exercises, and more.

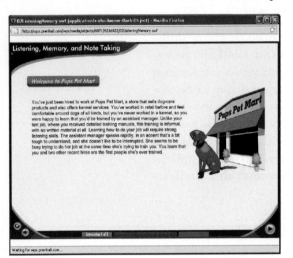

- **Interactive Case Studies**—Students can practice their decision-making skills with these interactive cases. Each case requires them to apply skills and strategies they've learned in the chapter—such as time management, critical thinking, and listening—to solve problems. At the end of the scenario, students receive constructive feedback relating to each choice they made as they worked through the case.
- **Goal Setting and Journaling tool**—Our unique Goal Setting and Journaling tool will help your students learn to set "SMART" long-term and short-term goals as they move through each chapter—and keep track of how well they are meeting those goals. The journaling activity will help them discover obstacles preventing them from attaining their objectives—and what will help them succeed. This tool's features allow you and your students to monitor their progress and identify areas for potential improvement. As the instructor, you also have the option of reviewing their journals for completion or content.

- **Comprehension test**—After reading a chapter, students take a post-test to check comprehension. Choose from multiple choice, true/false, fill in the blank, short answer, and essay questions, and results will be imported to Gradetracker.
- **Portfolio Exercises**—Students can build an electronic portfolio containing artifacts of their work with these classroom-tested exercises. Students demonstrate skill mastery with actual work that can be shared with future instructors or employers.
- **Weblinks**—Looking for current issues in student success and career development? Weblinks offer quick access to relevant, reliable links that update course content.

NOTE—A way to search for ALL media within the site is to use the *Index of Multimedia.* Students can choose from many icons, such as *Explore* or *Watch. Explore* refers to Interactive features such as our Time Management Activity: Interactive calendar; *Watch* links to Videos. Videos include study skills, workplace tips, and role-playing videos to help students see how other students cope with the demands of college or show how the course content relates to this class and beyond.

MyStudentSuccessLab is integrated into the text to reinforce the content! Wherever the **MSSL** icons appear in the margins, your students can follow the link instructions to access the **MyStudentSuccessLab** resource that corresponds with the chapter content. ***Activities & Exercises*** are assignable and give students the opportunity to understand each chapter's material by applying content in an engaging way.

Margin Note Icons for Exercises include:

- *Practice* identifies opportunities for students to demonstrate skill level and reflect on the reading.

- *Explore* points to multimedia interactive exercises that reinforce the material.

- *Interactive Reading* highlights features where students read and respond to specific material.

- *Case Study* spotlights features that focus on student real world scenarios with probing questions.

- *Profile* indicates exercises that aid students in developing their personal portfolio.

MyStudentSuccessLab is available as a supplemental package option, as well as for stand-alone purchase. It is available in CourseCompass, Blackboard, and WebCT course management platforms, as well as a version to use for other learning platforms.

MyStudentSuccessLab is easy to use and assign. It allows students to set their own pace, build self-awareness, and practice what *they* need to set personal goals and achieve success in college, career, and life. Visit www.mystudentsuccesslab.com to explore this exciting new online teaching resource, contact your local sales professional, or send an inquiry to Student.Success@pearson.com for additional support.

INSTRUCTOR SUPPORT

Resources to simplify your life and engage your students.

Book Specific

Print   Instructor's Manual with Test Bank

Computerized TestBank on CD

Technology

*"Easy access to online, book-specific **teaching support** is now just a click away!"*

Instructor Resource Center—Register. Redeem. Login. Three easy steps that open the door to a variety of print and media resources in downloadable, digital format, available to instructors exclusively through the Pearson/Prentice Hall Instructor's Resource Center. Click on "Educator," then click on "Download Instructor Resources" to access online resources.
http://www.prenhall.com

Are you teaching online, in a hybrid setting, or looking to infuse exciting technology into your classroom for the first time?

Then be sure to refer to the **MyStudentSuccessLab** section of this Preface to learn about our revolutionary resource that **helps students build college success and career development skills, and to *apply* what they learn.** **MyStudentSuccessLab** (www.mystudentsuccesslab.com) offers students a self-paced, interactive, virtual lab designed to offer *application* and *practice* of their skills. By developing strategies that work best for them, students experience greater relevance, motivating them to achieve success.

*"Choose from a wide range of **video resources** for the classroom!"*

Prentice Hall Reference Library: Life Skills Pack, 0-13-127079-6, contains all 4 videos, or they may be requested individually as follows:

- Learning Styles and Self-Awareness, 0-13-028502-1
- Critical and Creative Thinking, 0-13-028504-8
- Relating to Others, 0-13-028511-0
- Personal Wellness, 0-13-028514-5

Prentice Hall Reference Library: Study Skills Pack, 0-13-127080-X, contains all 6 videos, or they may be requested individually as follows:

- Reading Effectively, 0-13-028505-6
- Listening and Memory, 0-13-028506-4

- Note Taking and Research, 0-13-028508-0
- Writing Effectively, 0-13-028509-9
- Effective Test Taking, 0-13-028500-5
- Goal Setting and Time Management, 0-13-028503-X

Prentice Hall Reference Library: Career Skills Pack, 0-13-118529-2, contains all 3 videos, or they may be requested individually as follows:

- Skills for the 21st Century—Technology, 0-13-028512-9
- Skills for the 21st Century—Math and Science, 0-13-028513-7
- Managing Career and Money, 0-13-028516-1

Complete Reference Library—Life/Study Skills/Career Video Pack on DVD, 0-13-501095-0

- Our Reference Library of thirteen popular video resources has now been digitized onto one DVD so students and instructors alike can benefit from the array of video clips. Featuring Life Skills, Study Skills, and Career Skills, they help to reinforce the course content in a more interactive way.

Faculty Video Resources

- Teacher Training Video 1: Critical Thinking, 0-13-099432-4
- Teacher Training Video 2: Stress Management & Communication, 0-13-099578-9
- Teacher Training Video 3: Classroom Tips, 0-13-917205-X
- Student Advice Video, 0-13-233206-X
- Study Skills Video, 0-13-096095-0
- Faculty Development Workshop (DVD), 0-13-227192-3

Current Issues Videos

- ABC News Video Series: Student Success 2/E, 0-13-031901-5
- ABC News Video Series: Student Success 3/E, 0-13-152865-3

MyStudentSuccessLab PH Videos on DVD, 0-13-514249-0

- Our six most popular video resources have been digitized onto one DVD so students and instructors alike can benefit from the array of video clips. Featuring Technology, Math and Science, Managing Money and Career, Learning Styles and Self-Awareness, Study Skills, and Peer Advice, they help to reinforce the course content in a more interactive way. They are also accessible through our MSSL and course management offerings and available on VHS.

*"Through partnership opportunities, we offer a variety of **assessment** options!"*

LASSI—The LASSI is a 10-scale, 80-item assessment of students' awareness about and use of learning and study strategies. Addressing skill, will, and self-regulation, the focus is on both covert and overt thoughts, behaviors, attitudes, and beliefs that relate to successful learning and that can be altered through educational interventions. Available in two formats: Paper, 0-13-172315-4, or Online, 0-13-172316-2 (Access Card).

Noel Levitz/RMS—This retention tool measures Academic Motivation, General Coping Ability, Receptivity to Support Services, PLUS Social Motivation. It helps identify at-risk students, the areas with which they struggle, and their receptiveness to support. Available in Paper or Online formats, as well as Short and Long versions. Paper Long Form A: 0-13-0722588; Paper Short Form B: 0-13-079193-8; Online Forms A, B & C: 0-13-098158-3.

Robbins Self Assessment Library—This compilation teaches students to create a portfolio of skills. S.A.L. is a self-contained, interactive, library of 49 behavioral questionnaires that help students discover new ideas about themselves, their attitudes, and their personal strengths and weaknesses.

Readiness for Education at a Distance Indicator (READI)—READI is a Web-based tool that assesses the overall likelihood for online learning success. READI generates an immediate score and a diagnostic interpretation of results, including recommendations for successful participation in online courses and potential remediation sources. Please visit www.readi.info for additional information. 0-13-188967-2

Pathway to Student Success CD-ROM, 0-13-239314-X

The CD is divided into several categories, each of which focuses on a specific topic that relates to students and provides them with the context, tools and strategies to enhance their educational experience.

*"Teaching tolerance and discussing **diversity** with your students can be challenging!"*

Responding to Hate at School—Published by the Southern Poverty Law Center, the Teaching Tolerance handbook is a step-by-step, easy-to-use guide designed to help administrators, counselors, and teachers react promptly and efficiently whenever hate, bias, and prejudice strike.

*"For a terrific one-stop shop resource, use our **Student Success Supersite!**"*

Supersite—www.prenhall.com/success—Students and professors alike may use the Supersite for assessments, activities, links, and more.

*"For a truly tailored solution that fosters campus connections and increases retention, talk with us about **custom publishing**."*

Pearson Custom Publishing—We are the largest custom provider for print and media shaped to your course's needs. Please visit us at www.pearsoncustom.com to learn more.

STUDENT SUPPORT

Tools to help make the grade now, and excel in school later.

*"Today's students are more inclined than ever to use **technology** to enhance their learning."*

Refer to the **MyStudentSuccessLab** section of this Preface to learn about our revolutionary resource that **helps students build college success and career development skills, and to *apply* what they learn.** MyStudentSuccessLab (www.mystudentsuccesslab.com) offers students a self-paced, interactive, virtual lab designed to offer *application* and *practice* of their skills. By developing strategies that work best for them, students experience greater relevance, motivating them to achieve success.

*"**Time management** is the #1 challenge students face." We can help.*

Prentice Hall Planner—A basic planner that includes a monthly and daily calendar plus other materials to facilitate organization. Paperback, 8 1/2 x 11.

Premier Annual Planner—This specially designed, annual 4-color collegiate planner includes an academic planning/resources section, monthly planning section (2 pages/month), and weekly planning section (48 weeks; July start date), which facilitate short-term as well as long-term planning. Spiral bound, 6 x 9. Customization is available.

*"**Journaling** activities promote self-discovery and self-awareness."*

Student Reflection Journal—Through this vehicle, students are encouraged to track their progress and share their insights, thoughts, and concerns. Paperback, 8 1/2 x 11. 90 pages.

*"Our **Student Success Supersite** is a one-stop shop for students to learn about career paths, self-awareness activities, cross-curricular practice opportunities, and more!"*

Supersite—at www.prenhall.com/success.

*"Learning to adapt to the **diverse** college community is essential to students' success."*

10 Ways to Fight Hate—Produced by the Southern Poverty Law Center, the leading hate-crime and crime-watch organization in the United States, this guide walks students through 10 steps that they can take on their own campus or in their own neighborhood to fight hate everyday. 0-13-028146-8

*"The **Student Orientation Series** includes short booklets on specialized topics that facilitate greater student understanding."*

S.O.S. Guides help students understand what these opportunities are, how to take advantage of them, and how to learn from their peers while doing so. They include:

- Connolly: *Learning Communities,* 0-13-232243-9
- Hoffman: *Stop Procrastination Now! 10 Simple and SUCCESSFUL Steps for Student Success,* 0-13-513056-5
- Watts: *Service Learning,* 0-13-232201-3
- Jabr: *English Language Learners,* 0-13-232242-0

begin

"Talent alone won't make you a success. Neither will being in the right place at the right time, unless you are ready. The most important question is: 'Are you ready?'"

Johnny Carson

The Goal of Cornerstone and Our Commitment to You

Our goal in writing *Cornerstone* is to help you discover your academic, social, and personal strengths so that you can build on them and use them to enhance your performance. Another goal of *Cornerstone* is to provide **concrete and useful tools** that will help you identify and overcome areas where changes might be necessary. We believe that in helping you identify and transform areas that have challenged you in the past, you can ***discover your true potential, learn more actively, and have the career you want and deserve***.

We know that your **time is valuable** and that you are pulled in countless directions with work, family, school, previous obligations, and many other tasks. For this reason, we have tried to provide only the most concrete, useful strategies and ideas to help you succeed in this class and beyond.

Collectively, we have spent over 50 years gathering the information, advice, suggestions, and activities on the following pages. This advice and these activities have come from trial and error, colleagues, former students, instructors across America, and solid research.

We wish you luck in your journey.

—Robb and Pat

We hope that you will enjoy them, learn from them, and most of all, use them to move closer to your dreams.

Important Chapter Features and *WHY* We Have Included Them in Your Text

Feature: The Big Why

THE BIG **WHY**

WHY read and work through this chapter? *WHY* will I ever be asked to use this stuff on self-responsibility? *WHY* will a chapter on adjusting to college and goal setting help me with my classes, at work, with my family, and beyond? *WHY* is this information such a big deal?

This feature is intended to help you understand WHY this chapter is included in the text and WHY the information in the chapter will be important to your overall success as a student. *The Big Why . . . from Another Perspective* shares what former students gained from reading the chapter.

Feature: Scan and Question (Based on SQ3R)

SCAN AND QUESTION

In the preface of this book (and in more detail in Chapter 6), we discuss how to use the **SQ3R Study Method**. This mnemonic stands for Scan, Question, Read, Recite, and Review. *Scanning* asks you to look over the chapter before reading it. Look at the headings, charts, photos, and call-out boxes. *Questioning* asks you to create study questions from the major headings. Take a few moments and scan this chapter. As you scan, **list five questions** you can expect to learn the answers to while reading and studying Chapter 1.

Example:
- What are the basic truths about the culture of college? (from page 12)
- Why must goals be measurable? (from page 24)

My Questions:

1. _____
_____ from page _____

2. _____
_____ from page _____
3. _____
_____ from page _____
4. _____
_____ from page _____
5. _____
_____ from page _____

Reminder: At the end of the chapter, come back to this page and answer these questions in your notebook, text margins, or online chapter notes.

You may be asking, "*What does SQ3R mean and what could it possibly have to do with me, my text, this course, and my success?*"

The answer: SQ3R (**S = Scan or Survey, Q = Question, 3R = Read, Recite, Review**) is one of the most successful and widely used learning and study tools ever introduced.

This simple, yet highly effective mnemonic (memory trick) asks that **before you actually read the chapter**, you look over the contents, check out the figures and photos, look at section headings, and review any graphs or charts. This is called **SCANNING.** Step two, **QUESTION,** asks that you jot down questions that you think you will need to answer about the chapter's content in order to master the material. These questions might come from charts or figures, but most commonly they come from the chapter's section headings. Examine the example below from a section heading from: *Criminal Justice: A Brief Introduction,* Sixth Edition, by Frank Schmalleger (2006).

of September 11, 2001, it went on to say that "these figures have been removed" from the reported data.[64] Crimes that result from an anomalous event, but which are excluded from reported data, highlight the arbitrary nature of the data-collection process itself.

Special Categories of Crime ◄

crime typology

A classification of crimes along a particular dimension, such as legal categories, offender motivation, victim behavior, or the characteristics of individual offenders.

A **crime typology** is a classification scheme that is useful in the study and description of criminal behavior. All crime typologies have an underlying logic, and the system of classification that derives from any particular typology may be based on legal criteria, offender motivation, victim behavior, the characteristics of individual offenders, or the like. Criminologists Terance D. Miethe and Richard C. McCorkle note that crime typologies "are designed primarily to simplify social reality by identifying homogeneous groups of crime behaviors that are different from other clusters of crime behaviors."[65] Hence one common but simple typology contains only two categories of crime: violent and property. In fact, many crime typologies contain overlapping or nonexclusive categories—just as violent crimes may involve property offenses, and property offenses may lead to violent crimes. Thus no one typology is likely to capture all of the nuances of criminal offending.

From this section heading, you might ask:

(1) *What are the categories of crime?* (2) *Why do they matter?* (3) *What is crime typology?* or (4) *When are categories of crime most often used?*

After writing these questions from the section heading, you will read this section and answer those questions. This technique gives you more focus and purpose for your reading. We included this feature in *Cornerstone* to help you become a more active reader with greater comprehension skills in all of your other classes. This technique is fully discussed in Chapter 6.

Feature: Open the Door: Tips for Career Success

This boxed feature will appear in every chapter. Within the box, concrete suggestions, advice, and tips are offered to help you with one of the major topics in the chapter. We put them in this easy-to-read box so that you can access them more easily.

Feature: Successful Decisions

SUCCESSFUL DECISIONS

After the first week of classes, Devon was very disheartened about the difficulty of his classes. He did not think that he was going to have so much reading or homework and he never thought the instructors would be so demanding. He considered dropping out. It was just

looked at his current financial situation, his dead-end job, and his desire to work in a health profession. Dropping out would never get him there.

He decided to "dig in" and try harder. He went by the tutoring center and found a study group. He changed his attitude and adopted the motto,

We included this feature to give you examples of real-life situations faced by many students today. Each *Successful Decisions* box allows you to read the situation and see how this student chose to deal with the issue.

Feature: From Ordinary to Extraordinary

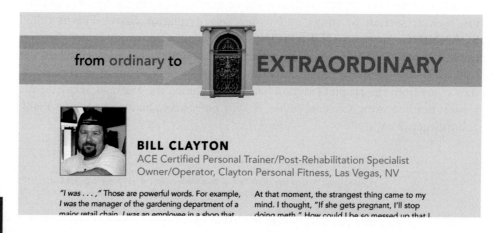

from ordinary to **EXTRAORDINARY**

BILL CLAYTON
ACE Certified Personal Trainer/Post-Rehabilitation Specialist
Owner/Operator, Clayton Personal Fitness, Las Vegas, NV

"I was . . . ," Those are powerful words. For example, I was the manager of the gardening department of a major retail chain. I was an employee in a shop that

At that moment, the strangest thing came to my mind. I thought, "If she gets pregnant, I'll stop doing meth." How could I be so messed up that I

This feature will appear in every chapter. We searched the country to find "ordinary" people who have overcome astronomical personal, physical, emotional, and/or financial odds to move ahead and do extraordinary things. This feature is included to remind you that it does not matter where you are at this moment in your life; what matters is WHAT you want, how BADLY you want it, and how HARD you're willing to work for it.

Feature: Did You Know?

In each chapter you will find stories from **famous people** who had humble or difficult beginnings and chose NOT to let circumstances keep them down. This feature is included to serve as a motivator to you when things get tough. Few people, famous or "ordinary," took the easy road to success.

Feature: Essential Cornerstones

Throughout each chapter, you will see boxes like this one. Each one asks you to reflect on one of the ten Essential Cornerstones introduced in Chapter 1. Feel free to make notes in the margin to respond to the questions posed in the boxes.

ESSENTIAL CORNERSTONE
VISION
How can having a clear vision of your future help you become a more optimistic person?

Feature: Passages—An Activity for Critical Thinking and Career Development

At the end of each chapter you will find a critical thinking activity called **Passages**. This activity asks you to use information you have learned from the chapter, classroom discussions, peers, and personal experience to put the ten Essential Cornerstones to work for you.

Area of Change	What needs to Change?	Where can help be found?	Which Cornerstone are you addressing? (List at least three)
Study Skills	I need to learn how to take better notes in class and while reading my text. I also need to know how to study from those notes more effectively.	My instructor for my student success class Tutorial center Study group or study partner	**Knowledge:** I am learning how to acquire more knowledge in all of my classes. **Adaptability:** I am learning how to adapt to harder classes than I had in high school. **Accountability:** I am learning how to be more responsible for my own education.
Personal Motivation			
Time Management			
Communication Skills (listening, writing, speaking)			
Money Management			

A Word About *USING* Cornerstone

We encourage you to read this text (and every text) with great care so that you can learn from the ideas presented within its pages. We also encourage you to USE this book:

- Write in the margins
- Circle important terms
- Highlight key phrases
- Jot down word definitions in the margins
- Dog-ear the pages
- Write questions in the white spaces provided

By treating this book like your "foundation to success," you will begin to see remarkable progress in your study practices, reading comprehension, and learning skills. Review the following page from another *Cornerstone* text to see how a "used" text might look.

cussion. If your body, mind, and soul are to function in a healthy manner, then your approach to wellness should be balanced. You need to explore and develop a holistic approach to wellness.

THE MIND'S EFFECT ON WELLNESS

The mind is an incredibly complex organ. The health industry has not begun to tap the awesome power the mind has over a person's physical health. Very basic studies have shown that the mind is a vital link to physical health. Your emotions play a tremendous role in how you approach your overall wellness program. Your emotional well-being impacts all aspects of your general wellness and therefore is the platform for all health. Christopher Reeve once discussed the importance that his mental state played in his recovery from what people thought would be a life-ending fall in 1990. Instead Reeve, although remaining a quadriplegic until his death in 2005, was able to continue acting, directing, and producing and was a very influential activist in the field of stem cell research.

People who are mentally healthy possess these qualities:

▸ Have a positive sense of self-worth
▸ Are determined to make an effort to be healthy
▸ Can love and have meaningful relationships
▸ Understand reality and the limitations placed on them
▸ Have compassion for others
▸ Understand that the world does not revolve around them

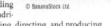

Ignoring your mental health can be dangerous. When was the last time you took a mental health break?

© BananaStock Ltd.

DEPRESSION AND ANXIETY DISORDERS

Depression is a term used to describe feelings ranging from feeling blue to utter hopelessness. The use of "I'm depressed" to mean "I'm sad" or "I'm down" is a far cry from the illness of clinical depression. Depression is a sickness that can creep up on an individual and render that person helplessly lost if it is not detected and properly treated. Signs of depression include the following (Donatelle and Davis, 2002):

▸ Lingering sadness
▸ Inability to find joy in pleasure-giving activities
▸ Loss of interest in work or school
▸ Unexplainable fatigue
▸ Sleep disorders, including insomnia or early-morning awakenings
▸ Loss of sex drive
▸ Withdrawal from friends and family
▸ Feelings of hopelessness and worthlessness
▸ Desire to die

DID YOU KNOW?

Sheryl Crow, singer, songwriter, and activist was diagnosed with breast cancer at age 44 just after the debut of her Grammy-nominated Wildflower CD was released. Those closest to Crow stated that it was her commitment to a holistic approach to living that kept her centered during her recovery from surgery.

© Steve Azzara/Corbis

Good luck in your journey. College will be one of the most rewarding and beneficial times of your life. Here's to new beginnings.

ROBERT M. SHERFIELD, PH.D.

Robert Sherfield has been teaching public speaking, theatre, and student success and working with first-year orientation programs for more than 25 years. Currently, he is a professor at the College of Southern Nevada, teaching student success, professional communication, public speaking, and drama. He is also an adjunct faculty member at The University of Nevada–Las Vegas in the William F. Harrah College of Hotel Administration, where he teaches classes in professional and career development.

Robb was named **Educator of the Year** at the College of Southern Nevada. He twice received the **Distinguished Teacher of the Year Award** from the University of South Carolina Union, and he has received numerous other awards and nominations for outstanding classroom instruction and advisement.

Robb's extensive work with student success programs includes experience with the design and implementation of these programs—including one program that was presented at the International Conference on the First-Year Experience in Newcastle upon Tyne, England. He has conducted faculty development keynotes and workshops at more than 250 institutions of higher education across America. He has spoken in 46 states and several countries.

In addition to his coauthorship of *Cornerstone: Opening Doors to Career Success,* he has authored or coauthored *Solving the Professional Development Puzzle: 101 Solutions for Career and Life Planning* (Prentice Hall, 2009); *Cornerstone: Discovering Your Potential, Learning Actively, and Living Well* (Prentice Hall, 2008); *Roadways to Success* (Prentice Hall, 2001); the trade book *365 Things I Learned in College* (Allyn & Bacon, 1996); *Capstone: Succeeding Beyond College* (Prentice Hall, 2001); *Case Studies for the First Year: An Odyssey into Critical Thinking and Problem Solving* (Prentice Hall, 2004); *The Everything Self-Esteem Book* (Adams Media, 2004); and *Cornerstone: Building on Your Best for Career Success* (Prentice Hall, 2006).

Robb's interest in student success began with his own first year in college. Low SAT scores and a low high school ranking denied him entrance into college. With the help of a success program, Robb was granted entrance into college, and he went on to earn five college degrees, including a doctorate. He has always been interested in the social, academic, and cultural development of students, and he sees this book as his way to help students enter the world of work and establishing lasting, rewarding careers.

Visit **http://www.robertsherfield.com**.

PATRICIA G. MOODY, PH.D.

Patricia G. Moody is dean emeritus of the College of Hospitality, Retail, and Sport Management at the University of South Carolina, where she served on the faculty and in administration for more than 30 years. Pat was honored as **Distinguished Educator of the Year** at her college and as **Collegiate Teacher of the Year** by the National Business Education Association. She was also a top-five finalist for the **Amoco Teaching Award** at the University of South Carolina. She received the prestigious **John Robert Gregg Award**, the highest honor in her field of over 100,000 educators.

Pat has coauthored many texts and simulations, including *Solving the Professional Development Puzzle: 101 Solutions for Career and Life Planning; Cornerstone: Discovering Your Potential, Learning Actively, and Living Well; 365 Things I Learned in College; Capstone: Succeeding Beyond College; Case Studies for the First Year: An Odyssey into Critical Thinking and Problem Solving;* and *Cornerstone: Building on Your Best for Career Success.*

A nationally known motivational speaker, consultant, and author, Pat has spoken in almost every state, has been invited to speak in several countries, and frequently keynotes national and regional conventions. She has presented her signature motivational keynote address, ***"Fly Like an Eagle,"*** to tens of thousands of people, from Olympic athletes to corporate executives to high school students.

As the dean of her college, Dr. Moody led international trips to build relationships and establish joint research projects in hospitality. Under her direction, faculty members in her college began a landmark study of Chinese tourists.

Pat now travels the country delivering workshops, keynotes, and presentations on topics such as change, working in the new global community, student motivation, and emotional intelligence. She also serves as a personal coach for business executives.

ACKNOWLEDGMENTS and GRATITUDE
Professional Acknowledgments

We would like to thank the following individuals for their support:

Dr. Michael Richards, president, College of Southern Nevada; Dr. Darren Divine, interim vice president, College of Southern Nevada; Professor Rose Hawkins, interim dean, College of Arts and Letters; Professor John Ziebell, interim department chair—English; Professor Kathy Baker, assistant chair—English; Kate Sawyer, Lincoln Educational Services; Karen McGrath, PIMA Medical Institute; Al Dornbach, ITT Technical Institute—Bensalem, PA; Doug Paddock, Louisville Technical College; Tara Wertz, MTI College; and Debra McCandrew, Florence Darlington Technical College.

Our fondest gratitude to the following **faculty and friends**, who recommended students for **The Big WHY:**

Melanie Deffendall, Delgado Community College; Debra McCandrew, Florence Darlington Technical College; Al Dornbach, ITT Technical Institute, Bensalem, PA; Doug Paddock, Louisville Technical College; Tara Wertz, MTI College; and Todd Phillips, East Central College.

We offer our heartfelt thanks to our **nominators** and **contributors** for **"from Ordinary to Extraordinary: True Stories of Personal Triumph":**

William (Bill) Clayton, Lydia Lebovic, Vivian Wong, Maureen Riopelle, H. D. Roma, Dr. Dino Gonzalez, Chef Odette Smith-Ransome, Leo G. Borges, Matthew Karres, Catherine Scheligh, Melanie Deffendall, Antionette Payne, and Karen McGrath.

And thanks to our **students** who shared their real-life stories for **The Big WHY:**

Darby Stone, College of Southern Nevada, Monica Miller, Delgado Community College, La Dondo Johnson, Houston Community College, Oscar Bowser, Midlands

Technical College, E. J. Grant, East Central College, Sheena Moses, Florence Darlington Technical College, William Paddock, Louisville Technical College, Michelle Lecroy, MCI College, Eric Despinis, ITT Technical Institute, Griffin Jones, Park Point University, Michelle Lecroy, MTI College.

Our Wonderful and Insightful Reviewers

For the second edition: Kenneth E. Bass Sr., Medical Careers Institute; Jean Fennema, Lincoln Educational Services; Steve Forshier, Pima Medical Institute; Angela D. Jones, Art Institute of California–San Francisco; Kate Sawyer, Lincoln Educational Services; Edward M. Tucker, Lincoln College of Technology; Tara Wertz, MCI College; and Sharon L. Youngue, Art Institute of Phoenix.

For previous editions: Christian M. Blum, Bryan and Stratton College; James Briski, Katherine Gibbs School; Pela Selene Terry, Art Institute of New York City; Christina Donnelly, York Technical College; Connie Egelman, Nassau Community College; Amy Hickman, Collins College; Beth Humes, Pennsylvania Culinary Institute; Kim Joyce, Art Institute of Philadelphia; Lawrence Ludwig, Sanford-Brown College; Bethany Marcus, ECPI College of Technology; Kate Sawyer, Pittsburg Technical Institute; Patricia Sell, National College of Business and Technology; Janis Stiewing, PIMA Medical Institute; June Sullivan, Florida Metropolitan University; Fred Amador, Phoenix College; Kathy Bryan, Daytona Beach Community College; Dorothy Chase, Community College of Southern Nevada; JoAnn Credle, Northern Virginia Community College; Betty Fortune, Houston Community College; Doroteo Franco Jr., El Paso Community College; Cynthia Garrard, Massasoit Community College; Joel Jessen, Eastfield College; Peter Johnston, Massasoit Community College; Steve Konowalow, Community College of Southern Nevada; Janet Lindner, Midlands Technical College; Carmen McNeil, Solano College; Joan O'Connor, New York Institute of Technology; Mary Pepe, Valencia Community College; Bennie Perdue, Miami-Dade Community College; Ginny Peterson-Tennant, Miami Dade Community College; Anna E. Ward, Miami-Dade Community College; Wistar M. Withers, Northern Virginia Community College; and Marie Zander, New York Institute of Technology. Joanne Bassett, Shelby State Community College; Sandra M. Bovain-Lowe, Cumberland Community College; Carol Brooks, GMI Engineering and Management Institute; Elaine H. Byrd, Utah Valley State College; Janet Cutshall, Sussex County Community College; Deborah Daiek, Wayne State University; David DeFrain, Central Missouri State University; Leslie L. Duckworth, Florida Community College at Jacksonville; Marnell Hayes, Lake City Community College; Elzora Holland, University of Michigan, Ann Arbor; Earlyn G. Jordan, Fayetteville State University; John Lowry-King, Eastern New Mexico University; Charlene Latimer; Michael Laven, University of Southwestern Louisiana; Judith Lynch, Kansas State University; Susan Magun-Jackson, The University of Memphis; Charles William Martin, California State University, San Bernardino; Jeffrey A. Miller; Ronald W. Johnsrud, Lake City Community College; Joseph R. Krzyzanowski, Albuquerque TVI; Ellen Oppenberg, Glendale Community College; Lee Pelton, Charles S. Mott Community College; Robert Rozzelle, Wichita State University; Penny Schempp, Western Iowa Community College; Betty Smith, University of Nebraska at Kearney; James Stepp, University of Maine at Presque Isle; Charles Washington, Indiana University–Purdue University; and Katherine A. Wenen-Nesbit, Chippewa Valley Technical College.

Our Creative and Supportive Team at Pearson/Prentice Hall

Without the support and encouragement of the following people at Prentice Hall, this book would not be possible. Our sincere thanks to Nancy Forsyth, Robin Baliszewski, Jeff Johnston, Sande Johnson, Amy Judd, and Connie James. Your constant belief in us over the years has been a most precious gift. We are lucky to know you and are better people because of you. Thank you!

We also thank the following friends at Pearson/Prentice Hall for their support, dedication, and miraculous hard work: Jenny Gessner, Toni Payne, Brenda Rock, Lynda Cramer, Walt Kirby, Debbie Ogilvie, Alan Hensley, Pam Jeffries, Barbara Donlon, Cathy Bennett, Meredith Chandler, Jeff McIlroy, Steve Foster, Meghan McCauley, and Matt Mesaros.

CORNERSTONE

Opening Doors to
Career Success

thrive

"The greatest reward of an education is to be able to face the world with an open mind, a caring heart, and willing soul."

R.M. Sherfield

thrive

Discovering Your Potential, *Nurturing* Change, and *Thriving* Through Goal Setting

THE BIG WHY

WHY read and work through this chapter? WHY will I ever be asked to use this stuff on self-responsibility? WHY will a chapter on adjusting to college and goal setting help me with my classes, at work, with my family, and beyond? WHY is this information such a big deal?

THE BIG WHY
from another perspective

Name:	Mark
Institution:	Spartanburg Methodist College, Spartanburg, SC
Age:	18
Major:	Associate of Arts—Theatre and Speech

I am the son of textile workers. Both of my parents worked in a cotton mill for over 30 years. My hometown is in the rural south about 35 miles from the nearest metropolitan area. I attended a small high school and had never been a good student. Because of my poor performance through the years, working full-time, and family commitments, I decided to attend a community college and then transfer to a four-year college.

I finished high school with a D– average and my SAT scores and class rank were in the lowest 25th percentile. In fact, I was denied entrance to the community college. The college granted me provisional acceptance only if I enrolled in, and successfully completed, a summer preparatory program. I graduated high school on a Friday night and began my college studies the very next Monday morning enrolled in the prep program. I never realized what lay ahead.

My first class that semester was English. Professor Brannon walked in, handed out the syllabus, called the roll, and began to lecture. Lord Byron was the topic for the day. The class ended and, after an hour's break, I headed across campus for history. Professor Wilkerson entered with a dust storm behind her. She went over the syllabus and, before we had a chance to blink, she was involved in the first lecture. "The cradle of civilization," she

began, "was Mesopotamia." We all scurried to find notebooks and pens to begin taking notes. I could not believe I was already behind on the first day.

One minute before class ended, she closed her book, looked directly at us, and said, "You are in history now. You elected to take this class and you will follow my rules. You are not to be late, you are to come to this class prepared, and you are to do your homework assignments. If you do what I ask you to do, you will learn more about Western civilization than you ever thought possible. If you don't keep up with me, you won't know if you are in Egypt, Mesopotamia, or pure hell! Class dismissed!"

Without a moment to spare, I ran to the other end of campus for my next class. I walked into the room in a panic, fearing I was late. To my surprise, the instructor was not yet in class. We *waited almost 15 minutes before the professor entered.* "You need to sign this roster and read Chapter 1 for Wednesday," he said. "You can pick up a syllabus on your way out." *I was shocked. Was the class over?*

On the 30-mile trip home, my mind was filled with new thoughts . . . *Lord Byron, Mesopotamia, professors who talked too fast, professors who did not talk at all,*

(continued on page 6)

4

> "I have no clue as to how my story will end.
> But that's alright. When you set out on a journey and night covers the road,
> that's when you discover the stars."
> —Nancy Willard

This chapter, indeed this whole book and course in which you are enrolled, is about helping you become the best college student and life-long learner that you can possibly be. Quite simply, this chapter is included to help you discover your strengths and build on them, and to help you identify areas where you might need to change your actions or behaviors by setting realistic goals. This chapter is about learning to thrive and survive in college.

Discovering your potential, adjusting to college life, and setting and working toward your **goals** can be essential keys to your success in college and beyond. This chapter can help you:

- Adjust to life as a student

- Determine how your education can help you beyond the classroom
- Understand the demands and realities of your instructors and institution
- Comprehend the differences between high school, college, and career
- Eliminate harmful roadblocks and negative attitudes
- Create positive changes by setting and working toward realistic, measurable goals

We hope this chapter will be an exciting introduction to a life filled with learning, growing, and new opportunities. Enjoy the ride. You'll never be the same!!

SCAN AND QUESTION

In the preface of this book (and in more detail in Chapter 6), we discuss how to use the **SQ3R Study Method.** This mnemonic stands for Scan, Question, Read, Recite, and Review. *Scanning* asks you to look over the chapter before reading it. Look at the headings, charts, photos, and call-out boxes. *Questioning* asks you to create study questions from the major headings. Take a few moments and **scan this chapter.** As you scan, **list five questions** you can expect to learn the answers to while reading and studying Chapter 1.

Example:
- What are the basic truths about the culture of college? (from page 12)
- Why must goals be measurable? (from page 24)

My Questions:

1. _____
_____ from page _____

2. _____
_____ from page _____

3. _____
_____ from page _____

4. _____
_____ from page _____

5. _____
_____ from page _____

Reminder: At the end of the chapter, come back to this page and answer these questions in your notebook, text margins, or online chapter notes.

(continued from page 4)

tuition, parking, and the size of the library. I knew that something was different, *something had changed in me.* I couldn't put my finger on it. It would be years later before I would realize that the change was not my classes, not my schedule, not the people, not the professors—but me; *I had changed.* In one day, I had tasted something intoxicating, something that was addictive. *I had tasted a new world.*

I had to go to work that afternoon at the mill, and even my job and my coworkers had changed. I had always known that I did not want to spend the rest of my life in the factory, but this day the feeling was stronger. My job was not enough, my family was not enough, the farm on which I had been raised was not enough anymore. *There was a new light for me, and I knew that because of one day in college, I would never be the same.* It was like tasting Godiva chocolate for the first time—Hershey's kisses were no longer enough. It was like seeing the ocean for the first time and knowing that the millpond would never be the same. *I couldn't go back. What I knew before was simply not enough.*

My name is Robert *Mark* Sherfield, and 31 years later, as I coauthor your *Cornerstone* text, I am still addicted to that new world. College changed my life, and I am still changing—with every day, every new book I read, every new class I teach, every new person I meet, and every new place to which I travel, I am changing.

By reading and engaging in this chapter, you will begin to discover the many possibilities that exist for you on a personal and professional basis. Looking forward is very important, but looking back is too. Looking back at your past adversities and challenges while planning for your future is an important tool in self-discovery. This chapter will help you begin to evaluate your strengths and identify areas where change may be necessary. We wish you good luck and good fortune on your journey.

YOUR EDUCATION, YOUR CAREER, THE NEW WORLD ECONOMY, AND YOU!

Complex Title, Simple Truth

Composer, singer, and activist Bob Dylan once wrote, "***The times, they are a-changin.***" Truer words have never been spoken—especially for anyone living at this moment. This is not your daddy's economy. It is not your mama's workplace, and it certainly is not your grandfather's job market. To glide over this simple truth *could be the most costly decision of your life.*

"New world economy," you might say. *"Who cares?"*

"China? Who cares about China or Russia or Dubai, Macau, or Saudi Arabia? I live in Kansas."

"An iPhone? A BlackBerry? I can't even afford my bus ticket this month," you may be thinking.

"A $9.5 trillion U.S. debt doesn't concern me. I'm no politician and I can't fix it. I just want to get a job and provide for my family," you may secretly reason. (A trillion is followed by twelve zeros . . . that's $9,500,000,000,000 we owe to other countries; that is, every man, woman, and child in America owes over $32,000 each.)

While you may not be alone in your thinking, you would be very wrong and exceptionally foolish to think that today's American profile does not concern you. Yes, it may be true that you are simply trying to get a certificate in Medical Assisting to work in a small medical office in Spokane, Washington, or to obtain a degree in Criminal Justice to work at the police department in Union, South Carolina. However, no certificate, no degree, no job, and certainly no person will be exempt from the changes and challenges upon us.

Consider the following FACTS:

- China's economy is growing at roughly 10 percent a year, triple that of the United States.
- The fastest growing segment of the American population is 85 and older.
- Over 40 million Americans do not have health insurance.
- Identity theft is up 2,000 percent in the past five years.
- By 2010, the average home will have 100 computers embedded in all types of appliances, communication devices, and amenities.
- Ninety percent of the U.S. budget is spent on entitlements and the military.
- The United States is experiencing a severe water shortage with no end in sight (water shortages will affect two-thirds of the world's population by 2025).
- Russia's economy is growing by 7–8 percent per year. The Russians are not "on their knees" anymore, economically or militarily.
- The largest casinos, malls, and hotels in the world used to be in America. Now, they are all abroad.
- Twenty-five percent of all bankruptcies in the United States are filed by people under the age of 25.
- The world has used all of the "cheap" oil. Prices may go up and down, but oil will not be "cheap" again.
- The United States (and indeed the world) has no reasonable energy replacement at this time.
- By 2010, over 75 percent of new jobs will require postsecondary education or training.
- America ranks 26th among industrialized nations in math and science achievement.

The world is changing so rapidly, it is important that you learn as much as possible and keep up with changes in your profession.

"So, where does this leave me," you might be asking? It leaves you in an exciting, vulnerable, challenging, scary, and wonderful place. We did *not* include these facts to scare you or to turn you off, but rather to give you a jolt, to open your eyes to the workforce you're about to enter. We included them to encourage you to use *every tool* available, *every resource* possible, *every connection* imaginable, and *every ethical means* possible to prepare yourself for this rapidly changing world. The present and the future may not be as rosy as you had hoped for, but it is here, it is real, and it is yours.

> "The real key to success is not just getting an education, but keeping one."
>
> —Unknown

You are going to have to prepare for a workforce that is constantly changing, global, innovative, trendy, exceptionally fast, volatile, detached and sometimes unpredictable—yes, even at that medical office in Spokane, Washington, and that small sheriff's department in Union, South Carolina. No workplace will be immune from the changes facing our world today, and your very survival depends on being prepared and knowing how to quickly adapt and change.

In this new economy, you are going to be asked to deal with things that your parents could never have imagined. Gone are the days when you worked for one company for 30 years, climbed the ladder, and retired with a pension and a gold watch. Most pension

The college experience is different for every person.

plans are history; gold watches are too expensive; and if you are under 45 at this moment, Social Security may not be an option for you either.

In his book *The 2010 Meltdown*, Edward Gordon (2005) writes, "Simply stated, today in America, there are just too many people trained for the wrong jobs. Many jobs have become unnecessary, technically obsolete . . . or worse yet, the job/career aspirations of too many current and future workers are at serious odds with the changing needs of the U.S. labor market (p. 17)." However, all is not lost to you or your future. People who are highly skilled, possess superb oral and written communication skills, know how to solve problems, and can work well with others will *be in high demand* for many years to come.

Careers in the following areas are projected for high growth in the coming decade: **health sciences** (includes dental assistants, home health aides, physician assistants, medical assistants, occupational therapy, physical therapist); **aviation** (airplane mechanics and air traffic controllers); **skilled trades** (plumbing, electricians, mechanics); **teachers** (K–12 and college); **technologists** (aerospace and GPS engineers, water and sanitation engineers, transportation services, systems analysts, programmers, interactive media designers, software engineers, desktop publishing); and **management, marketing, and public relations** (business managers, human resource directors, advertising and public relations).

Whether we like it or not, a massive transformation is going on all around us in this country, as well as all over the world. Thriving in the coming years is going to be more difficult than in the past and will require certain new and different abilities and attitudes. This new world we are entering is indeed a world where many people will be highly successful and others will simply be left behind. And it is happening NOW! Without possessing the abilities and skills listed below, you will have little or no chance of succeeding. Today's students must master new ways of thinking and producing while they are in school, skills that will carry over to the workplace. Consider the skills and abilities needed for success in the new millennium (Figure 1.1).

By learning to develop these enduring skills, you will be able to carry them with you on your first job, on your tenth job, and well into your future.

THE M & M THEORY
Your Money and Your Mama!

What is the M & M Theory? It is quite simple. We all pay attention to and try to protect the things that matter most to us. Your "**m**oney and your **m**ama" are simply symbolic of what you care about. Most people do care what happens to their families, their income, their friends, their careers, the environment, and many of the alarming facts mentioned above.

However, in the hustle and bustle of finding day care, studying for classes, working a full-time job, cleaning the house, helping the kids with homework, and trying to prepare a meal from time to time, we lose sight of some of the most important things in our lives. Never forget this important fact: *Your EDUCATION is important, too*. It is important to your future on many levels—culturally, socially, intellectually, and in preparing you for the future. Your education is a part of the M & M Theory because it involves your money—the future financial health for you and your family.

FIGURE 1.1   Ten Essential Cornerstones for Personal and Professional Success

PASSION—The ability to show the world a person who is passionate about your mission and who has aligned your goals with your education, talents, experiences, and skills. A person who cares not only about your own success, but about the world and your surroundings—a person who sees yourself as "a citizen of the world."

MOTIVATION—The ability to find the inner strength and personal drive to get up each day and face the world with an "I can, I Will" attitude. The ability to develop a strong personal value and belief system that motivates you when the going gets tough. The ability to know who you are and never let anyone steal your identity or erode your personal ethics.

KNOWLEDGE—The ability to become highly skilled in a profession or craft that will enable you to make a good living for you and your family in a rapidly changing workplace and to use life-long learning to maintain your marketable skill sets. The ability to master important academic information beyond your major field in areas such as math, science, psychology, history, technology, economics, and communication, and to practically apply that information in an evolving and highly technical work environment.

RESOURCEFULNESS—The ability to know WHERE to find information and resources that will help you be successful in your academic studies and your chosen profession. The ability to look and seek for new opportunities, options, and outcomes. The ability to imagine new ways of solving old problems.

CREATIVITY—The ability to use creativity and innovation in solving problems that will enable you to anticipate new and emerging issues, to communicate and use what you know and what you have learned and discovered to answer critical questions and solve complex and demanding problems.

ADAPTABILITY—The ability to make good choices based on future opportunities and a changing workplace and to constantly reinvent yourself as change brings about necessity and opportunity.

OPEN-MINDEDNESS—The ability to accept and appreciate a highly diverse workplace and the inherent differences and cultures that will be commonplace. The ability to listen to others with whom you disagree or with whom you may have little in common and learn from them and their experiences. The ability to learn a new language, even if your mastery is only at a primitive, broken, conversational level.

COMMUNICATION—The ability to develop and maintain healthy, supportive personal and professional relationships and to build a solid network of well-connected professionals who can help you and who YOU can help in return.

ACCOUNTABILITY—The ability to accept responsibility and be accountable for all aspects of your future including your psychological well being, your spiritual well being, your relationships, your health, your finances, and your overall survival skills. Basically, you must develop a plan for the future that states, "If this fails, I'll do this," or "If this job is phased out, I'll do this," or "If this resource is gone, I'll use this," or "If this person won't help me, this one will."

VISION—The ability to guide one's career path in a new-world, global economy and to understand and take advantage of the inherent impact of worldwide competition—regardless of where you live or the size of your company.

According to one of the leading research sources in higher education, *The Chronicle of Higher Education* (August 2007), first-year students had a variety of reasons for attending college such as: "To learn about things that interest me"; "To get training for a specific career"; and "To be able to get a better job." However, 71.0 percent of those polled stated that his/her reason for attending college was "To be able to make more money" (p. 19).

Depending on how you approach this new venture, it will be one of the most exciting and important times of your life—regardless of your age, interests, past experiences, or reasons for attending. Higher education can bring rewards of the mind and of the soul, and yes, rewards of a more lucrative future.

> "The real object of education is to give you resources that will endure as long as life endures."
>
> —S. Smith

FIGURE 1.2   Education, Pay, and Unemployment Statistics of Full-Time Workers, 25 and Over

Unemployment Rate	Degree	Mean Earnings
1.35%	Professional Degree	$122,480
1.40%	Doctorate Degree	$108,563
1.85%	Master's Degree	$80,407
2.20%	Bachelor's Degree	$66,133
3.15%	Associate Degree	$47,196
3.85%	Some College, No Degree	$44,488
4.35%	High School Graduate	$37,424
7.40%	Less than High School Graduate	$28,539

Source: Department of the Census, Department of Labor, 2008.

According to the U.S. Census Bureau in its annual report, *Education and Training Pay* (2007), people with college degrees can earn considerably more than those who do not have a degree. For instance, those with bachelor's degrees average approximately $29,000 *more per year* in earnings than those with only high school educations. People with associate's degrees average approximately $10,000 more per year in earnings than those with only high school educations. For a complete look at earning power of U.S. citizens 25 and older, look at the Annual Education, Pay, and Unemployment Chart in Figure 1.2.

By focusing on money in this section, we do not mean to suggest that the only reason for attending college is to make more money. As a matter of fact, we feel that it is a secondary reason. Many people *without college degrees* earn huge salaries each year. However, as the data in Figure 1.2 suggests, traditionally, those with college degrees earn *more* money and experience *less* unemployment. Basically, college should make the road to financial security easier, but college should also be a place where you learn to make decisions about your values, your character, and your future. College can also be a place where you make decisions about the changes that need to occur in your life so that you can effectively manage and prosper in an ever-changing world.

CAREER COLLEGE AND YOU

The Partnership of a Lifetime!

Right now, you're one of almost four million first-year students enrolled in higher education in America. Some have enrolled to gain the skills and/or degree necessary to enter a great career field. Some are here for retraining, and some are here to complete a dream begun years ago. Some of your classmates may have recently lost a job, and they are here to get skills and expertise that were not available 10 or 15 years ago. Regardless of your reason, you've made the first step and, just like Mark in the opening story, your life will never be the same.

FIGURE 1.4 continued

	HIGH SCHOOL	COLLEGE	WORK
PERSONAL RESPONSIBILITY AND ATTITUDE	**Expectations:** • Teachers may coach you and try to motivate you • You are required by law to be in high school regardless of your attitude or responsibility level **Penalties:** • You may be reprimanded for certain attitudes • If your attitude prevents you from participating you may fail the class	**Expectations:** • You are responsible for your own learning • Professors will assist you, but there is little "hand holding" or personal coaching for motivation • College did not choose you, you chose it and you will be expected to hold this attitude toward your work **Penalties:** • You may fail the class if your attitude and motivation prevent you from participating	**Expectations:** • You are hired to do certain tasks and the company or institution fully expects this of you • You are expected to be positive and self-motivated • You are expected to model good behavior and uphold the company's work standards **Penalties:** • You will be passed over for promotions and raises • You may be reprimanded • You may be terminated
ETHICS AND CREDIBILITY	**Expectations:** • You are expected to turn in your own work • You are expected to avoid plagiarism • You are expected to write your own papers • Poor ethical decisions in high school may result in detention or suspension **Penalties:** • You may get detention or suspension • You will probably fail the project	**Expectations:** • You are expected to turn in your own work • You are expected to avoid plagiarism • You are expected to write your own papers • You are expected to conduct research and complete projects based on college and societal standards **Penalties:** • Poor ethical decisions may land you in front of a student ethics committee or a faculty ethics committee or result in expulsion from the college • You will fail the project • You will fail the class • You may face deportation if your visa is dependent on your student status	**Expectations:** • You will be required to carry out your job in accordance with company policies, laws, and moral standards • You will be expected to use adult vision and standards **Penalties:** • Poor ethical decisions may cause you to be severely reprimanded, terminated, or in some cases could even result in a prison sentence

understanding of both, take a few moments and jot down your personal strengths and areas of transition.

My Greatest Strengths/Talents	Things I Need to Change in My Life
_____	_____
_____	_____
_____	_____
_____	_____

Now, choose one of the things above that you have identified as needing to change in your life. _____

After reviewing your strengths and talents, determine how you can use them to help you bring this change about in your life. (Example: If you listed **courageous** as being one of your strengths, how can your **personal courage** help you deal with one of the items listed on the right?)

_____

_____

_____

_____

ELIMINATING ROADBLOCKS
What to Do If Your Emotions, Fears, Friends, or Self-Talk Try to Derail You

Try as you might, sometimes harmful emotions, fear of the unknown, and that nagging little voice inside your head (negative self-talk) can cause you problems. Negative self-talk usually appears when you are afraid, uneasy, hurt, angry, depressed, or lonely. By the time you read this, you may have experienced these feelings. When you experience change, your body, mind, and soul typically go through a process of physical and emotional change as well. Learning to recognize these symptoms in order to control them can help you control the stress that can accompany change.

Many people report that when they encounter a major life change, they experience:

- Nervousness
- Stress
- A sense of being on the edge
- Fear
- Fatigue
- Guilt
- Homesickness
- Denial
- Anger
- Depression

These feelings are normal when you go through a powerful change, *but remember, they are temporary*. If any of these feelings become overwhelming or life-threatening, seek counseling, talk to your friends, go to your advisor, or speak with your professors. These people are your support group; use them. No one is going to look down on you or criticize you for feeling depressed or edgy—they've experienced the same things you're feeling now.

Your attitude is yours. It belongs to you. You own it. Good or bad, happy or sad, optimistic or pessimistic, it is yours and you are responsible for it. However, your attitude is greatly influenced by situations in your life and by the people with whom you associate. Developing a winning, optimistic attitude can be hard yet extremely rewarding work. Motivated and successful people have learned that one's attitude is the mirror to one's soul.

> ### ESSENTIAL CORNERSTONE
> ### VISION
> How can having a clear vision of your future help you become a more optimistic person?

Optimism has many benefits beyond helping you develop a winning attitude. Researchers have found that people who are optimistic live longer; are more motivated; survive cancer treatment at a greater rate; have longer, more satisfying relationships; and are mentally healthier than pessimists. This would suggest that developing and maintaining a winning, optimistic attitude can help you have a longer and more satisfying quality of life. It would also suggest that by thinking positively, your motivation level increases and you are able to accomplish more.

Listen to yourself for a few days.   Are you more of an optimist or a pessimist? Do you hear yourself whining, complaining, griping, and finding fault with everything and everybody around you? Do you blame others for things that are wrong in your life? Do you blame your instructors for your bad grades? Is someone else responsible for your unhappiness? If these thoughts or comments are in your head, you are suffering from the ***"I CAN'T Syndrome"*** (**I**rritated, **C**ontaminated, **A**ngry, **N**egative **T**houghts). This pessimistic condition can negatively influence every aspect of your life, from your self-esteem to your motivation level to your academic performance, to your relationships, and your career success.

If you want to eliminate ***I CAN'T*** from your life, consider the following tips:

- ☐ Work every day to find the good in people, places, and things.
- ☐ Discover what is holding you back and what you need to push you forward.
- ☐ Visualize your success—see yourself actually being who and what you want to be.
- ☐ Locate and observe positive, optimistic people and things in your life.
- ☐ Make a list of who helps you, supports you, and helps you feel positive—then make a point to be around them more.
- ☐ Take responsibility for your own actions and their consequences.
- ☐ Force yourself to find five positive things a day for which to be thankful.

You've seen the difference between an optimist and a pessimist. They are both everywhere—at work, at school, and probably in your own family. Think of the optimist for a moment. You've probably sat next to him or her in one of your classes or seen him or her at work—the person who always seems to be happy, motivated, bubbling with personality, organized, and ready for whatever comes his or her way. They greet people as they enter the room, they respond in class, they volunteer for projects, and they have a presence about them that is positive and lively. You may even look at him or her out of the corner of your eye and ask, "What is he on?"

Positive, upbeat, and motivated people are easy to spot. You can basically see their attitude in the way they walk, the way they carry themselves, the way they approach people, and the way they treat others.

Learn from them as you move through the days and months ahead. Choose your friends carefully. Seek out people who have ambition, good work habits, positive attitudes, and high ethical standards. Look for those who study hard, enjoy learning, are goal oriented, and don't mind taking a stand

> "You gain strength, experience, and confidence by every experience where you stop to look fear in the face. You must do the thing you think you cannot.
> —Eleanor Roosevelt

when they believe strongly about something. Befriend people who have interests and hobbies that are new to you. Step outside your comfort zone and add people to your circle of friends who are from a different culture, are of a different religion, or who have lived in a different geographic region. You'll be happily surprised at how much enrichment they can bring to your life.

Be weary, however, of *"the others."* The ones you need to avoid. Whiners. Degraders. Attackers. Manipulators. Pessimists. Back-stabbers. Abusers. Cowards. Two-faced racists, sexists, ageists, homophobics, ethnocentrists. These people carry around an aura so negative that it can almost be seen as a dark cloud above them. They degrade others because they do not like themselves. They find fault with everything because their own lives are a mess. They do nothing and then attack you for being motivated and trying to improve your life. We call them ***contaminated people.***

Examine the two lists below. As you read through the lists, consider the people with whom you associate. Are the majority of your friends, family, peers, and work associates positive or contaminated?

POSITIVE PEOPLE are those who	CONTAMINATED PEOPLE are those who
☐ Bring out the best in you	☐ Bring out the worst in you
☐ Find the good in bad situations	☐ Find the bad in every situation
☐ Are gracious and understanding	☐ Are rude and uncaring
☐ Build people up	☐ Sabotage people, even loved ones
☐ Support your dreams	☐ Criticize your hopes and plans
☐ Make you feel comfortable and happy	☐ Make you feel uneasy, nervous, and irritable
☐ Tell you the truth and offer constructive criticism	☐ Are two-faced and always use harsh language to "put you in your place"
☐ Are open minded and fair	☐ Are narrow and ethnocentric
☐ Are patient	☐ Are quick to anger
☐ Are giving	☐ Are jealous and smothering
☐ Love to learn from others	☐ Know everything already

As you think about the list above and the people in your life, ask yourself, "Do I surround myself with more positive or contaminated people?" As you consider your friends, family, classmates, and work associates, use the space below to compare and contrast one *positive person* with one *contaminated person* in your life.

Positive Person _____

His/Her Attributes _____

_____

_____

Contaminated Person _____

His/Her Attributes _____

_____

_____

Compare and Contrast _____

_____

_____

_____

_____

How can an optimistic attitude help you in your career? _____

_____

_____

_____

_____

BECOMING WHO YOU WANT TO BE

Bringing About Positive Change Through Goal-Setting

Positive change can be brought about in several ways, but the most effective way is through goal setting and having a "change plan." Simply allowing others to force changes on you or not knowing how to deal with the changes over which you have no control can be detrimental to your success. The relationship between successful change and goal setting is a powerful one in that it gives you tools to control your own life. This section will help you learn more about setting and evaluating your goals.

> "Decide you want it more than you're afraid of it."
>
> —Bill Cosby

Beginning the Process of Change

Think about what you really want or what you need to change in your life. More importantly, think about why you want "this thing" and what it is going to mean to your life. By thinking about what you want, what needs to change, and where you want to be, goals become easier. Goal setting itself is relatively easy—it is the personal **commitment** that requires detailed attention, hard work, and unbridled hope. Many people make goals, and to succeed in meeting them they define their goals in concrete, measurable terms, they work toward them daily, they have a specific, clear plan of how to attain them, and they know when they want the goal to be reached. The most vital step toward reaching your goal is making a personal commitment to yourself that you are going to achieve it and then committing all of your possible resources toward the completion of that goal.

As you begin to think about your life, your future and your goals, think about setting a goal in at least two of the following categories:

- Personal or self-improvement
- Academic
- Family
- Community service
- Social
- Health
- Financial
- Spiritual
- Career

You are likely to achieve goals that relate to your own personal value system and that are truly important to you.

Characteristics of Attainable Goals

The following characteristics will help you in your quest to bring about change through effective goal setting. Goals should be:

- **Reasonable**   Your goal should be a challenge for you, but also within reason of your abilities.
- **Believable**   To achieve a goal, you must really believe it is within your capacity to reach it.
- **Measurable**   Your goal needs to be concrete and measurable in some way. Avoid such terms as "gonna earn a lot" and "wanna lose some."
- **Adaptable**   Your goals may need to be adapted to changing circumstances that may be happening in your life.
- **Controllable**   Your goals should be within your own control; they should not depend on the whims and opinions of anyone else.
- **Desirable**   To attain a difficult goal, you must want it very badly. You should never work toward something just because *someone else* wants you to pursue it.

How to Write Your Goals to Bring About Positive Change

"I will pass my next math test with a B or better" is an example of a short-term goal. *"I will purchase my first home by the time I am ___ years old"* is probably a long-term goal. During your college years, more of your goals may be short term than long term, but you can certainly begin setting both. Goals can be lofty and soaring, but great goals can also be as simple as *"I will spend two hours at the park with my children tomorrow afternoon."*

Well-written, exciting, and effective goals include:

- A goal statement with a target date
- Action steps
- A narrative statement
- An "I Deserve" statement
- A personal signature

The **goal statement** should be specific and measurable; that is, it should entail some tangible evidence of its achievement and it should have a **target date;** a timeline for accomplishing your goal. Your goal statement MUST also use an action verb. An example of a goal statement with an action verb and target date is: *"I will* lose 10 pounds in 6 weeks" or *"I am going to* join a campus club by the fifth week of this term." This is a much more powerful statement than: "I am thinking about joining a club" or "I wanna have a new car."

After you write the goal statement, you'll need to create **specific action steps** that explain exactly what you are going to do to reach your goal. There is no certain number of steps; it all depends on your goal and your personal commitment. An example of action steps for weight loss might be: (1) join the campus health center, (2) meet with a personal trainer on campus, (3) set an appointment with a nutrition counselor in the health center, (4) and so on.

Open the Door
Tips for Career Success

Consider the following strategies for adjusting to change in the days to come:

- Approach change with an open mind.
- If you haven't done so, take an afternoon and explore all the resources on your campus such as the library, the academic support center, counseling and advising office, etc.
- Don't be afraid to ask people in your class or your instructors questions about things that are confusing or unclear.
- So you won't fall behind, adjust your study habits to accommodate more rigorous assignments.
- Join a club, organization, or study group so you can start building a network of friends.
- If you are not technologically savvy, find out if there are any resources that can help you catch up.

from ordinary to EXTRAORDINARY

BILL CLAYTON

ACE Certified Personal Trainer/Post-Rehabilitation Specialist
Owner/Operator, Clayton Personal Fitness, Las Vegas, NV

"I was . . . ," Those are powerful words. For example, *I was* the manager of the gardening department of a major retail chain. *I was* an employee in a shop that prints and mails inserts and flyers. *I was* a rock band drummer for several bands. *I was* a crystal meth addict. Yes . . . *I was!*

It seems strange to write that now, but the term "I was . . . " is impossible to erase. My friends and clients often ask me how I managed to go from the life of a meth addict to a personal trainer. The journey was a strange one and often difficult.

I began playing the drums when I was six years old and by the time I was eight, I had my first garage band. Writing and playing music were my only passions. They were my life. After high school, I worked many odd jobs, but my love of performing never waned.

In my twenties, I had a band that steadily played gigs and I was living the life of a rocker. We traveled. We sang. We partied. We traveled some more and we partied some more . . . and more. Before I really realized what was happening with me, I had become addicted to meth. It was my life. I hung around people who used with me and they became my family.

I met Kathy, the woman I would eventually marry, while performing with my band. She and I hit it off even though she knew of my addiction. One evening after we were married, Kathy and I were talking and she mentioned that she would like to have children one day, I wanted children, too.

At that moment, the strangest thing came to my mind. I thought, "If she gets pregnant, I'll stop doing meth." How could I be so messed up that I would work to abolish my addiction for a child not yet born, *but* I would not consider trying to stop *just for me?* That was my wake-up call. I knew I had to change my life. I was 29 years old.

I was one of the lucky ones. I was able to stop "cold turkey" on my own. I know that others are not so lucky. I began to look at my life and tried to determine what I wanted to do. I had to seriously evaluate every aspect of who and what I was. I knew that I had to set goals to get my life back on track.

I had been in a life-threatening motorcycle accident years earlier and remembered the great care I received from my physical therapist. So I began to look at PT programs and that is when I found the personal trainer program at our local college. Something about this was very attractive to me. Again, I was lucky. I happened to find my passion and my life's vocation without much struggle.

Today, after working through my addiction, surviving a divorce, and mourning the death of my mom, I can say without a doubt that I am one of the luckiest people on earth. Because I was willing to change and stay committed to finding a better life, I found my true soul mate; I own my own gym; hold certifications from every major fitness and rehabilitation organization in America; and count each day as a true gift.

To help you get started, use this goal setting sheet as template for this and future goals. Additional goal sheets can be found in the Appendix of this book.

Name _____

Goal Statement (with Action Verb and Target Date) _____

_____

_____

Action Steps (concrete things you plan to do to reach your goal)

1. _____

2. _____

3. _____

4. _____

Narrative Statement (how your life will look when you reach your goal) _____

_____

_____

_____

_____

_____

_____

I deserve this goal because:

1. _____

_____

2. _____

_____

I hereby make this commitment to myself.

_____   _____

My Signature   Date

The next step is to write a **narrative statement** about what your goal accomplishment will mean to you and how your life will change because of reaching this goal. For example, if your goal is to lose 50 pounds, paint a "verbal picture" of how your life is going to look once this goal has been reached. Your verbal picture may include statements such as: "I'll be able to wear nicer clothes." "I'll feel better." "I'll be able to ride my bicycle again." "My self-esteem will be stronger." If your goals don't offer you significant rewards, you are not likely to stick to your plan.

Next, write down two reasons why you deserve this goal. This is your **"I Deserve It Statement."** It may seem simple, but this is a complex question. Many people do not follow through on their goals because deep down, they don't feel they deserve them. The narrative statement helps you understand how your life will look once the goal is met but your "I deserve statement" asks you to consider *why* you deserve this goal. Considering the goal above of losing 50 pounds, your "I deserve it statement" might read: *"I deserve to lose 50 pounds because I deserve to be healthy. I deserve to live a long life to be with my partner and my children."*

Finally, *sign your goal statement*. This is an imperative step in that *your signature* shows that you are making a personal commitment to see this goal to fruition. This is your name. Use it with pride.

When you have accomplished your goal, you will find that it is somewhat addictive. The feeling that you get from reaching an important milestone in your life is incredible, and many people begin the goal setting process again. Successful people never get to a target and sit down; they are always becoming. They reach one goal and begin dreaming, planning, preparing for the next accomplishment. Goal setting and follow-through are major components of your personal staying power as a college student. Goal setting is also a powerful tool to help you build healthy self-esteem and discover your real potential. Chapter 2 will help you look more deeply at your life and how to enhance your self-concept.

Evaluating Your Goals and Plans

Now that you have set your goal(s) and begun the work toward reaching your goal(s), consider the following questions as a way to evaluate your goal(s) and progress.

- Do I really want to achieve this goal enough to pay the price and to stick with it?
- What is the personal payoff to me if I achieve this goal, and what is the payoff to society and the good of other people?
- Who will notice if I achieve this goal? Does that matter to me?
- How realistic is this goal? Is it over my head for this stage of my development?
- Do I need to reduce my expectations so I won't be disillusioned in the beginning, and then increase the difficulty of my goal only after I have reached the first steps?
- Can I control all the factors necessary to achieve this goal?
- Is this goal specific and measurable?
- Does this goal contribute to my overall development? Is this goal allowing me to spend my time in the way that is best for me right now?
- How will I feel when I reach this goal? Will I be proud?
- Will the people who love me be proud that I accomplished this goal?

THINK ABOUT IT

Reflecting for Success

The transition from one place to another is seldom easy, even when the change is what you want. Entering college has given you the opportunity to assume new roles, develop new friendships, meet new people, work under different circumstances, and perhaps adjust

did you know?

Tim McGraw, recording artist and country music sensation, has recorded almost a dozen CDs, has 23 number one hits, and has sold 32 million CDs to date. However, his first series of singles failed so badly that he was told to give up his dream of becoming a country recording artist. One producer even told him, "You'll never make it, son. Go on home and find yourself a job."

"A possibility was born the day you were born, and it will live as long as you live."

—R. Burak

your lifestyle. It has also given you the opportunity to reflect on your strengths and consider areas where you might need to change. These changes form the very essence of the college experience; they create wonderful new experiences and help you discover who you really are and what you have to offer the world.

As you reflect upon this chapter, keep the following pointers in mind:

- ☐ Evaluate your reason(s) for attending college and what it means to your life.
- ☐ Use goal setting to help you direct changes in your life.
- ☐ Don't just let change happen; get involved in your own life and learning.
- ☐ Learn and grow from your past adversity and challenges.
- ☐ Focus on the positive by eliminating your negative self-talk.
- ☐ Keep your sense of humor.
- ☐ Talk to friends and family. Share your experience.
- ☐ Be courageous by facing your fears.
- ☐ Be objective.

passages
An Activity for Critical Thinking and Career Development

On page 9 of Chapter 1, and inside the front cover, you read **The Ten Essential Cornerstones for Personal and Professional Success.** They are:

Passion	Motivation
Knowledge	Resourcefulness
Creativity	Adaptability
Open-mindedness	Communication
Accountability	Vision

The following chapter-end activity will ask you to use several of these Essential Cornerstones to identify and actually bring about positive change in your life.

Four Steps: (1) Considering information from this chapter, your peers, classroom discussions, and your personal experience, think about what changes need to occur in each of the following areas to ensure your success. (2) Using the following chart, identify exactly what needs to change in this area. (3) Identify a place or person on campus or in the community where you can get help with this change. (4) Write in one or more of the **Essential Cornerstones** you are addressing by bringing about this change. *One example for Study Skills has been provided for you.*

Area of Change	What needs to Change?	Where can help be found?	Which Cornerstone are you addressing? (List at least three)
Study Skills	I need to learn how to take better notes in class and while reading my text. I also need to know how to study from those notes more effectively.	My instructor for my student success class Tutorial center Study group or study partner	**Knowledge:** I am learning how to acquire more knowledge in all of my classes. **Adaptability:** I am learning how to adapt to harder classes than I had in high school. **Accountability:** I am learning how to be more responsible for my own education.
Personal Motivation			
Time Management			
Communication Skills (listening, writing, speaking)			
Money Management			

PREPARING FOR SUCCESS

Refer to page 5 of this chapter and answer the questions you developed from headings. You should also be able to answer the following questions if they were not on your list:

1. Why is it important to understand the new world economy and be ready for changes in the coming years?

2. Why is change important to growth?

3. What is a narrative statement?

4. How can goal setting help you achieve your educational dreams?

5. Why is open-mindedness important in your college education?

chapter two

engage

"To be successful you need to find something to hold on to, something to motivate you, something to inspire you."

Tony Dorsett

engage

Cultivating Your *Personal Motivation* and *Academic Passion*

THE BIG WHY

WHY will I ever be asked to use this stuff? *WHY* will a chapter on motivation and academic passion help me in college, at work, with my family, and beyond? Why is it important to know about persisting in college? *WHY* is engagement such a big deal?

THE BIG WHY

from another perspective

Name:	Monica Miller
Institution:	Delgado Community College, New Orleans, LA
Age:	47
Major:	Hospitality Management

After August 29, 2005, I learned the meaning of self-motivation and persistence . . . especially persistence. Hurricane Katrina changed the way so many people live and the way so many people think about themselves. "Hanging on" and learning to motivate yourself for another day became a way of life, even for many people who thought they did not have the strength to do so. By having a chapter on motivation, engagement, and persistence in Cornerstone, you can learn some of the techniques to help you become more motivated, stronger, and endure even when it seems the odds are against you.

My whole life has been about self-motivation, persisting, growing stronger, and holding on. I am a single parent, a college student, and an abuse survivor. I've been unemployed, without an education, and worked full- and part-time in many areas. I was also a professional model for 16 years. I've taken giant steps and baby steps, forward steps and backward steps, and through it all, I learned that motivation and learning to help yourself are vital to your survival. I also learned that when you learn more about yourself and who you are and what you have to offer, you can help other people, too. I have learned that when you help yourself "hold on," you are also serving as a role model to help others "hold on."

In college, persisting or "holding on" will allow you to reach your dreams. You're going to face many challenges, but by learning some of the ins and outs of college life at the beginning of your college career, you will be ready to deal with most of the challenges that come your way. From financial aid to building healthier self-esteem to getting along with your professors, "holding on" will become a daily adventure and this chapter can help you become a student who will not "let go."

> "If you want to achieve worthwhile things in life, you must become a worthwhile person in your own self-development."
> —Brian Tracy

Success is built on motivation and self-engagement—the ability to absorb yourself in your own life, your own goals, your own beliefs, values, judgments, purpose, and behaviors. *Engagement* means that you have made a commitment to give your best to the endeavors you have chosen to undertake. You can read about motivation, study how others became motivated, and even emulate those whom you perceive as motivated but, the only person, place, or thing that can ever give you *internal motivation* is you. And, you have the power to make decisions that will help you remain in college and get your degree.

Dropping out of college is not uncommon. As a matter of fact, over 40 percent of the people who begin college never complete their degrees. Don't be mistaken in thinking that they dropped out because of their inability to learn.

Many leave because they made serious and irreparable mistakes early in their first year. Some students leave because they did not know how to manage their time, because they could not manage their money, because they couldn't get along with an instructor, or because they put partying above academics. And still, some leave because they simply could not figure out how "the system" worked and frustration, anger, disappointment, and fear got the best of them. Don't be led to believe that you have to be one of those students.

This chapter can help you:

- Understand the relationship between self-discovery and motivation.
- Grasp the relationship between motivation and personal/professional success.
- Examine your values, beliefs, and what makes you tick.

SCAN AND QUESTION

Take a few moments and **scan this chapter**. As you scan, **list five questions** for which you can expect to learn the answers while reading and studying Chapter 2.

Example
- What does the word character mean? (from page 39)
- What are the five characteristics of self-esteem? (from page 44)

My Questions

1. _____

_____ from page _____

2. _____

_____ from page _____

3. _____

_____ from page _____

4. _____

_____ from page _____

5. _____

_____ from page _____

Reminder: At the end of the chapter, come back to this page and answer these questions in your notebook, text margins, or online chapter notes.

- Evaluate your self-image and work to build healthier self-esteem.
- Understand the impact of your attitude on motivation and self-esteem.
- Make the most of your relationships with instructors and advisors.

- Use personal decorum to best advantage.
- Learn the strategies to persist in college.

We hope the information herein will help you find the means necessary to become more involved in your own learning and your personal development.

THE POWER AND PASSION OF MOTIVATION

Two Perspectives to Consider

Motivation can change your life! *Read that statement again. Motivation can change your life!* Ask any successful business person. Ask your favorite athlete or actor. Ask your classmates who pass every exam, project, or paper with an A. It is their burning desire—their aspiration to succeed, to live a motivated life, and reach their goals—that changed their lives and got them to where they are today. Motivation is a force that can transform your attitude, alter the course of your performance, intensify your actions, and illuminate your future. Motivation can help you live a life that reflects your true potential.

If you have a need or desire to change your motivation level or attitude toward personal and academic success, there are steps you can take to help you with this goal. Some of the steps described in this chapter will be easy and others will greatly challenge you, but taken seriously, each step can assist you in discovering who you really are, what you want in life, and help you find the motivation you need to change.

"The moment you begin to do what you really want to do, your life becomes a totally different kind of life."

—B. Fuller

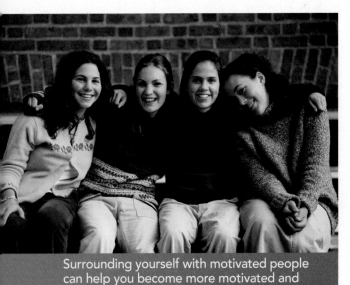

Surrounding yourself with motivated people can help you become more motivated and engaged.

There are two types of motivation: **external and internal**. *External motivation* is the weaker of the two because, as the title suggests, there are *external forces or people* causing you to do something. You do not own it. External motivators may be things or people such as your parents, spouse, or partner pushing you to complete your degree; your work supervisor telling you to do "x, y, or z" or you will be fired; or even your instructors giving you an exam to make sure you have read Chapter 2. You may do the things asked, but the reason for doing them is external.

Internal motivation is yours. It is *energy* inside of you—pushing YOU to go after what YOU want. Internal motivation is a strong and driving force because you own it. There are no external forces or people telling you that you must do it—it comes from your desire *to be something, to do something, to have something, or attain a goal that is near and dear to you.* Successful people live in the world of internal motivation or find ways to convert external motivation into internal motivation.

A simple example of this conversion may be that your current degree requires you to take classes in which you cannot understand their value or purpose. You may ask yourself, *"Why would a student majoring in criminal justice have to take two classes in college math?"* The class is hard, math is not your thing, the chapters are frustrating and difficult to read, and math has little to do with your interests, career goals, or overall life plan.

The challenge for you is to find an internal reason to move forward—a rationale for how math is going to help you, now and in the future. This is called internalizing.

By converting this external motivation (a requirement for your degree) into internal motivation (something that can help you), the math class will become easier because you have found a way to link it to your success, your goals, your money, your health, your family, or your overall life plan.

By internalizing, you see that good math skills can help you land a work-study job with the department chair for Criminal Justice. You find that good math skills can help you create an effective personal budget plan and help you save money. You find that the more you learn about the logic and process of math, the easier it is to solve problems and think more critically, thus helping you perform better in other classes. By silencing your negative self-talk about math, you are able to internalize the rewards of the class and own the outcome. You have made a conversion.

The following sections in this chapter will give you the framework to convert external motivators into internal motivators and help you become a more engaged person. The advice and strategies are included to assist you in discovering what you actually want out of life and focusing on what type of person you want to be. Also, our intention is to help you make the connection between self-discovery, clarifying your values, strengthening your character, and intensifying your motivation. This connection will help you convert external motivation into internal motivation.

> **ESSENTIAL CORNERSTONE**
>
> ## OPEN-MINDEDNESS
>
> How can being more open-minded help you internalize and "see" your goals?

THE CORNERSTONES FOR MOTIVATION AND RENEWAL

Twelve Powerful Tips and Strategies for Increasing Your Motivation, Discovering Your Inner Strength, and Persisting in College

"I am a winner."

"I fail at everything I do."

"I am a dedicated person."

"I don't really care about anything."

"I am a giving person."

"Life is about looking out for number one—me!"

"I am proud of my name."

"What's in a name?"

As you can see by the different perspectives above, your attitude and perspective on how you approach life, relationships, problems, and goals can mean the difference between being a motivated, inspired, and successful person or a weary, doubtful, and unsuccessful person.

As you scanned this chapter and its section headings, you may have asked yourself, what do *contaminated people* or *character* or *attitude* have to do with my motivation? The answer is simple. **Everything.** The reason that we have included this TWELVE-Point Plan in this chapter is to help you see that by focusing on you—becoming a person who knows where you're going, what you want, and what you have to offer, your motivation and passion for learning and growing will flourish. By knowing more about yourself, your institution, and your instructors, you can establish a clearer vision of your true potential.

POINT # 1

Overcome Your Doubts and Fears

"Successful people are the ones who can lay a firm foundation with the bricks others have thrown at them."

—David Brinkley

Success is a great motivator, but fear can be equally persuasive. Fear probably motivates more people than anything else. Unfortunately, fear motivates most people to hold back, to doubt themselves and to accomplish much less than they could have without the fear.

One of the biggest obstacles to reaching your potential may be your own personal fears. If you are afraid, you are not alone; everyone has fears. Isn't it interesting that *our fears are learned.* As a baby, you had only two fears: a fear of falling and a fear of loud noises. As you got older, you added to your list of fears. And, if you are like most people, you let your fears dominate parts of your life, saying things to yourself like: "What if I try and fail?" "What if people laugh at me for thinking I can do this?" or "What if someone finds out that this is my dream?"

You have two choices where fear is concerned. You can let fear dominate your life, or you can focus on those things you really want to accomplish, put your fears behind you, and *"go for it."* The people who are most successful in their fields admit they have fears, but they also confess that they work daily to overcome them because their desire to achieve and experience success is greater than the fear.

Dr. Robert Schuller, minister, motivational speaker, and author, once asked, ***"What would you attempt to do if you could not fail?"*** This is an important question for anyone, especially those trying to increase his or her motivation level. In the spaces below, work through this idea by answering the questions truthfully. We have adapted and expanded this question for the purpose of this exercise.

---

1. What would you attempt to do or what would your college major be if you could not fail? _____

_____

_____

2. Beyond the answers, *"I'm afraid"* or *"Fear,"* WHY are you not doing this "thing"? _____

_____

_____

_____

3. What has not doing this "thing" cost you? In other words, how have you suffered or what damages have been done to your life because you have not done this "thing"?

_____

_____

_____

4. On a scale of 1 to 10 (10 being the strongest), how often do you dream or think about doing this "thing"? 1   2   3   4   5   6   7   8   9   10

(continued)

5. If you did this "thing" and were successful at it, predict how your life would change? Be specific. _____

_____

_____

_____

_____

6. List five things (action steps) that you could begin doing today (by yourself or with another person), that could put you on the road to begin doing this "thing."

☐ _____

☐ _____

☐ _____

☐ _____

☐ _____

Consider using one of the goals sheets in the Appendix to develop an entire goal strategy to bring this "thing" to fruition in your life.

POINT # 2

Identify and Clarify What You Value in Life

If you have been highly motivated to accomplish a goal in the past, this achievement was probably tied to something you valued a great deal. Most of what you do in life centers on what is truly important to you. This is why it is important to identify and then clarify what you value in your life—what matters to you.

Values, self-esteem, motivation, and goal setting are all mixed up together, making it difficult to separate one from the other. **The things you work to accomplish** are directly connected to those things, ideas, and concepts that you value. Therefore, your ATTITUDE and ACTIONS are tied to your VALUES. If you value an attitude or belief, your actions will be centered on these ideals. If you love to spend time with your friends and this is valuable to you, you will make the time for this on a daily basis. Why? Because your friendships are a fundamental part of your value system. You like it so you are motivated by it and you do it. It is that simple. *Our values influence our actions.*

You were not born with your basic values. Your values were learned over the years and were shaped to a great extent by your parents, the school you attended, the community where you grew up, and the culture that nourished you. Because of your unique, personal background, you have

> "The greatest discovery of my generation is that we can alter the course of our lives simply by altering our attitude."
>
> —William James, Psychologist

What do you value right now? Time in class? Time with friends or family? Work? The chance for growth and future opportunities?

"Our souls are not hungry for fame, comfort, wealth, or power. These rewards create almost as many problems as they solve. Our souls are hungry for meaning, for the sense that we have figured out a way to live so that our lives matter."

—H. Kushner

developed a set of unique, personal values. To make sound decisions, set appropriate goals that are right for you, and manage your priorities accordingly, you must identify those things in your life that you hold in esteem.

Many of our values lay in our unconscious mind. They were put there by things we've heard, items we've read, music we've listened to, TV shows we've watched, and by what we may have seen others do. We may not even know that we value something until it is threatened or removed. Until you clarify what it is that YOU really value, you may be working to accomplish goals or pursuing career choices that someone else values, not you.

By having vague or poorly clarified values, you may be working toward something, believe something, or acting in a way that is not really who you are. This can cause you to wander aimlessly and become frustrated; eventually destroying your motivation level. **Values bring direction to your life and help you stay motivated.**

Below, you will find a wide and varied list of items. Read over them carefully and circle the ones you value in others and in you. Be careful and selective. DO NOT just randomly circle words. As a criteria for each word you circle ask yourself, "Can I defend why I value this in my life?" and "Is this truly something *I value* or something I was told to value and never questioned why?" If you value something and it is not on the list, add it to the spaces at the bottom.

Honesty	Stability	Hobbies	Books
Frankness	Affection	Punctuality	Respect
Sincerity	Open-mindedness	Reliability	Trustworthiness
Frugality	Wit / humor	Spontaneity	Devotion
Spirituality	Justice	Creativity	Caring
Attentiveness	Friendliness	Energy	Intellect
Fine dining	Conversational	Money	Security
Positivism	Beauty	Devotion	Enthusiasm
Organization	Commitment	Foresightedness	Giving
Control	Learning	Listening	Success
Athletic ability	Comfort	Knowledge	Courage
Safety	Thoughtfulness	Independence	Partying
Love	Fun	Excitement	Speaking
Reading	Friendship	Writing	Teamwork
Time alone	Family	Dependability	Walks
Exercise	Time with friends	Phone calls	Integrity
Service to others	Problem solving	Empowerment	Tolerance
Imagination	Modesty	Strength	Power
Winning	Self-esteem	Food	Change
Self-improvement	Goals	Risk taking	Optimism
Successful career	Forgiveness	Fairness	Direction in life
Working	Motivation	Trust	Mentoring
_____	_____	_____	_____
_____	_____	_____	_____
_____	_____	_____	_____
_____	_____	_____	_____

Now that you have circled or written what you value, choose the five that you value the most. In other words, if you were allowed to value ONLY five things in life, what five would you list below?

LIST   **RANK**

☐ _____   _____

☐ _____   _____

☐ _____   _____

☐ _____   _____

☐ _____   _____

In the space to the right of each value, rank them from 1 to 5 (1 being the least important to you, your life, your relationships, your actions, your education, and your career).

Examine Value #1. Where did this value originate? _____

_____

_____

Defend why this is the one thing you value more in life than anything else.

_____

_____

_____

How does this one value motivate you? _____

_____

_____

_____

POINT #3

Take Pride in Your Name and Personal Character

At the end of the day, the end of the month, the end of your career, and the end of your life, your name and your character are all that you have. Taking pride in developing your character and protecting your good name can be two powerful, motivational forces.

"*My name?*" you may ask. "*What does my name have to do with anything?*"

Imagine for a moment that you are working with a group of students on a project for your Anatomy class. The project is to receive a major grade, and you and your group will present your findings to a group of 100 students at a campus forum. Your group works hard, develops an effective research tool to gather information, and builds a product of which everyone is exceptionally proud. When you present the project, your group receives a standing ovation and earns an A. The name of each group member is read aloud as you stand to be recognized. Your name and project are also posted in a showcase. You are proud. Your hard work paid off. Your name now carries weight with your peers, and among the faculty. It feels good.

Protecting your reputation may seem "old fashioned," but taking pride in your name and character are two extraordinary traits.

LYDIA HAUSLER LEBOVIC

Jewish Holocaust Survivor
Auschwitz Concentration/Extermination Camp
Auschwitz, Poland, 1944

"Sweet Sixteen." Isn't that the moment of joy for so many female teens today? It is a milestone date when childhood passes and young adulthood arrives. One can legally drive and in many states, "Sweet Sixteen" signifies the age of consent.

My "Sweet Sixteen" was very different. Yes, I was dating, had a somewhat rebellious relationship with my mother, and socialized with friends, but in the countryside around me, World War II raged. In 1944 when I was 16, my family and I were ordered to pack 20 pounds of personal belongings and told that we

Lydia Lebovic, center, Auschwitz, 1944

were being taken to "the Ghetto," a holding area for Jews in my hometown of Uzhorod, Czechoslovakia, now a part of Ukraine. I understood that the situation was not good and that things were changing, but I had no real idea of how my life would forever be altered in the coming weeks, months, and years.

After two weeks in "the Ghetto," my family, friends, neighbors, and I were ordered onto cattle cars—60 to 80 per car—and told that we were being taken to Hungary to work in the corn and wheat fields. So there, in the darkness of night, our journey began—young, old, weak, strong, nursing mothers, and babies—all in the same cattle car with no water and only two buckets to use for a bathroom.

After two days of travel, the train stopped and the doors of the cattle car opened. My mother recognized that we were not in southern Hungary, but rather on

Conversely, your group slacks off; the project is poorly prepared and received by the audience and your instructor. Your group earns an F on the project. Your name is associated with this project and your name and grade are posted with every other group's. Yours is the only group to receive an F. It doesn't feel good.

Your name and your character are tied together in that one overlaps the other. If you have pride in your name, you will act in ways, and treat others in ways, that bring credit to your name. If you constantly act in a way that reflects your strong, reputable character, people will recognize this by your name. Your name carries weight when people respect you, your actions, and your work.

Basically, it comes down to this: ***Every time you make a choice, every time you complete a project, every time you encounter another person, you define your character and your name.*** Both are exclusively yours and you are responsible for their well being. If you are truly concerned about building

"Your character is determined by how you treat people who can do you no good and how you treat people who can't fight back."

—Abigail Van Buren

the Hungary/Poland border in the north. She took us aside in the car and told us of her suspicion—that we were being taken to Auschwitz concentration camp. After another two days on the train, we arrived at Auschwitz in the early dawn hours.

The doors of the cattle cars opened and the men were quickly separated from the women and the children from the adults. We were put into lines of five and marched forward. In front of every line was an SS officer. Quickly, I was pushed to the right and my mother and sister were pushed to the left. Little did I know at that point that those shoved to the right would be put to work and those shoved to the left would be dead by the evening. I never saw my mother or sister again after that moment. I never said goodbye. I was "Sweet Sixteen."

After the separation, my group was taken to a very large building and told to undress. We were completely shaven, sponged from head to toe with a bleach-like substance, showered, and given a uniform. We were then marched to the barracks where we would sleep 12–14 to a bed with 600 to 800 people per barracks. The black and white photo was taken as we marched toward the barracks from the shower facility and now hangs in the National Holocaust Museum in Washington, DC.

Some of the Jewish girls who had been in the camp for a while were considered "foremen." I remember approaching one such female. I asked her, "When do I get to see my mother and my sister?"

She took me by the arm and pointed me toward the billowing chimney of the crematory, "*You see that smoke? You see that ash? You smell that flesh burning? That's your mother. That's your sister.*" She walked away. I did not believe her at the time, but she was absolutely right. This realization remains the most distressing of all events in my life—past and present—that my mother and sister died in such a horrific manner. Gassed and cremated.

I remained in Auschwitz until I was shipped to the labor camp, Bergen-Belsen, in Germany. We were liberated on April 15, 1945. Upon liberation, I began working for the British Red Cross. Later that year, I was reunited with a friend of my brother and we were married in November of 1945. We moved to Chile in 1947 and then to Los Angeles, California, in 1963.

I now travel the nation speaking about the events of my life and delivering the message, "NEVER AGAIN." I write this essay to you for many reasons, but specifically to let you know this: The Holocaust did not ruin me. They did not destroy me. They did not destroy my belief in love. They did not destroy my faith in people. They did not destroy my religion or values. The events made me a stronger, more compassionate person. I went on to become a loving wife and mother, a successful businesswoman, and eventually a devoted grandmother. *I refused to be ruined.*

I encourage you to use the adversity in your life to make you stronger, more compassionate, more caring, and more helpful to mankind.

strong character and having credit to your name, this will be a force that motivates you. By taking your character and name into account when you submit projects, encounter people, and work in your profession, you are constantly motivated to do your very best to protect (or build) them both. You are motivated to ensure that your name and character are not damaged by giving less than you are capable of giving.

Character, from the Greek *charakter* (which means "to stamp," "to scratch or mark," or "to engrave") refers to the attributes that make up or distinguish you as an individual. In essence, your character is how your soul is "marked" or "engraved," and this is directly related to your ethical and moral behavior. You have a choice as to how your soul is engraved.

Who can you think of in your personal life or in the national spotlight that has reputable character and people think highly of him or her when they hear his or her name? _____

_____

Why is this person's character and name in good standing? _____

_____

_____

_____

What qualities does he or she possess that you admire? _____

_____

_____

Choose one and describe how you can bring this quality to fruition in your life. _____

_____

_____

_____

POINT #4
Cultivate and Protect Your Ethics and Integrity

Who are you when no one else is looking? Think about these questions: What if there were no rules or laws to govern your behavior? What if there were no consequences or ramifications for any of your actions? Let's pretend for a moment that you could never go to jail or face fines or be shunned for your words, actions, behaviors, or thoughts. If these statements came to pass, what would your life—or the lives of those you love—look like? This is one of the best ways to offer a practical definition of ethics. Basically, ethics is the *accepted* moral code or standard by which we all live, and that code is communicated many ways, including through our relationships with others. Codes of ethics vary from culture to culture, country to country, and group to group, but each carry with them certain rules by which members of that culture, country, or group are expected to follow.

Ethics, however, is about **much, much more** than following the law, adhering to your society's accepted code, or following your religion's teachings. Society, religion, and laws will usually contain ethical standards, but as argued in the article "What Is Ethics?" (Velasquez, 1987), entire societies can become corrupt and following that society's "moral" standard can have dire consequences. Nazi Germany is a perfect example of this situation. Consider America's slavery laws prior to the Civil War. Few people would now suggest those laws were "ethical." And think about the Christian Crusades, in which hundreds of thousands of people were murdered in the name of religion. Was that ethical?

Think back in history for a moment (and you won't have to think back too far), and consider some national and international leaders, entertainers, sports figures, or even local professionals who, at the height of his or her "fame" made paramount ethical mistakes that cost him or her dearly. Richard Nixon. Michael Vick. Barry Bonds. Bill Clinton. Martha Stewart. Prince Harry. O. J. Simpson. Each of these people, to varying degrees, failed to maintain the *accepted* moral code of his or her community and the consequences were grave. From jail sentences to public shame, each suffered a demoralizing defeat and a tarnished public image due to their ethical errors.

"Have the courage to say no. Have the courage to face the truth. Do the right thing because it is right. These are the magic keys to living your life with integrity."

—Clement Stone

there are several things that you need to do. First, be truthful with yourself and examine the amount of time you spent on the project. Did you really give it your best? Next, review the requirements for the assignment. Did you miss something? Did you take an improper or completely wrong focus? Did you omit some aspect of the project? Did you turn the project in late?

Next, consider the following questions, as they can contribute to your total understanding of material, projects, and expectations.

<table>
<tr><td>ESSENTIAL CORNERSTONE</td></tr>
<tr><td>ACCOUNTABILITY</td></tr>
<tr><td>How can accepting responsibility for your grades help you become more accountable in the future?</td></tr>
</table>

- ☐ Did you attend class regularly?
- ☐ Did you come to class prepared and ready for discussion?
- ☐ Did you ask questions in class for clarification?
- ☐ Did you meet with the instructor during office hours?
- ☐ Did you seek outside assistance in places such as the writing center or math lab?
- ☐ Did you ask your peers for assistance or join a peer study/focus group?

These activities can make the difference between success and failure with a project or a class.

If you are truly concerned about the grade, talk to your instructor about the assignment. Ask him or her what is considered to be the most apparent problem with your assignment, and ask how you might improve your studying or preparing for the *next* assignment.

Above all, don't get into an argument over the grade. In 99 percent of the cases, this will not help. Also, make sure that *the instructor is your first point of contact*. Unless you have spoken with him or her *first* and exhausted all options with him or her, approaching the department chair, the dean, the vice president, or the president will more than likely result in your being sent directly back to the instructor.

Accepting Criticism as a Growth Opportunity

If you receive a grade or comment than is less than you desired, think about the following tips for accepting criticism:

- Try to remember—the comment, criticism, or grade is about a paper or project, *not about you personally*.
- Don't freak out—staying composed can help you think and act appropriately.
- If you are confused about the criticism, ask the instructor to explain his or her comment in greater detail.
- Listen before you respond—don't attack the person offering the criticism.
- Be open-minded—ask for help in making the project or paper more appropriate next time.
- Don't make excuses.
- *Valid, constructive* criticism can help you grow—take the advice and make it work for you next time.

POINT #12

Work Hard to Persist

It is estimated that each year, nearly 40 percent of the people who begin their college studies do not enroll for a second year. The national college dropout rate for public two-year colleges is 48 percent. The average college dropout rate for public four-year colleges is 32 percent (ACT 2000).

> "In order to be successful, you have to last."
>
> —Anonymous

SUCCESSFUL DECISIONS

JoAnne was a very shy lady who had been out of school for 27 years. When she entered her first class, she was stunned to see so many younger people and to learn that everyone seemed to have more in depth computer skills than she did.

Horrified that her first assignment was to include a chart created in Microsoft Excel, she thought about dropping the class. *"How am I going to ever* *learn how to turn data into a chart and insert it into a document by next week,"* she thought. She even heard a classmate grumbling about dropping the class, too.

Determined that she was not going to be beaten, JoAnne decided to go to the computer lab and ask for help. Within an hour, she had learned how to make a simple chart and paste it into a document.

JoAnne made a *successful decision.*

The age-old scare tactic for first-year students—"Look to your left, look to your right; one of those people will not graduate with you"—is not far from the truth. But the good news (actually, the great news) is that you do not have to become a statistic. You do not have to drop out of classes or college. You have the power to earn your degree or certificate. Sure, you may have some catching up to do or face a few challenges, but the beauty of college is that if you want help, you can get help.

Below, you will find some powerful, helpful tips for persisting in college. Using only a few of them can increase your chances of obtaining your degree. Using all of them virtually ensures it!

- Visit your advisor or counselor frequently and establish a relationship with him or her. Take his or her advice. Ask questions. Use your advisor as a mentor.
- Register for the classes in which you place. It is unwise to register for Math 110 if you placed in Math 090 or English 101 if you placed in English 095. It will only cost you money, heartache, time, and possibly a low GPA.
- Use every academic service that you need that the college offers, from tutoring sessions to writing centers; these are essential tools to your success.
- Work hard to learn and understand your "learning style." This can help you in every class in which you enroll. Chapter 7 will assist you with this endeavor.
- Work hard to develop a sense of community. Get to know a few people on campus such as a special faculty member, a secretary, another student, or anyone that you can turn to for help.
- Join a club or organization. Research proves that students who are connected to the campus through activities drop out less.
- After reading Chapter 1, "Thrive," concentrate on setting realistic, achievable goals. Visualize your goals. Write them down. Find a picture that represents your goal and post it so that you can see your goal every day.
- Work hard to develop and maintain a sense of self-esteem and self-respect. The better you feel about yourself, the more likely you will reach your goals.
- Learn to budget your time as wisely as you budget your money. You've made a commitment to college and it will take a commitment of time to bring your degree to fruition.
- If you have trouble with an instructor, don't let it fester. Make an appointment to speak with him or her and work through the problem. Be respectful.
- If you get bored in class or feel that the class is not going to benefit you, remember that it is a required class and you will always have a few boring classes during your college career. Stick to it and it will be over soon.
- If you feel your instructor doesn't care, it may be true. Some don't. This is where you have to apply the art of self-management.

- Find some type of strong, internal motivation to sustain you through the tough times—and there will be tough times.
- Focus on the future. Yes, you're taking six classes while your friends are off partying, but in a few years, you'll have something that no party could ever offer, and something that no one can ever take away . . . your very own college degree.
- Choose optimism. Approach each day with a positive and upbeat attitude, even if it is Tuesday and you have your two hardest classes. Today is the day you're going to have a breakthrough!
- Move beyond mediocrity. Anyone can be average. If college were easy, everybody would have a college degree. You will need to learn to bring your best to the table for each class.
- Focus on your career choice. Can you do what you want to do without a college degree? That is perhaps the most important question when it comes to persistence. Can you have what you want, do what you want, be who you want to be without this degree?

Surround yourself with people who are going places, who love to learn, and who have a passion for the future. It can be contagious.

As instructors, we wish you every success imaginable. Use us as resources, contact us, ask us questions, trust us, visit us, and allow us to help you help yourself.

THINK ABOUT IT

Reflections for Success

Motivation can change your life. Healthy self-esteem can change your life. Developing a strong and lasting set of ethical standards can change your life. *You* can change your life. This chapter has been about self-discovery and defining what you value, what role your attitude plays in your motivation, how to surround yourself with positive, optimistic people, and how to build your integrity and character. By focusing on YOU and determining what is important to your college studies, your career, your relationships, and your personal life, you can develop a vision of your future. If you can see your future, *really see it*, then you are more likely to be motivated to achieve it. Remember, we are motivated by what we value. As you continue through the quarter or semester and work toward personal and professional motivation, consider the following ideas:

- ☐ Convert external motivators into internal motivation.
- ☐ Use the power of positive thinking and surround yourself with positive people.
- ☐ Step outside your comfort zone.
- ☐ Use your values to drive your life-statement.
- ☐ Clear up your past by forgiving those who hurt you.
- ☐ Do one thing every day to strengthen your self-esteem.
- ☐ Turn negative thoughts into positive energy.
- ☐ Don't give in to defeat.
- ☐ View adversity as a stepping-stone to strength.
- ☐ Picture yourself as optimistic and motivated.

Good luck to you as you begin developing the motivation and positive attitude you need to be successful in your studies and beyond.

"The thing always happens that you believe in; and the belief in a thing makes it happen."

—Frank Lloyd Wright

passages
An Activity for Critical Thinking and Career Development

On page 9 of Chapter 1 and inside the front cover, you read **The Ten Essential Cornerstones for Personal and Professional Success.** They are:

Passion	Motivation
Knowledge	Resourcefulness
Creativity	Adaptability
Open-mindedness	Communication
Accountability	Vision

The following chapter-end activity will ask you to use several of these **Essential Cornerstones** to help you put your Guiding Statement into action.

Copy your Guiding Statement as written on page 49 of this chapter:

_____

_____

_____

How will your Guiding Statement help you . . .

Become more open minded? _____

_____

_____

_____

_____

_____

_____

Increase your self-motivation and passion for learning? _____

_____

_____

_____

_____

_____

Network and connect with other people? _____

_____

_____

_____

_____

_____

An old quote says, "*No man is an island.*" Basically, this is true. You would literally have to be shipwrecked on an island to be free of relationships with other humans, but you would still have relationships with nature, the animals, birds, and reptiles on the island. People simply do not live alone. We are constantly communicating even when we think we may not be and even when we are not trying to do so. This is one of the beauties and curses of communication.

The ability to know yourself and how to communicate with others; to understand them, to work with them, and to manage conflicts that may arise are some of *the most* valuable tools you will ever learn how to use. Effective communication determines so much about the quality of your life including aspects of your relationships, your romances, your career, your future, your friends, your values, your ethics, and, indeed, your character. *This chapter can help you:*

- Understand the power and magnitude of communication
- Learn the essential skills of interpersonal communication
- Understand the role and power of ethics and personal character
- Understand and enhance your Emotional Intelligence
- Learn why relationships are important
- Develop positive and rewarding communities
- Learn about cultures that differ from your own
- Learn how to appreciate other cultures
- Navigate and learn how to manage conflict

Addressing various aspects of interpersonal communication, emotional intelligence, and relationships is important to your success as a student, employee, and citizen. This chapter examines these topics so that can learn to communicate and relate with others more effectively and ultimately, achieve your true potential.

SCAN AND QUESTION

Take a few moments and **scan this chapter**. As you scan, **list five questions** you can expect to learn the answers to while reading and studying Chapter 3.

Example
- What does interpersonal communication really mean? (from page 62)
- What is Emotional Intelligence? (from page 66)

My Questions:

1. _____

_____ from page _____

2. _____

_____ from page _____

3. _____

_____ from page _____

4. _____

_____ from page _____

5. _____

_____ from page _____

Reminder: At the end of the chapter, come back to this page and answer these questions in your notebook, text margins, or online chapter notes.

INTERPERSONAL COMMUNICATION

Just What Is It, Anyway, and What's the Big Deal?

Communication is not something we do **to people**, rather it is something that is done **between people**. Communication can take on a variety of forms such as oral speech, the written word, body movements and even yawns. All of these actions communicate something to another person. When thinking about your interpersonal communication encounters, remember this: **Communication cannot be stopped.**

> "Interpersonal communication is important to our life happiness. When our involvements are satisfying, we find ourselves happier in general."
>
> —D. G. Myers

Almost every single moment of every single day of every single week, you are involved in some type of communication activity. The activity may be speaking, listening, or writing, but those are not the only types of communication. You also receive a great deal of information from the Internet, Webcasts, TV, billboards, music, video games, cell phones, BlackBerries, and print material such as newspapers and magazine articles. Many types of communication are all around you every day.

Yes, communication can and does involve speaking (sometimes public speaking), but more often than not, communication can be the simple act of speaking with a friend or coworker, listening to someone, or watching a person's nonverbal body language. Each of these acts makes up the communication spectrum. Collectively, they are often referred to as interpersonal communication.

Basically, the communication process involves **six elements**: the source, the message, the channel, receiver, barriers, and feedback. Consider Figure 3.1.

Barriers (represented by the red lines in Figure 3.1) are things that can interfere with the source, the message, the channel, or the receiver. They can occur anywhere

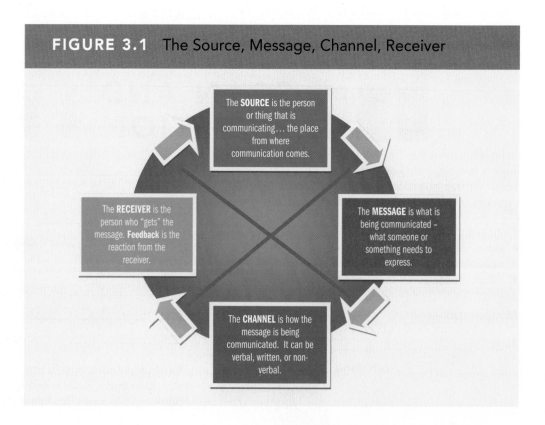

FIGURE 3.1   The Source, Message, Channel, Receiver

The **SOURCE** is the person or thing that is communicating… the place from where communication comes.

The **MESSAGE** is what is being communicated – what someone or something needs to express.

The **CHANNEL** is how the message is being communicated. It can be verbal, written, or non-verbal.

The **RECEIVER** is the person who "gets" the message. **Feedback** is the reaction from the receiver.

within the communication process and can include things like external noise, internal noise (self-talk), interference, and poor communication habits. Your emotions, experiences, social norms, communication expectations, and prejudices can also be barriers to effective communication.

Feedback in any response from the listener.

Interpersonal communication is "a dynamic form of communication between two (or more) people in which the messages exchanged significantly influence their thoughts, emotions, behaviors, and relationships" (McCornack, 2007). The messages in interpersonal communication are not static like the words in a book, a written letter, or a text message; they are fluid and constantly changing, causing your relationships to change along with them. Interpersonal communication is a powerful force that helps us build effective, meaningful relationships. When we feel a connection to another person and strive to see their viewpoints and understand their emotions and points of view, this takes us closer to them. Interpersonal communication can help us with this endeavor.

> ### ESSENTIAL CORNERSTONE:
>
> ## COMMUNICATION
>
> How can becoming more adept at developing positive relationships help you with your career aspirations?

McCornack (2007) suggests that there are three interpersonal communication goals: Self-presentation, Instrumental, and Relationship. *Self-presentation* goals help us present ourselves to others in a particular fashion and help others see us as we wish to be seen. *Instrumental* goals help us present information in a way so that we get what we want or need from another person. Finally, **Relationship** goals help us build meaningful, lasting, and effective relationships with other people.

Later in this chapter, we will discuss how to use interpersonal communication to your best advantage in understanding others, learning from others, celebrating cultures, building lasting relationships, and dealing with eventual conflicts.

WHY IS INTERPERSONAL COMMUNICATION IMPORTANT?
The Story of One Wild Boy

You do NOT have a choice. If you are in the presence of another human being, you are communicating. Period! Silence is communication. Smiling is communication. Reading a newspaper is communication. Turning your back to the wall and hiding your face from everyone is communication. It is just the law of nature—if you are around one or more people, you are communicating with them. With that said, understanding the impact of effective communication can help you in the interview, on the job, and with every type of personal and professional relationship throughout your life.

Interpersonal communications is about enriching and building positive and lasting relationships.

Consider this: nothing in your life is more important than effective communication. Nothing! Your family is not. Your friends are not. Your career is not. Your religion is not. Your money is not. "*Why?*" you may ask. "*That is a harsh statement.*" We make this assertion because without effective communication, you would not have a relationship with your family and friends. You would not have a career or money or even religious beliefs. Communication is that important. In fact, it is so important that communication gives us our identity. That's right. Without communication, *we would not even know that we were human beings.*

Take into account the true story of the Wild Boy of Aveyron. This story has been documented in many science, psychology, sociology, and communication texts over the years. In January of 1800, a gardener in Aveyron, France, went out one morning to collect vegetables for the day. To his surprise, he heard an unusual moaning and groaning. Upon further inspection, he found a "wild boy" squatting in the garden eating vegetables as an animal might do. This boy showed no signs or behaviors associated with human beings. He appeared to be 12–14 years old, but stood just a little more than four feet tall. He had scars and burns on his body and his face showed traces of smallpox. His teeth were brown and yellow and his gums were receding. It can only be assumed that when he was an infant, he was abandoned in the woods and left to die. It has also been suggested that someone may have tried to kill him as an infant because of the long scar across his trachea (Lane, 1976).

> "I see communication as a huge umbrella that covers and affects all that goes on between human beings."
>
> —Joseph Adler

When he was found, he could not speak and barely stood erect. "*He had no sense of being a human in the world. He had no sense of himself as a person related to other persons*" (Shattuck, 1980). Because of his lack of communication and contact with other humans, he had no identity, no language, no self-concept, and no idea that he was even a human being in a world of human beings. Of course, he had no religious beliefs or relationships. *That* is how **powerful** communication is in our world today—it gives us our identity. It lets us know we are HUMAN!

Communication is also important for many other reasons such as:

- Survival
- Establishing relationships and building friendships
- Relating to family members
- Gaining knowledge
- Finding enjoyment and succeeding at work
- Entertainment
- Expressing opinions and explaining details
- Articulating our desires and wishes
- Promoting health and stress reduction
- Motivating and influencing others
- Managing conflict and overcoming adversity

The more you learn about all types of human communication, the stronger you become in each of the areas above and the more effective and powerful your communication efforts become.

THE POWER OF WORDS

The benefits and value of written, oral and interpersonal communication cannot be measured. The power of words has changed nations, built and demolished civilizations, preserved and destroyed traditions, freed and enslaved masses, and prevented and caused destruction. Think of the powerful words written or spoken by Dr. Martin Luther King Jr., Josef Stalin, Maya Angelou, Booker T. Washington, Franklin Roosevelt, the Khmer Rouge, Frederick Douglass, George W. Bush, Hillary Clinton, Steven Spielberg, Adolf Hitler, and Princess Diana. Good or bad, right or wrong, appropriate or inappropriate, their words changed many lives.

> "People may forget what you say. People may forget what you do. But, people NEVER forget how you make them feel."
>
> —Anonymous

Think about a time when someone said something hurtful to you. Do you remember how those words made you feel? You may have been having a perfectly fine day, but when you heard those words your day was ruined. Conversely, think of a time when you were down and out and someone said something positive to you. Do you remember how this changed your outlook? *That* is how powerful words can be.

Numerous studies have reported that clear communication is imperative for one's success. In the marketplace of ideas, the person who communicates clearly is also the person who is seen as thinking clearly. Effective communication skills not only help you secure a job but are also necessary to help you keep a job, get along with others, and move up the career ladder. The ability to communicate tops the list of skills that are sought after by employers all over America . . . and beyond. A survey by the Advanced Public Speaking Institute (2007) found that executives who earn more than $250,000 per year believed that their communication skill was the number one factor that carried them to the top. Other surveys reveal that the most important thing a college graduate can learn to do is communicate well. This includes understanding interpersonal communication and the power of words.

The communication between two people can be very positive or powerfully negative, depending on the words you use.

YOUR SELF-CONCEPT

How You Feel About YOU Determines How You Communicate with and Feel About Others

Consider this: The words you say to others come from the way you look at and think of yourself. Yes, your self-concept drives many, if not most, of your actions, including your communication efforts and treatment of others. "Your self-concept is your image of who you are. It's how you perceive yourself; your feelings and thoughts about your strengths and weaknesses and your abilities and limitations" (DeVito, 2006). Self-concept develops from our experiences, our gender, our sexual orientation, our religion, our socioeconomic background, our association with others, and our evaluations of our own thoughts and behaviors.

> "We evaluate people based on how we feel about ourselves. We like in others the traits we like in ourselves, and we dislike in others the traits we dislike in ourselves."
>
> —S. McCornack

Having healthy self-esteem and a positive self-concept is not so much about "feeling good" as it is "feeling right." There is a huge difference between the two. "Feeling *good* cannot make you feel right, but feeling *right* can make you feel good" (Sherfield, 2004). This feeling of "right" has nothing to do with right versus wrong, but much to do with feeling authentic, genuine, and real inside. Having a positive self-concept is much like slipping into an old recliner. When you sit down in it, it just feels comfortable—it feels like you are "home." Sure, there may be other chairs in your house that sit well and may even be comfortable, but nothing fits you like *your* chair. This chair feels beyond good to you; it feels right.

Whether you feel right about yourself or not, your self-concept does determine how you interact and communicate with others. "Your awareness of your self, self-esteem, and self-concept all shape your interpersonal communication" (McCornack, 2007).

Examine the Self-Fulfilling Prophecy chart in Figure 3.2.

FIGURE 3.2 Your Self-Concept

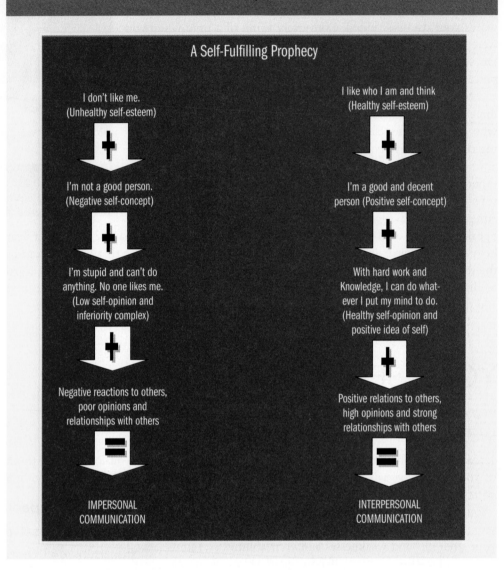

YOUR EMOTIONAL INTELLIGENCE (EI)

Understanding How EI Affects your Communication Efforts, Self-Concept, and Relationships

If you have ever heard the old saying "Think before you act," you were actually being told to use your emotional intelligence.

Everyone knows that **IQ** (Intelligence Quotient) is important to success in college, work, and life. Many experts also believe that **EI** (Emotional Intelligence) is just as important to being successful because it helps people cope with social and emotional demands in daily life. "Emotional intelligence is the single most influencing variable in personal achievement, career success, leadership, and life satisfaction" (Nelson and Low, 2003).

Exactly what is EI? EI includes all the skills and knowledge necessary for building strong, effective relationships. EI includes the ability to motivate oneself, to manage one's own personal emotions and impulses, to control one's emotions when involved in relationships, and to understand and interpret personal emotions and feelings, as well as those of others. Simply stated, EI is understanding how you and others feel and managing those feelings in a rational manner that is good for both parties.

We all have emotions and feelings that influence our actions significantly. "Emotions are strong feelings and physiological changes that prepare the body for immediate action" (Nelson and Low, 2003). It is important to master emotional intelligence skills in order to direct your feelings and emotions in an appropriate manner.

Your emotions can manifest themselves in a wide range from happiness to sadness, serenity to anger, and apathy to passion. You need to be able to recognize each of these emotions and employ appropriate skills for dealing with them whether you are feeling these emotions personally or someone else is. Some other often-experienced emotions are fear, joy, surprise, hate, sorrow, and rage. The most common emotions are known as primary emotions and include sadness, happiness, fear and anger. These emotions are universally recognized by people of most cultures. By recognizing these basic emotions, we can usually determine how to relate to another person.

We actually have a comprehensive emotional system that includes **emotions** (how we react), the **thinking or logical mind** (one that is logical and makes sound decisions), **the emotional mind** (the one that feels and tends to act impulsively and sometimes illogically), **passion** (the heart) and the **amygdala (**the remembering component). Emotions originate in the brain. If you have emotional intelligence skills, your thinking mind and emotional mind should function interactively, making it more likely that you will make sound, rational decisions. In other words, you will *think* before you *act*. Ideally, these two minds operate in harmony, creating balance between the thinking mind and the emotional mind, but if the emotional mind overshadows the thinking mind, a person might make highly emotional decisions that can be viewed as irrational.

The amygdala, a set of nuclei in the brain, is part of the limbic system that is responsible for regulating emotions. The amygdala is most commonly associated with the emotions of fear and anxiety (Wisegeek.com, 2008). This part of the emotional system can hijack your body and cause your heart to beat faster, your breathing rate to dramatically increase, and your reflexes to be increased.

THE AMYGDALA

Don't let this word or concept frighten you. If you have never heard "amygdala," (pronounced ah-MIG-da-la), you're not alone. Most people have not. But, this concept is important for you to understand the overall aspects of EI. The amygdala is simply a part of the emotional system and can cause us to go into default behavior based on what we remember from a similar experience. Do I use **fight** or **flight?** Basically, the amygdala is there to protect us when we become afraid or emotionally upset. When influenced by the amygdala, everything becomes about us. We become more judgmental. We don't stop to think about generational differences or the other person's feelings or the relationship. The

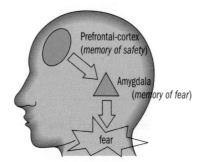

amygdala can trigger an emotional response before the cortical centers of the brain have had time to understand what is happening, and this situation causes us to have problems with others.

The amygdala remembers frustrations, fears, hurt feelings, previous anger. The tension from these experiences causes the amygdala to go into default behavior—we feel before we think—and this can create a potentially explosive situation. The chemicals released by the amygdale stay in our system for three to four hours, keeping us in a defensive mode for an extended period in which the thinking mind does not rationally consider what is happening.

If there is an argument, confrontation, or disagreement, in many cases neither person will hear the other very clearly because both have an amygdala and they are perhaps both in a defensive, fighting mode, using no logical thinking patterns. When such a situation arises, it is important that at least one of the people use his or her thinking mind to rationally analyze the scenario and make a wise decision.

The most important thing to know about the amygdala is that it remembers experiences (frustrations, fear, anger) and causes us to prepare for "fight or flight." Therefore, if you had a bad experience several years ago and are placed in a similar situation, the amygdala will remember and trigger emotions that cause the body to respond. Everything becomes about you with no thoughts of the other person's feelings. These feelings often cause people to bypass their thinking brain (logic) and to respond with angry words or actions. You need to be aware of this function and learn to manage reflex behaviors that are tied to the past but are triggered by a present experience.

It is also important to know that these feelings can stay in the body for three to four hours, keeping you in a defensive mode that could easily cause you to get in an argument with someone who had nothing to do with the previous experience or the current disagreement you just had. Because everyone has an amygdala, neither person in an argument may hear the other unless they have learned to control their emotions using rational thinking.

Think about one experience you've had in which your negative emotions took over. Perhaps it was anger, fear, sorrow, hatred, or rage. What was the situation and where were you when it happened? _____

_____

_____

_____

What were the negative consequences to you (or someone else) because of your emotions?

_____

_____

_____

How would you react differently today? Why? _____

_____

_____

_____

Emotions are not like thoughts. Rather than creating rational thought patterns, emotions cause you to react. Reacting can become a habitual pattern if you allow your emotions to control your actions. If you REACT instead of ACTING AFTER MAKING LOGICAL DECISIONS, your relationships will not be very effective and people will begin to see you as a "hot head" or "trouble maker" and your interpersonal communication efforts will suffer.

There are four dimensions of emotional intelligence, according to Nelson and Low (2003):

- Interpersonal skills
- Leadership skills
- Self-management skills
- Intrapersonal skills

To function at your highest level, you need to employ emotional intelligence in each area.

The **interpersonal** dimension relates to how assertive you are in dealing openly and honestly with people and in expressing your true feelings in a direct, respectful manner. This dimension includes the need to control your anger as well as overcoming any tendencies you might have to show deference to everyone's else's ideas rather than expressing your own in a positive, assertive manner.

The **leadership** dimension includes mastering business and personal skills of empathy, listening, and decision making. When developing leadership skills, it is important to be able to trust others and to act in such a way that people trust you. You cannot become an effective leader if people don't trust you. You cannot develop a skill that is more important to your personal and professional success than empathetic listening. Listening is discussed in detail in Chapter 8.

> "Empathy is your pain in my heart."
> —Indian proverb

Self-management skills are closely related to motivation. Motivation is all about directing oneself to achieve goals. This category includes drive strength, commitment ethic, time management, and positive change (Nelson and Low, 2003). Drive is simply your ability to direct your energy and ambitions toward doing what is necessary to reach your goals. Commitment relates to your ability to finish the job whether it is a short-term task or a long-term project. Time management, as it relates to emotional intelligence, is your ability to organize tasks, assignments, and goals around a personal time schedule and to complete a variety of assignments in a timely manner. "Successfully intelligent people carefully formulate strategies for problem solving. In particular, they focus on long-range planning rather than rushing in and then later having to rethink their strategies" (Sternberg, 1996).

The **intrapersonal** dimension is all about how you feel inside about yourself. In a nutshell, it is about your self-esteem. Self-esteem, in the context of relationships, is about exuding confidence and positive feelings when you interact with others. No one can anoint you with self-esteem. It has to be earned by paying the price to be very good at something. Working smart and hard usually equate to success in reaching established goals. With success comes self-esteem.

Becoming an EI Master

Have you ever known people whom you consider to be exceptional at building positive, loving, caring relationships? They succeed in business and in life and seem to do so with little effort. They demonstrate the capacity to recognize their own feelings and those of others, to motivate themselves and others, and to perform their work in an outstanding manner, treat everyone fairly, and have empathy and compassion for others.

Think of one person you admire because of relationship building ability. Name several characteristics you admire about this person:

1. _____
2. _____
3. _____
4. _____
5. _____

Which of these characteristics would you most like to emulate? List the top three in the space below:

1. _____
2. _____
3. _____

Now design a personal plan for developing these characteristics. As you design your plan, think about what emotional concerns you have that need to be addressed. What are strengths that you have already developed that will enable you to accomplish this plan? What are self-talk statements that you can employ to boost your confidence? Discuss any negative emotions that you often feel (anger, fear, sorrow) that need to be addressed in your plan. Finally, discuss how you will begin to express healthy emotions at school, work, and at home. **Use your Goal Sheets found in the Appendix of this book to develop your EI Plan.**

"Many people prefer emotions to reasoning."

—M. Beyle

Because emotional intelligence skills and knowledge are so important to your success in all areas of your life, you are encouraged to read extensively about this subject and to design your own plan for dealing with emotional concerns. To begin this process, take the following assessment to determine where you stand at the moment with regards to your emotional intelligence.

THE EMOTIONAL RESPONSE ASSESSMENT

(© 2008, Sherfield and Moody.)

Consider the following 16 questions. Place a check mark beside the statements that sound like something you would say, something you feel, or something with which you agree. Be totally honest with yourself.

_____ 1. I often feel as if people are out to "get me."

_____ 2. I am easily frustrated by the behavior of others.

_____ 3. I am often annoyed by the attitudes, values, and beliefs of my family and friends.

_____ 4. Basically, people are not very kind or good to each other.

_____ 5. Most people are immoral and sinful and often lie.

_____ 6. Sometimes, people just have to be rude to others to get their attention.

_____ 7. When people are mean to me, I get mean right back at them. They deserve it.

_____ 8. When people are wrong, they are wrong! Period. No excuse.

_____ 9. I hate inconsiderate people.

_____ 10. When someone cuts me off in traffic or pulls out in front of me, I feel like I just have to "get them back."

(continued)

_____ 11. Sometimes, intimidation is necessary.

_____ 12. If I'm sad or angry or mad, I show it. There is no need to try to hide it.

_____ 13. There is nothing wrong with being defensive or aggressive. You have to protect yourself.

_____ 14. Verbal aggression is better than hitting someone.

_____ 15. Who cares if you're from another culture or country. You're in America now. Assimilate and act like an American.

_____ 16. Once you betray me, that is it! I'll never, ever trust you again.

Now, add up the number of check marks.   TOTAL _____

1–3   You have a low degree of hostility and your emotional intelligence is high.

4–9   You have a moderate degree of hostility and your emotional intelligence needs to be monitored quite frequently.

10–16   You have a high degree of hostility and your emotional intelligence skills need to be constantly monitored to ensure fairness and equality to others.

EMOTIONAL MANAGEMENT

Understanding and Managing Emotions for a Happy, Productive, and Rewarding Life

We discuss emotional management in this chapter on communications because a person's emotions have a great deal of impact on how we communicate and relate to others. Emotional management covers a broad spectrum of all the essential emotions that are required for good interpersonal relationships and interactions with others. The spectrum of human emotions ranges from depression to joy and empowerment.

> "Take advantage of every opportunity to practice your communication skills so that when important occasions arise, you will have the gift, the style, the sharpness, the clarity, and the emotions to affect other people."
>
> —Jim Rohn

While the spectrum includes highly desirable feelings like optimism, hopefulness, enthusiasm, and happiness, the range of feelings also includes emotions that are undesirable, emotions that if left unchecked can cause serious problems at school, at work, at home, and in relationships. Some of the emotions on the darker side of the spectrum include depression, guilt, unworthiness, and a feeling of powerlessness.

Most people experience the less desirable emotions at one time or another. Problems arise, however, when one feels these emotions most of the time. Such deep-seated emotions that have lasted for a long time need to be discussed with a professional counselor. Treatment of negative emotions may be necessary before a person can move forward and become able to experience the joy and optimism that the bright side of emotions bring. Some of these emotions can be crippling at work and in other relationships if they have existed for a long time with no treatment to bring them under control.

The purpose of discussing emotional management in this chapter is to have you understand the broad range of emotions you might experience, as well as making you aware that people with whom you are interacting are also experiencing these same emotions. As you prepare to move into the workforce, you need to be aware of the emotional spectrum in others and know that you may work with people who have difficulty managing their emotions. You may have experiences with supervisors and colleagues who are having problems controlling their emotions in a healthy manner. Although you cannot control colleagues' and supervisors' behavior, you can understand why they react the way they do and perhaps learn to adjust your actions and reactions accordingly at work.

If you have relationships or interactions with people away from work who are not supportive of you and who are inhibiting and threatening and perhaps even physically abusive, you need to move away from these people. No matter how much you might care about a person, if he or she is abusive to you in any way, you need to run—not walk—away from that person because this type of behavior often escalates. If you personally have difficulty controlling rage or anger, you might want to explore anger management sessions, which can help you address this behavior. Again, there are counseling centers on your campus to help you understand and make decisions related to abusive behavior. The important point is to get help in dealing with emotional behavior that is out of control.

To become the successful, happy person you want to be and to have lasting interpersonal relationships, you must learn to manage the entire spectrum of your personal emotions from the extreme **negative side** to the extreme **positive side**. This spectrum ranges from the darker side of your emotions or extreme negative pole to the optimistic side or extreme positive pole. Study the spectrum of emotions illustrated in the figure below. Think about which of these emotions you experience frequently and where you are located most of the time on this emotional continuum.

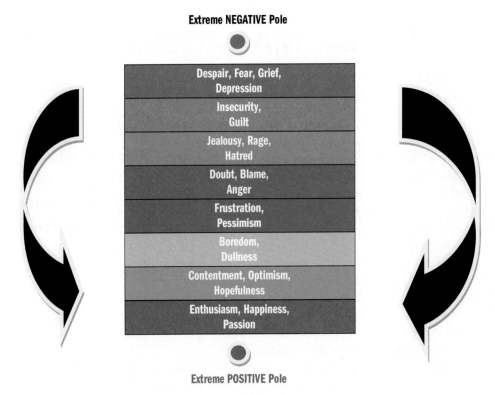

Extreme NEGATIVE Pole

| Despair, Fear, Grief, Depression |
| Insecurity, Guilt |
| Jealousy, Rage, Hatred |
| Doubt, Blame, Anger |
| Frustration, Pessimism |
| Boredom, Dullness |
| Contentment, Optimism, Hopefulness |
| Enthusiasm, Happiness, Passion |

Extreme POSITIVE Pole

The darkest part, which we will refer to as the extreme negative pole, includes the emotions of despair, grief, depression, and fear. When we are experiencing these emotions, we feel disconnected and powerless to help ourselves. Some of these emotions may be temporary and may subside after a while. Depression, on the other hand, may require counseling in order a person to heal and move forward. With some people, these emotions can be managed on some days and become out of control on others. Typically, an emotionally healthy person is positioned at the bottom of the spectrum or at least no further to the top than the emotions of boredom and dullness. Ideally, you will be positioned in a spectrum ranging from contentment to passion most of the time.

As you can see, the management of your personal emotional spectrum can impact you greatly at work. This relatively new concept is being given a great deal of attention in the corporate world. Faced with a declining pool of highly skilled employees, companies are paying more attention to the tactics used by their managers. Not only will you find it helpful and necessary to manage your emotions at work, but you also will be able to apply emotional management techniques at home with family and with friends and associates.

If you become a manager or supervisor, it will be very important for you to have a mature, positive emotional management system because you will encounter many situations in which you need to maintain control of your emotions. As an employee, you may deal with a supervisor who does not know how to manage emotions, and you will no doubt find this frustrating. In some organizations you might encounter bullying, intimidation, poor communication, stress, unrealistic expectations, and internal conflict as the norm. Some

> "The degree of one's emotions varies with one's knowledge of the facts."
>
> —Bertrand Russell

managers believe using these tactics is the best way to manage people. To be able to deal with a manager like this, you will have to call on your strongest emotional management techniques, and in some cases, you might simply have to find another job. Before quitting a job, talk to your supervisor's manager, and calmly and rationally describe your supervisor's behavior toward you. Most companies do not want this kind of behavior demonstrated toward their employees.

Listed below are several general points that can assist you in managing your personal emotions whether as an employee or as a manager.

GUIDELINES FOR EMOTIONAL MANAGEMENT AT SCHOOL, WORK, AND BEYOND

(© 2008, Sherfield and Moody.)

- **Face each day with an "I feel great attitude."** No one wants to hear about your headache, congestion or problems. When you wake up in the morning, tell yourself "I feel great" before you ever get out of bed. Most people have already had 25–30 negative thoughts before they even get in the shower. Your brain is a powerful computer, and you can program it to have a good day. You can control your emotions! This day you are experiencing is a day of your life that you can never get back. Have as much fun, be as productive as you can, and do something that makes giving that day up worthwhile.

- **Hear both sides of an argument before you say anything, make a decision or take an action.** There are always two sides of a story, and in many cases, both parties may be partially right. After you have heard both sides of the argument, bring the two parties together, share with them what you have gleaned from their conversations and try to find a resolution to the problem that makes both of them satisfied. People don't have to like each other, but they have to find ways to work together.

- **Practice a win–win philosophy at all times.** Try to help other people feel like winners. Share the glory of an accomplishment by recognizing everyone who contributed. Never take sole credit for a job in which other people participated. If you are a supervisor or team leader, brag on your people. You are getting the glory anyway because you are their leader. You can't lead if people won't follow, and if you don't treat people right, you will be marching out front all by yourself.

- **Avoid letting your personal feelings about a person color your decisions.** If you like a person, you might be tempted to assign more credibility or weight to their opinions than someone else. If you dislike someone, you might be inclined to discount their opinions and not give them proper respect. Liking or disliking a person is not a good reason to use when making a decision that might impact you, as well as others. Try to put aside your personal feelings when making a decision.

- **Learn to inject humor into tense situations.** When tempers are flaring and people are obviously losing control, infusing a bit of humor can often diffuse arguments and help people get back on an even keel. Poking fun at yourself can often work wonders. John Kennedy, an excellent communicator, was a master at this skill.

(continued)

- **Never, never, never lose control!** If you feel intense anger coming on and realize you are about to say or do something you will regret, take a deep breath and gain control; take a walk; get away from the situation until you have gained control. Stop for a moment and think about the cost of your words to yourself or to someone to whom they are directed. Remember, you cannot take words and actions back. You can apologize, but your words are always out there waiting to rear their heads again in another difficult situation. You can't really take back hostile words. You do not want to be perceived as a hothead.

- **If you are about to lose control, breathe calmly and ask yourself, "Is this a reaction caused by something from the past rather than an action I want to take at this time?"** Remember how the amygdala works and be aware that someone may have triggered an unpleasant experience from the past that is causing your anger to escalate out of control.

- **Watch out for "emotional numbness."** Think before you speak or act. How will your words impact other people, your studies, your job, your boss, your future at the company? Put yourself in other people's places. Where are they coming from? What has happened before that you need to consider before speaking? This does not mean that you should not express yourself assertively and openly; it just means to be careful about the use of accusations and inflammatory words that you spoke while not having your brain in gear.

- **Avoid negative stereotyping and putting people into negative categories.** If you find yourself saying things like, "All women are emotional," or "All Asians stick together and don't see anyone else's side," or "All men are unable to show emotions," you are putting groups of people into categories. Go out of your way to get to know individuals. They are most likely not who they appear to be once you understand them and why they do and say what they do.

- **Never see someone through someone else's eyes.** This is a great piece of advice that can be invaluable to you at work and in your personal relationships. Just because your best friend doesn't like Jack, this does not mean that you can't. Your friend might be right—perhaps Jack is a loud-mouthed, arrogant bully. On the other hand, maybe your friend did something to cause Jack to treat him this way. Get to know people before you form opinions or pass judgment. Remember this statement because it is true: "Everyone wants to be understood."

- **Learn to keep a tight rein on any emotional "hotspots" that you know you have like anger, rage, jealousy.** If you can't control yourself when driving and often succumb to road rage, for example, you might make a mistake that could haunt you forever. What if you lost your temper like this when your boss was in the car with you and realized that you have a control problem? What if you totally lose control and drive your car into the back of someone else's vehicle and cause them serious injury? What if your child sees you behaving in this manner and embraces your behavior as his own? If someone at work says something that triggers an unhappy experience from the past, don't let your amygdala take control and cause you to say or do things you will regret and cannot take back.

- **Communicate often and clearly, operate as much as possible from a position of transparency, and listen to people when they need to be heard.** Good communicators share the news—good and bad—and they do it in a timely manner. A policy of "There are no secrets" is a great way to operate. Put yourself in the place of people receiving your message. If there is a way to misconstrue a message, someone usually will, and then the rumor mill is off and running. Quickly dispel rumors and misinformation. Never allow misinformation to circulate and fester if you know this is happening.

- **Strive to treat people so well that you can always put your head on your pillow and sleep well knowing that you have not been underhanded, rude, or unfair.** You can't control other people. You can control only you! Although you may be tempted to retaliate, to spread half-truths or to let them go unchecked, or to use underhanded tactics to get back at someone, control your urges. This type of control is perhaps the hardest of all. It is very difficult not to retaliate against someone who has deliberately hurt you.

As you can see, emotional management includes all your relationships and dealings with other people, whether at home, at school, at work, or in your community. Learning to control your emotions and keep yourself focused on the right side of the emotional spectrum demonstrates growth and maturity and may indicate that you are ready for a promotion.

WHY ARE RELATIONSHIPS IMPORTANT?

How Interpersonal Communication and Emotional Management Shapes or Breaks Our Bonds

To function in a happy and healthy manner, human beings need one another—and they need to communicate with one another. Everything we learn in this life comes through and from our relationships with others. We need each other to help us laugh, cry, learn, work, provide for the survival of the species, and even to help us die when the time comes.

Throughout our lives, we experience myriad relationships. We are someone's son or daughter, we may be someone's brother or sister, and we probably will be someone's friend and someone's lover, as well as someone's helpmate through life. Each of these relationships has its own individual dynamics, but all successful relationships have some similarities.

Work hard to manage your emotions, keeping them on the positive side of the Emotional Spectrum.

RELATIONSHIPS WITH FAMILY

Almost everyone has a family in one form or another, be it a biological family, an adoptive family, or one pulled together from friends and loved ones. There is nothing that promises that any one of these families will be any more functional than the other. They can either help you succeed or help you fail. The power you give them to control your life is up to you. Regardless of what your choices might be, a family can be either your biggest fan or number one critic.

When dealing with your family (regardless of its makeup), here are a few pointers:

> "Stepping on one's feeling hurts just as badly as stepping on one's toes . . . and lasts a lot longer."
>
> —Anonymous

- Remember that honesty is the best policy—all of us, at one time or another, have tried lying to our parents, friends, or loved ones and paid the price for it. Just remember the old saying, "Honesty without love is brutality." Honesty needs to be tempered with compassion.
- Talk things out with family members when you have differences or arguments; remember, you have two ears and one mouth. Use them in that proportion.
- Know that family is forever, whether it's the one you were born into or the one you have chosen. Your connections are powerful and should not be taken lightly or abused because of a whim or a passing bad mood.
- Accept the fact that words spoken cannot be unspoken. This is not to say you won't be forgiven, but forgiving is different from forgetting. The wounds your words cause may last a lifetime, so choose them carefully.

Healthy relationships with family and friends can help you celebrate good times and manage bad times.

EXTRAORDINARY

VIVIAN WONG, FOUNDER
Global Trading Consortium
Greenville, SC

In the early '60s, I was a very young woman and a new wife when my husband began talking about coming to America. We dreamed of living in our own house with a yard rather than a flat as we did in China. We were working as front desk clerks in a Hong Kong hotel, when fate intervened in the person of Robert Wilson, who was in China marketing his Barbeque King grills. We told him about our dream, and he decided to help us. Many people would have never followed through, but Mr. Wilson gave us $100 and told us to get photos made and to purchase passports. He promised to work on a visa for us. It took a year for us to finally be granted a trainee visa, and we headed to Greenville, SC, to work for Mr. Wilson, leaving our little girl behind with her grandparents.

In Greenville we trained to learn to sell Barbeque King grills in China. After about ten months, we were very homesick for China so we went home. We realized after we got to Hong Kong that our hearts were really in America, because now we were homesick for Greenville. Without even realizing it, Greenville and America had become our home. Mr. Wilson brought us back and, this time, we brought our little girl.

In 1967 we were blessed with twin girls, and in 1968 we were given a permanent visa and U.S. citizenship. I often say, "We spent the first twenty years in America simply trying to earn a meager living and put food on the table." We began to look around to try to figure out what kind of edge we had that we could use to start our own business in Greenville, because we

RELATIONSHIPS WITH FRIENDS

It has been said that a very lucky person has three to four good friends at any given time. True friends are hard to find, and even harder to keep! Many of us approach friendship as if it just happens, and, in some cases, it does. Think about your best friend. How did you meet?

"The worst solitude is to be destitute of sincere friendship.

—Francis Bacon

Probably by chance. Perhaps fate brought you together. Sometimes circumstances can cause you to drift apart.

Why is it important to build strong friendships? Friendships can bring you comfort, understanding from another person, and loyalty, and they give you someone to talk with about joys and sorrows. You can share your hopes and dreams and fears with good friends. Another reason for developing friendships is to have people with whom you share common interests and who allow you to have uninhibited joy and fun. Really good friends bring joy into your life. Close and trusted friends are among the most important members of your personal community. When making friends, consider adding people to your life who:

☐ Treat you well and equally
☐ Have ambition and courage

didn't want to work for other people the rest of our lives. In 1970, with Mr. Wilson as a partner, we opened our first business, a Chinese restaurant, but before we opened, my husband spent two years in Washington, DC, training for restaurant ownership. Others followed in 1975 and 1976 and 1988. By now, I could put food on the table, and I wanted to do something other than sell egg rolls.

I became very interested in commercial real estate and began to learn everything I could and branched out into real estate. Most people will tell you that the main thing to know about real estate is location, location, location. I would say, "Timing, timing, timing." If you purchase a property, you have to be sure the timing is right for someone to want to lease it or buy it. I was fortunate in that I have an eye for good properties and a head for business. I operate on a "gut feeling," and I believe in paying cash for property.

Because I owned the land, I was able to partner with others to build hotels. Today I own several hotels in America, and I am starting a chain in China with my brother. This chain will be called Hotel Carolina and is aimed at business travelers. We found a niche that had not been tapped—a clean, reasonable three-star hotel for business travelers who couldn't afford five-star accommodations. We also own and operate a large business park and foreign trade zone in

Greenville, SC. We are partners and franchisees of the Medicine Shoppe, China's first American pharmacy. In 2001 we started Pacific Gateway Capital to help people in China get a foothold in the U.S. and to open the lines of communication and trade between Greenville and China. My next 20-year project is the Global Trade Center which we opened in Greenville in 2003. We have helped all our siblings, in-laws, many chefs and cooks to come to this country. Once they are here they petition to bring their families. We have been instrumental in bringing several hundred people to the U.S., and I am proud that we were able to help so many people.

Today I am a partner in three banks located in Greenville, Atlanta, and Myrtle Beach. People ask me how I know how to own and manage such a disparate collection of businesses. My answer is simple, "I know how to connect the dots; this is what I do best." I also believe strongly in networking and communicating with partners and people who know how to get things done. I have partners all over the world in a great variety of businesses. I have developed the vision, action plans and good teams to make things happen. I take nothing for granted!

We have been very blessed to live in America and now to open businesses in our native land. In this wonderful country, we have succeeded beyond our wildest dreams! So can you!

☐ Have healthy work habits and a strong work ethic
☐ Have pride in his/her character and reputation
☐ Enjoy college and learning new things
☐ Are outgoing and adventurous
☐ Understand their goals and mission in life

RELATIONSHIPS WITH DIVERSE OTHERS

One of the biggest advantages of going to college is the fact that you will most likely study in an international community—a place where people bring different perspectives, ideas, values, and beliefs than your own. If you approach diverse populations with an open mind and heart, you can benefit greatly from the exposure to people who are different from you.

"You have to move to another level of thinking, which is true of me and everybody else. Everybody has to learn to think differently, think bigger, to be open to possibilities."

—Oprah Winfrey

did you know?

Dith Pran was born in 1942 in Cambodia. He learned English and French and worked for the U.S. government as a translator, then with a British film crew, and as a hotel receptionist. In 1975, after meeting a *New York Times* reporter, he taught himself how to take pictures.

After U.S. forces left Cambodia, he stayed behind to cover the fall of Phnom Penh to the communist Khmer Rouge. Then he was forced to stay while foreign reporters were allowed to leave. From this point, Dith witnessed many atrocities and had to hide the fact that he was educated or knew any Americans. He pretended to be a taxicab driver. Cambodians were forced to work in labor camps, and Dith was not immune. He endured four years of starvation and torture before Vietnam

(continued)

The Power of an Open Mind

To experience other people and to receive the benefits of knowing someone, enter all relationships with an open mind. If you have a derogatory mind-set toward a race, an ethnic group, a sexual orientation, or a religion, for example, you have internal barriers that can keep you from getting to know who a person really is.

Learning to interact with people from different cultures is a matter of keeping an open mind and looking at each person as an individual, not as a race, a class, or a religion. We cannot help but be influenced by what we have been taught and what we have experienced, but we can overcome prejudices and biases if we view people as individuals. If you intend to grow as an educated person and as a human being, you will need to expand your capacity to accept and understand people from different cultures inside and outside your own country.

You Are a Culture of One

During our formative years, each of us develops a unique set of values, beliefs, and customs. We are virtually programmed, based on who raises us, our race, our nationality, where we live, where we go to school, our religion or lack of religion, our friends, our relatives, and our experiences and opportunities. Like fingerprints, no two people with their beliefs, customs, and experiences are exactly alike. This amazing phenomenon is what makes human beings interesting.

Culture is learned. People are born into a culture, but their culture is not a physical trait, such as eye color or hair texture. You probably developed, or absorbed, most of your personal culture from your family. The process is almost like osmosis in plants; it is as though culture seeps gradually through your skin. Many of the beliefs and values you embrace have been passed from one generation to another.

In college, you are likely to find your values, beliefs, and actions changing as you meet new people and become involved in new situations and as your horizons broaden. Quite simply, your college experience enhances your understanding causing your cultural beliefs to change as a result. This change is known as *cultural adjustment*. You can, and should, expect to have your beliefs greatly tested—and perhaps adjusted—before you graduate.

Cultural adjustment doesn't mean that you must abandon your family, church, basic values, and friends. It may mean, however, that you need to re-evaluate why you feel the way you do about certain situations and certain groups of people. You may have been taught that people belonging to a certain group are not acceptable. As you learn and grow, you may find that they are not bad at all, just different from you. You may discover that this different culture is one to be celebrated. Even if the ones who taught you cultural biases were your parents, strive to be open minded and to accept people who are different from you. Judge people as individuals, not as a race, religion, or class.

CONFLICT IN RELATIONSHIPS IS INEVITABLE

Understanding It and Learning How You Deal with It

Many people intensely dislike conflict and will go to extreme measures to avoid it. On the other hand, some people seem to thrive on conflict and enjoy creating situations that put people at odds with each other. While in college, you certainly will not be sheltered from conflicts. In fact, on a college campus where a very diverse population lives and learns together, conflict is likely to arise on a regular basis. The simple truth is, conflict is pervasive throughout our culture, and you simply cannot avoid having some confrontations. Therefore, you should not try to avoid conflict; rather, you can use it to create better relationships by exploring workable solutions.

You may experience conflict in a classroom when another student takes issue with your opinions and continues to harass you about your ideas after the class is over. You could be placed on a team where conflicts arise among the members. Conflict among team members happens frequently if one or more members do not do their part of the work. A major conflict could erupt in the parking lot if someone thoughtlessly pulls into a parking space that you have been waiting for. You could even experience conflict with a faculty member because you intensely disagree with the grade he or she assigned you on a project. Conflict can occur in any relationship, whether it is your parents, your girlfriend or boyfriend, your best friend, a roommate, a spouse or partner, your children, or a total stranger.

Some of the causes of *relationship tensions* include:

- Jealousy
- Honesty
- Perceptions
- Dependency
- Culture (race, social status, gender, background, etc.)
- Sexual orientation
- Affiliations (politics, organizations, religions, etc.)
- Outside commitments
- Opinions, values, and beliefs
- Innate personality traits
- Emotions (passion, anger, fear, hostility, etc.)

As you consider conflicts in your life and relationships, take a moment and complete the Conflict Management Assessment to determine your awareness of issues related to conflict and managing conflict.

overthrew the Khmer Rouge and he escaped the camp. He coined the term "The Killing Fields" because of the number of dead bodies he encountered during his escape. He later learned that his three brothers and fifty members of his family were killed during the genocide. Dith escaped to Thailand in 1979 fearing for his life because of his association with Americans and his knowledge of what had happened. He moved to America in 1980. In 1984, the movie *The Killing Fields* was released detailing the horrors and triumphs of his life. He died of pancreatic cancer in 2008.

CONFLICT MANAGEMENT ASSESSMENT

(© Robert M. Sherfield, Ph.D., 2005, 2008)

Read the following questions carefully and respond according to the key below. Take your time and be honest with yourself.

1 = NEVER typical of the way I address conflict
2 = SOMETIMES typical of the way I address conflict
3 = OFTEN typical of the way I address conflict
4 = ALMOST ALWAYS typical of the way I address conflict

1. When someone verbally attacks me, I can let it go and move on.   1 2 3 4

2. I would rather resolve an issue than have to "be right" about it.   1 2 3 4

3. I try to avoid arguments and verbal confrontations at all costs.   1 2 3 4

4. Once I've had a conflict with someone, I can forget it and get along with
   that person just fine.   1 2 3 4

5. I look at conflicts in my relationships as positive growth opportunities.   1 2 3 4

6. When I'm in a conflict, I will try many ways to resolve it.   1 2 3 4

(continued)

7. When I'm in a conflict, I try not to verbally attack or abuse the other person.   **1 2 3 4**

8. When I'm in a conflict, I try never to blame the other person; rather, I look at every side.   **1 2 3 4**

9. When I'm in a conflict, I try not to avoid the other person.   **1 2 3 4**

10. When I'm in a conflict, I try to talk through the issue with the other person.   **1 2 3 4**

11. When I'm in a conflict, I often feel empathy for the other person.   **1 2 3 4**

12. When I'm in a conflict, I do not try to manipulate the other person.   **1 2 3 4**

13. When I'm in a conflict, I try never to withhold my love or affection for that person.   **1 2 3 4**

14. When I'm in a conflict, I try never to attack the person; I concentrate on their actions.   **1 2 3 4**

15. When I'm in a conflict, I try to never insult the other person.   **1 2 3 4**

16. I believe in give and take when trying to resolve a conflict.   **1 2 3 4**

17. I understand AND USE the concept that kindness can solve more conflicts than cruelty.   **1 2 3 4**

18. I am able to control my defensive attitude when I'm in a conflict.   **1 2 3 4**

19. I keep my temper in check and do not yell and scream during conflicts.   **1 2 3 4**

20. I am able to accept "defeat" at the end of a conflict.   **1 2 3 4**

Total number of 1s _____
Total number of 2s _____
Total number of 3s _____
Total number of 4s _____

If you have more 1s, you do not handle conflict very well and have few tools for conflict management. You have a tendency to anger quickly and lose your temper during the conflict.

If you have more 2s, you have a tendency to want to work through conflict, but you lack the skills to carry this tendency through. You can hold your anger and temper for a while, but eventually, it gets the best of you.

If you have more 3s, you have some helpful skills in handling conflict. You tend to work very hard for a peaceful and mutually beneficial outcome for all parties.

If you have more 4s, you are very adept at handling conflict and do well with mediation, negotiation, and anger management. You are very approachable; people turn to you for advice about conflicts and their resolution.

Candid discussions, and sometimes brutal honesty, are useful and necessary when you are addressing complex or difficult issues. However, be careful not to let emotions take over your objectivity.

Learning to manage conflict is a very important step in developing sound communication practices. Conflict exists between people in every organization, and there is no doubt that you will encounter some people who will not agree with you on some specific issue. If you can learn to stay calm, put yourself in the other person's shoes, and try to find a mutually beneficial solution, you will gain admiration and respect from your colleagues. In time, you might even begin to understand the person who appears to have a great deal of hostile feelings.

A series of important tips for developing a strong system that can guide your interpersonal communication decisions is listed below. These tips should be helpful as you work with certain difficult people who tend to create conflict.

SUCCESSFUL DECISIONS

In a student leadership council meeting, John made a suggestion that the council sponsor a fund raiser to secure funds to send the officers to a leadership retreat. His suggestion included having all members of the council participate in raising the funds even though only the officers would get to attend.

This suggestion set Barry off and he began to talk very animatedly with a loud, intimidating voice about how this would be unfair to everyone who worked and didn't get to attend the retreat. He stood up and towered over John and continued to use abusive language.

Rather than fuel Barry's argument, John remained calm, and in a very quiet, controlled, but firm voice, say, "Barry, I understand your feelings, but what you need to realize is that next year you will be an officer, and all of us will be working to send you and your team. Why don't we move to another agenda item and come back to this one after we have all had time to collect our thoughts." By staying calm, he gave Barry no good reason to keep the fight going.

John made a *successful decision*.

STANDARDS OF INTERPERSONAL COMMUNICATION

(© Robert M. Sherfield, Ph.D., 2007)

GENERAL TIPS FOR INTERPERSONAL COMMUNICATION

- You never know what type of day, month, year, or life a person has had . . . act accordingly.
- Ask people about themselves. This puts people at ease.
- Interpersonal communication involves a great deal of trust on your part.
- The healthier your self-esteem, the better you treat and respect others, so work to enhance your self-esteem. Never try to diminish another's self-worth in order to feel better yourself.
- Try to greet and treat everyone as nicely and thoughtfully as if he or she was your close, personal friend.
- Show empathy for others and most of the time, you will be treated the same.
- ALWAYS select and use your words carefully. Words are immensely powerful tools.
- Pay very close attention to your nonverbal communication such as gestures, facial expressions, clothing, proximity, posture, touch, and eye contact.
- Understand that first impressions are NOT always correct. Get to know the person and the situation.
- NEVER use your "power" or position to control a person just because you can.

LISTENING TO OTHERS

- Remember this fact: **Listening is HELPING**.
- The number one rule to effective listening is this: "STOP talking."
- Look at the other person's facial expressions.
- Concentrate on what the other person is saying. Give him or her your full attention.
- Eliminate distractions such as phones, other conversations, and outside noise.
- DO NOT judge the situation before you hear what is being said. Judging current situations on past experiences hampers listening. Put prejudices aside.
- Leave your emotions out of the situation. They can cloud your listening ability.
- Ask questions for clarification.
- Repeat what you have heard so that you are assured you heard it correctly.

(continued)

- Listen for what is NOT being said. Listen "between the lines."
- Avoid jumping to conclusions. Keep your cool and don't make immediate assumptions.

DEALING WITH DIFFICULT PEOPLE

- Don't become the same type of difficult person as the ones with whom you are dealing. Fighting fire with fire will only make the flame hotter. In most situations, you will need to be the cool one.
- Don't take the other person's attitude or words personally. Most of the time, they don't know you or your life. They are probably just letting off steam or expressing anger at something that has little to do with you.
- AVOID physical contact with others at every expense.
- If you must give criticism, try to do so with a positive tone and attitude. If possible, provide some positive comments to the person before you offer your criticism.
- Remember that everyone is sensitive about themselves. Avoid language that will set someone off.
- Don't save up a list of the person's faults and problems and "sandbag" him or her all at once.
- NEVER verbally attack the other person.
- Allow the other person to save face. In other words, don't beat the dead horse.
- If you have a problem with someone or someone's actions, be specific and let them know before it gets out of hand. They can't read your mind.
- Ask yourself, "If this were my last action on earth, would I be proud of how I acted?"
- If someone shows signs or becoming physically aggressive toward you, get help early, stay calm, talk slowly and calmly to the other person, and, if necessary, walk away to safety.

RESOLVING CONFLICT

- Remember that conflict will more than likely happen throughout your entire life. It is a natural occurrence, a natural force in life.
- Allow the other person to vent fully before you begin any negotiation or resolution.
- Try to see the world through the other person's eyes.
- Try to create win-win situations in which everyone can walk away having gained something. It is always best not to have a loser.
- Determine if the conflict is a "person" conflict or a "situation" conflict.
- Ask the other person or people what he or she needs. Try to understand the situation.
- Realize that you (or your company or office) may very well be in the wrong.
- Try to face the conflict head-on and quickly. To avoid conflict only makes it worse.
- OWN your words. If you're making a statement, let it come from YOU, not "them."
- Show your concern for the other person.
- Try with all your might to end on a positive note.

"The #1 Rule for Effective Interpersonal Communication: Be Nice. Be Nice. Be Nice."

The world is full of difficult people, but most of them can be dealt with if you keep a lid on your own hostility. The basic idea of resolving conflict is to get a handle on your own emotions. Remove threatening actions, words, and body language and be prepared to compromise so everyone leaves feeling like they won something. Think of conflict resolution as a way to gain a new friend instead of adding a new enemy. Never allow yourself to become the person you're trying to avoid.

THINK ABOUT IT

Reflections for Success

In today's fast-paced, ever-changing, cell-phone-addicted, text-message-crazy, pay-at-the-pump, "don't have to talk to anyone unless I want to," action-packed world, it is easy to forget that communication is paramount in so many areas of your life. From building healthy and useful relationships with your fellow students to talking to your instructors to learning from diverse others to managing conflict, no tool will ever give you more power to effect change than interpersonal communication skills.

Think of all that is "out there" to learn—not only from your texts and instructors, but also from people who have come from a world much different than your own. If you will open up your heart and mind to all of the possibilities, you will leave college a much more enlightened person than you were when you arrived. Rather than close out people who are different from you, embrace new and different cultures. While you don't have to be just like these new people, if you learn to listen, share, empathize, and communicate more effectively, you are certain to learn to appreciate and benefit from the many wonderful and varied relationships.

Remember, we are motivated by what we value. As you continue on in your studies and work toward personal and professional growth, consider the following ideas:

- ☐ Work every day to strengthen your interpersonal communication skills.
- ☐ Strive to have a positive self-concept and to be an optimist.
- ☐ Try to stay at the positive end of the Emotional Spectrum.
- ☐ Work to maintain a high level of Emotional Intelligence.
- ☐ Listen to people and try to understand them.
- ☐ Stand up against intolerance of any kind.
- ☐ Develop relationships with people from a variety of backgrounds.
- ☐ Learn to appreciate and grow from differences.
- ☐ Maintain close friendships.

> "The best relationship is the one in which your love *for* each other exceeds your *need* for each other."
>
> —Unknown

passages
An Activity for Critical Thinking and Career Development

On page 9 of Chapter 1, and inside the front cover, you read **The Ten Essential Cornerstones for Personal and Professional Success.** They are:

Passion	Motivation
Knowledge	Resourcefulness
Creativity	Adaptability
Open-mindedness	Communication
Accountability	Vision

Consider the following **ESSENTIAL CORNERSTONES.** Write a brief statement as to how each can be enhanced by (1) improving your interpersonal communication abilities, (2) expanding your cultural awareness, and (3) learning conflict management skills. Be certain to address all three areas.

Knowledge _____

_____

_____

_____

_____

_____

_____

Creativity _____

_____

_____

_____

_____

_____

_____

Open-mindedness _____

_____

_____

_____

_____

_____

_____

Accountability _____

_____

_____

_____

_____

_____

_____

Resourcefulness _____

_____

_____

_____

_____

_____

_____

Time and stress—partners in crime or helpful allies? You cannot get more of one, but you can certainly have more than your share of the other. In reality, one can define and drive the other. The more effectively you manage your time the less stress you will have in your life. Time, of course, is not the only thing in your life that can cause stress. Stress can be brought on by relationships, work, family issues, and money to name a few. However, by learning to more effectively manage your time, you can reduce this one factor that contributes to the stress level in your life. *This chapter can help you:*

- Learn to make an effective "to do" list
- Use a priority check-off system for your "to do" list
- Understand the cycle of procrastination
- Overcome procrastination
- Manage your time more effectively to reduce stress
- Identify the major stressors in your life
- Understand the effects of stress on your body and memory

By learning to manage your time and reduce your level of stress, you can concentrate on the important aspects of your education, and life in general—and become more productive.

SCAN AND QUESTION

Take a few moments and **scan this chapter**. As you scan, **list five questions** you can expect to learn the answers to while reading and studying Chapter 4.

Example
- Discuss five ways to avoid procrastination? (from page 91)
- Why is it important to create a to-do list every night? (from page 98)

My Questions

1. _____
_____ from page _____
2. _____
_____ from page _____

3. _____
_____ from page _____
4. _____
_____ from page _____
5. _____
_____ from page _____

Reminder: At the end of the chapter, come back to this page and answer these questions in your notebook, text margins, or online chapter notes.

TIME—YOU HAVE ALL THERE IS
Taking Control of Your Schedule and Using Your Time Wisely

Why is it that some people seem to get so much more done than most other people? They appear to always be calm and collected and have it together. Many people from this group work long hours in addition to going to school. They never appear to be stressed out, and they seem to be able to do it all with grace and charm. Uggh!

You are probably aware of others who are always late with assignments, never finish their projects on time, rarely seem to have time to study, and appear to have no concrete goals for their lives. Sometimes, we get the idea that the group mentioned above accomplishes more because they have more time or because they don't have to work or they don't have children or they are smarter or wealthier. Actually, all of these reasons may be true, but it doesn't change the basic, raw fact about time: We all have the same amount of time each week, and we decide how to spend most of it. Even if you are rich, you can't buy more time than the allotted 10,080 minutes that each of us is given every week. Time is so valuable that the last words of Queen Elizabeth I were, *"All my possessions for a moment of time."*

> "You have as many hours in the day as Monet, Beethoven, Henry Ford, Mother Teresa, and Charles Lindberg."
>
> —Anonymous

Time is an unusual and puzzling resource. You can't save it in a box until you need it. You don't feel it passing by like wind in your face. It has no color. If you are in a hurry or if you are pressured to reach a deadline, time seems to fly. If you are bored or have nothing to do, it seems to creep. Time is an invisible commodity. You can't get your arms around it, yet you know it exists.

Time management is actually about managing yourself, taking control. The sooner you get control of how you use your time, the quicker you will be on your way to becoming successful in college. Learning to manage your time is a lesson that you will use throughout your college career and beyond. Actually, you can't control time, but you can control yourself. Time management is self-management. Time management is paying attention to how you are spending your most valuable resource and then devising a plan to use it more effectively. This is one of the goals of this chapter.

Staying power begins with how you manage your time. Strive to build on your best in all areas of your life—school, work, family, and friends.

THE DREADED "P" WORD: PROCRASTINATION
Why It Is So Easy to Do and How to Beat It Once and for All

It's not just you! We all procrastinate, and then we worry and tell ourselves, "I'll never do it again if I can just get through this one project." We say things to ourselves like, "If I can just live through this paper, I will never wait until the last minute again." But someone comes along with a great idea for fun, and off we go. Or there is a great movie on TV, the kids want to play a game of ball, you go to the refrigerator for a snack, and before you know it, you reward yourself *with a break* before you have done your work.

The truth is simple: We all tend to avoid the hard jobs in favor of the easy ones. Even many of the list makers fool themselves. They mark off a long list of easy tasks while the big ones still loom in front of them. Many of us put off unpleasant tasks until our back is against the wall. So why do we procrastinate when we all know how unpleasant the results can be? Why aren't we disciplined and organized and controlled so we can reap the rewards that come from being prepared? Why do we put ourselves through so much stress just by putting things off?

> ## ESSENTIAL CORNERSTONE
> ### MOTIVATION
> How can internalizing your personal motivation help you with time management?

Procrastination is quite simply a bad habit formed after many years of practice. There are reasons, however, that cause us to keep doing this to ourselves. They involve:

- Superhuman expectations
- Trying to be a perfectionist
- Fear of not knowing how to do the task
- Lack of motivation and the inability to find internal motivation
- Fear of failing or fear of the task being too hard
- No real plan or goal for getting the task done

The biggest problem with procrastination, even beyond not getting the job, task, or paper completed, *is doing it poorly*. By putting the project off, you have cheated yourself out of the time needed to bring your best to the table and, most likely, you are going to hand over a project, *with your name on it*, that is not even close to your true potential. And to top it off, more stress is created by this vicious cycle of "I'll do it tomorrow—or this weekend." Consider the trap you get yourself into when you procrastinate (Figure 4.1).

20 WAYS TO BEAT PROCRASTINATION

- Face up to the **results of procrastination**; they can be monumental.
- **Concentrate on the rewards** of managing yourself and your time more effectively.
- Break up big tasks into **small ones**.
- Give yourself a **time limit** to accomplish a task.
- Set a regular, realistic time for study, and **stick to it**.
- Start the project with **positive, optimistic thoughts**.
- Set reasonable, concrete goals that you can reach in about **20–25 minutes**.
- **Face your fears**; look them right in the face and make a decision to defeat them.
- **Ask for help** from your professors, advisor, counselor, or other professionals.
- **Avoid whining and complaining** *and* people who whine and complain.
- Allow yourself **more time than you think you need** to complete a project.
- Actually **reward yourself** when you have accomplished an important body of work.
- Look at completing the project in terms of your **long-range goals** and your overall life plan.
- **Don't get involved** in too many organizations, accept too many commitments, or overextend yourself.
- **Just do it!** Force yourself to jump into the task.
- Start on the difficult, **most boring tasks first**.
- Find a **quiet place to study** and concentrate.
- Weed out your personal belongings and living space. Organization helps you manage your time and **get to work**.
- **Prepare to be successful** by getting ready the evening before.
- Take time to do the **things you love**—creating a healthy balance in your life.

Think of something that you have been putting off in one of the major areas of your life: academic, financial, household, and so on. Using three or four of the tips above,

FIGURE 4.1   A Day in the Life of The Procrastination Trap

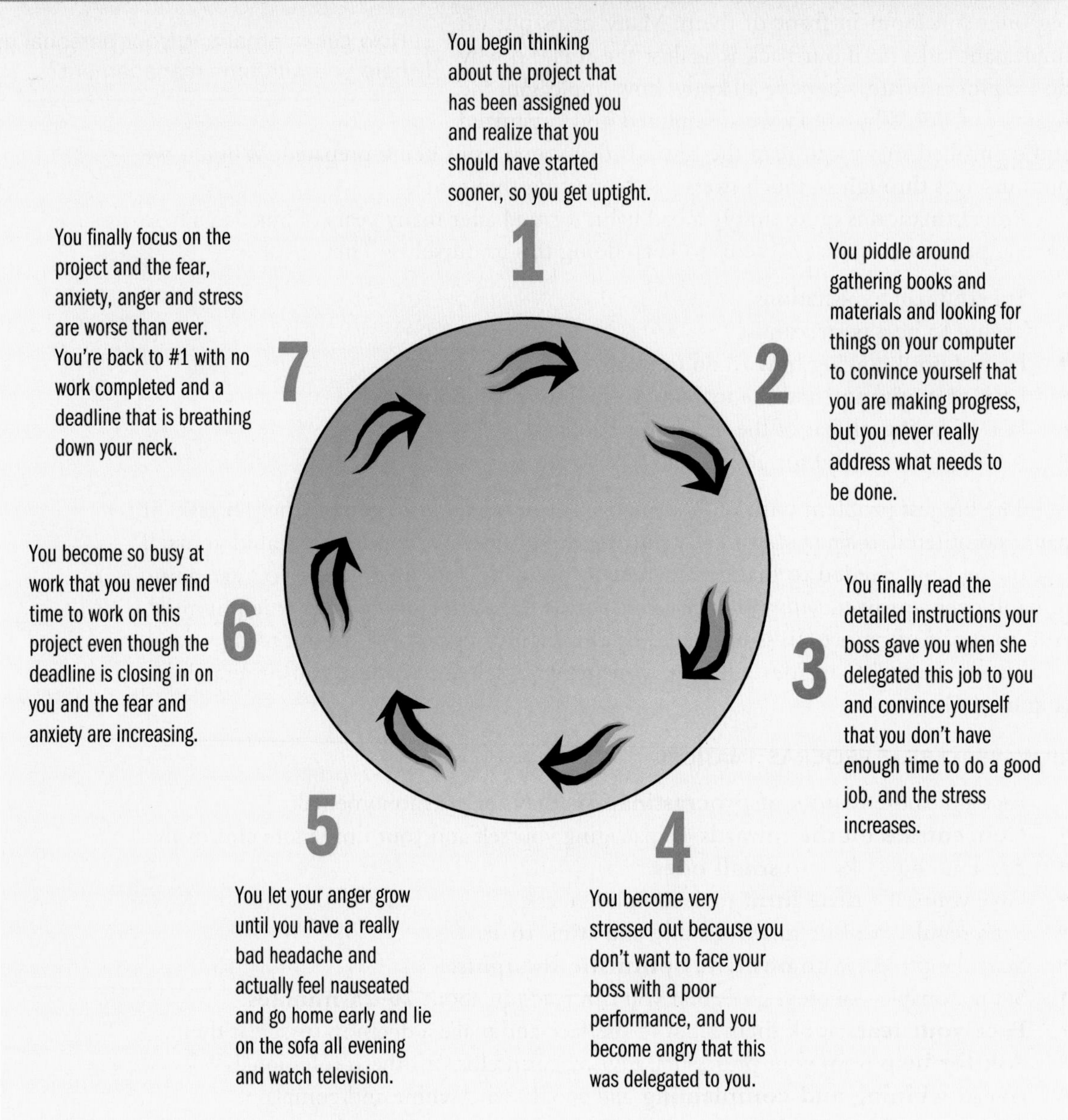

You begin thinking about the project that has been assigned you and realize that you should have started sooner, so you get uptight.

1

You piddle around gathering books and materials and looking for things on your computer to convince yourself that you are making progress, but you never really address what needs to be done.

2

You finally read the detailed instructions your boss gave you when she delegated this job to you and convince yourself that you don't have enough time to do a good job, and the stress increases.

3

You become very stressed out because you don't want to face your boss with a poor performance, and you become angry that this was delegated to you.

4

You let your anger grow until you have a really bad headache and actually feel nauseated and go home early and lie on the sofa all evening and watch television.

5

You become so busy at work that you never find time to work on this project even though the deadline is closing in on you and the fear and anxiety are increasing.

6

You finally focus on the project and the fear, anxiety, anger and stress are worse than ever. You're back to #1 with no work completed and a deadline that is breathing down your neck.

7

develop a plan for getting this important task done this afternoon. That's right—**THIS afternoon**. List at least five action steps to erase this project from your "to do" list.

_____

_____

_____

_____

_____

_____

_____

_____

EVALUATING HOW YOU SPEND YOUR TIME

Knowing Where Time Goes Means Getting to Enjoy More of It

So how do you find out where your time goes? The same way that you find out where your money goes—you track it. Every 15 minutes for one week, you will record exactly how you spent that time. This exercise may seem a little tedious at first, but if you will complete the process over a period of a week, you will have a much better concept of where your time is being used. Yes, that's right—for a week, you need to keep a written record of how much time you spend sleeping, studying, eating, working, getting to class and back, cooking, caring for children, watching television, doing yardwork, going to movies, attending athletic events, hanging out, doing laundry, whatever.

Take your plan with you and keep track of your activities during the day. To make things simple, round off tasks to 15-minute intervals. For example, if you start walking to the cafeteria at 7:08, you might want to mark off the time block that begins with 7:00. If you finish eating and return to your home at 7:49, you can mark off the next two blocks. You will also want to note the activity so you can evaluate how you spent your time later. Study the example that is provided for you in Figure 4.2.

In Figure 4.3, on pages 94–95, you will find a daily time log for you to use in this exercise. Remember to take these pages with you and record how you are spending your time during the day. As you progress through the week, try to improve the use of your time. When you finish this exercise, review how you spent your time.

FIGURE 4.2 How You Really Spend Your Time

Time	Activity	Time		Activity	Time
7:00	get up & shower	7:00		)	12:15
		7:15		)	12:30
	✕	7:30		Walked to Union	12:45
	Breakfast	7:45	1:00	Ate lunch	1:00
8:00	)	8:00		)	1:15
		8:15		)	1:30
	Read paper	8:30		Talked w/ Joe	1:45
	Walked to class	8:45	2:00	)	2:00
9:00	English 101	9:00		Went to book	2:15
		9:15		store	2:30
		9:30		Walked to	2:45
		9:45	3:00	my room	3:00
10:00		10:00		Called Ron	3:15
		10:15		)	3:30
		10:30		)	3:45
	Walked to class	10:45	4:00	Watched	4:00
11:00	History 210	11:00		Friends	4:15
		11:15		)	4:30
		11:30		Walked to	4:45
		11:45	5:00	library	5:00
12:00		12:00		)	5:15

FIGURE 4.3 Daily Time Sheets

Monday		Tuesday		Wednesday	
6:00	6:00	6:00	6:00	6:00	6:00
	6:15		6:15		6:15
	6:30		6:30		6:30
	6:45		6:45		6:45
7:00	7:00	7:00	7:00	7:00	7:00
	7:15		7:15		7:15
	7:30		7:30		7:30
	7:45		7:45		7:45
8:00	8:00	8:00	8:00	8:00	8:00
	8:15		8:15		8:15
	8:30		8:30		8:30
	8:45		8:45		8:45
9:00	9:00	9:00	9:00	9:00	9:00
	9:15		9:15		9:15
	9:30		9:30		9:30
	9:45		9:45		9:45
10:00	10:00	10:00	10:00	10:00	10:00
	10:15		10:15		10:15
	10:30		10:30		10:30
	10:45		10:45		10:45
11:00	11:00	11:00	11:00	11:00	11:00
	11:15		11:15		11:15
	11:30		11:30		11:30
	11:45		11:45		11:45
12:00	12:00	12:00	12:00	12:00	12:00
	12:15		12:15		12:15
	12:30		12:30		12:30
	12:45		12:45		12:45
1:00	1:00	1:00	1:00	1:00	1:00
	1:15		1:15		1:15
	1:30		1:30		1:30
	1:45		1:45		1:45
2:00	2:00	2:00	2:00	2:00	2:00
	2:15		2:15		2:15
	2:30		2:30		2:30
	2:45		2:45		2:45
3:00	3:00	3:00	3:00	3:00	3:00
	3:15		3:15		3:15
	3:30		3:30		3:30
	3:45		3:45		3:45
4:00	4:00	4:00	4:00	4:00	4:00
	4:15		4:15		4:15
	4:30		4:30		4:30
	4:45		4:45		4:45
5:00	5:00	5:00	5:00	5:00	5:00
	5:15		5:15		5:15
	5:30		5:30		5:30
	5:45		5:45		5:45
6:00	6:00	6:00	6:00	6:00	6:00
	6:15		6:15		6:15
	6:30		6:30		6:30
	6:45		6:45		6:45
7:00	7:00	7:00	7:00	7:00	7:00
	7:15		7:15		7:15
	7:30		7:30		7:30
	7:45		7:45		7:45
8:00	8:00	8:00	8:00	8:00	8:00
	8:15		8:15		8:15
	8:30		8:30		8:30
	8:45		8:45		8:45
9:00	9:00	9:00	9:00	9:00	9:00
	9:15		9:15		9:15
	9:30		9:30		9:30
	9:45		9:45		9:45
10:00	10:00	10:00	10:00	10:00	10:00
	10:15		10:15		10:15
	10:30		10:30		10:30
	10:45		10:45		10:45
11:00	11:00	11:00	11:00	11:00	11:00
	11:15		11:15		11:15
	11:30		11:30		11:30
	11:45		11:45		11:45
12:00	12:00	12:00	12:00	12:00	12:00

FIGURE 4.4   Daily Calendar

DAY Monday		Priority	Complete?
Time	**Task**		
6:00			Yes ___ No
6:30			Yes ___ No
7:00	Study for finance		Yes ___ No
7:30	↓		Yes ___ No
8:00	English 101		Yes ___ No
8:30			Yes ___ No
9:00	↓		Yes ___ No
9:30	Read Pg. 1–10 of Chem. Chapter		Yes ___ No
10:00	Management 210		Yes ___ No
10:30			Yes ___ No
11:00	↓		Yes ___ No
11:30	Finish Reading Chem. Chapter		Yes ___ No
12:00	↓		Yes ___ No
12:30	↓		Yes ___ No
1:00	Meet w/ Chemistry group (take lunch)		Yes ___ No
1:30			Yes ___ No
2:00			Yes ___ No
2:30	↓		Yes ___ No
3:00	Exercise at Golds		Yes ___ No
3:30			Yes ___ No
4:00	↓		Yes ___ No
4:30	go to grocery store & get B/day card		Yes ___ No
5:00	& drop off shirts		Yes ___ No
5:30			Yes ___ No
6:00			Yes ___ No
6:30	Dinner		Yes ___ No
7:00	↓		Yes ___ No
7:30	Internet Research for speech		Yes ___ No
8:00			Yes ___ No
8:30	↓		Yes ___ No
9:00	call Janice @ w/end		Yes ___ No
9:30			Yes ___ No

Now, take these tasks and schedule them into your daily calendar (see Figure 4.4). You would schedule category 1 first (MUST DO), category 2 next (NEED TO DO), and category 3 (FUN STUFF) next. Remember, NEVER keep more than one calendar. Always take it with you and always schedule your tasks immediately so that you won't forget them.

Planning and Organizing for Work

- Organize your materials at work as they are organized at home. If you have a desk in both places, keep your supplies in the same place in both desks. Simplify your life by following similar patterns at work and at home.
- Write directions down! Keep a notebook for repetitive tasks. Keep a calendar, and be on time to meetings.
- Learn to do paperwork immediately rather than let it build up. File—don't pile!
- Never let your work responsibilities slide because you are studying on the job. Employers always notice.

SUCCESSFUL DECISIONS

Darius is a single father of two young daughters. He and his wife divorced several years ago and he gained custody of Alice and Marianne.

Shortly after the divorce, Darius was laid off from his job as a construction foreman. He had been making a very good living, but now it was hard to make ends meet. He could not find another job that paid well enough to support the three of them.

Therefore, he decided to go back to school to pursue his dream of becoming a draftsman. His classes, along with his new part-time job, demanded much of his time. He found that he was spending much less time with his daughters than he had in the past—and he did not like this at all.

His daughters were cast in the school play and the performance was scheduled for Friday night—the same night as one of his drafting classes. He knew that he had a conflict on his hands. He knew that class was very important, but so was supporting his daughters.

He went to his drafting instructor, explained the situation, picked up his assignments for the next week, arranged for a classmate to send him the notes from the class, and attended his daughters' play.

Darius made a *successful decision*.

- Leave the office for lunch, breaks, and short walks.
- When you are given projects that require working with others, plan carefully to do your work well and on time.
- Keep a Rolodex file or use a Palm Pilot, your iPod or your cell phone for important phone numbers and addresses that you use frequently.
- Perform difficult, unpleasant tasks as soon as you can so you don't have them hanging over your head.
- When you plan your work schedule, allow for unexpected problems that might interfere with the schedule.
- Practice detached concern—care about your work but avoid taking it home with you.

Planning and Organizing for Home

- Organize as effectively at home as you do at work.
- If you have roommates, divide the chores. Insist on everyone doing his or her share.
- Plan a rotation schedule for major household chores and stick to it—do laundry on Mondays and Thursdays; clean bathrooms on Saturdays; iron on Wednesdays; and so on.
- Organize your closet and your dresser drawers. Get rid of clothes you don't wear.
- Put a sign by your telephone that reads "TIME" to remind yourself not to waste it on the phone.
- Establish a time for study hall in your home. Children do their homework, and you do yours.
- If you can't study at home because of children, drop-in visitors, or loud roommates, go to the library or study BEFORE you leave school.
- If you drive to class or work, fill up your tank ahead of time so you won't be late.
- Keep yourself physically fit with a regular exercise plan and nutritious meals.
- If you are a perfectionist and want everything in your home to be perfect, get over it!
- Get rid of the clutter in your garage, basement, closets, kitchen, bathroom, and so on.
- If you have a family, insist that all of you organize clothes in advance for school or work for several days.
- Put a message board in a convenient place for everyone to use.
- If your children are old enough to drive, have them run errands at the cleaners, post office, and grocery store.

- Carpool with other parents in your neighborhood.
- Delegate, delegate, delegate! You are not Superwoman or Superman. Tell your family you need help. Children can feed pets, make their own beds, fold clothes, vacuum, sweep, iron, and cut the grass if they are old enough.
- Schedule at least one hour alone with each of your children each week. Make this a happy, special time—a fun break!
- Make meals happy, relaxed times when each person's successes are shared and celebrated. Discuss current events.
- Plan special times with your spouse or partner if you have one so that he or she does not get fed up with your going to school.
- Tell your family and friends when you have to study; ask them to respect you by not calling or dropping by at this time.
- Post a family calendar where everyone can see it. Put all special events on it—for example, Janie's recital, Mike's baseball game, Jasmine's company party.
- Put fun days on this calendar so that your entire family has something to look forward to.

TOMORROW? WHAT DO YOU MEAN, IT'S DUE TOMORROW?

The Relationship Between Poor Time Management and Monumental Stress

There are probably as many stressors in this world as there are people alive. For some people, loud music causes stress. For others, a hectic day at the office with demanding people and malfunctioning equipment can cause stress. For others, that loud music and a busy day at the office is just what the doctor ordered. One thing is for sure, however, is that poor planning and "running out of time" are on most people's list of major stressors.

Most stress does not "just happen" to us. We allow it to happen by not planning our day or week. We allow our "to do" list to get out of hand, and before we know it, there is more on the list than can be done in a month. Because of poor planning and procrastination, we become anxious and nervous about not getting it all done. By planning and doing, we can actually lower our stress level and improve our general health and our memory.

> **ESSENTIAL CORNERSTONE**
>
> ### CREATIVITY
>
> How can managing your time more effectively, thus reducing stress, help you become a more creative person?

Medical research has shown that exposure to stress over a long period can damage your body. Stress can also have an effect on your memory. When you are stressed, your brain releases cortisol, which affects the neurons in your brain. Over time, cortisol can be toxic and damage parts of the hippocampus—the part of the brain that deals with memory and learning. Therefore, learning to control stress through managing your time more effectively can be a key to better memory.

Stress: What Is It, Anyway?

The word *stress* is derived from the Latin word *strictus,* meaning "to draw tight." Stress is your body's response to people and events in your life; it is the mental and physical wear and tear on your body as a result of everyday life. Stress is inevitable, and it is not in itself bad. It is your response to stress that determines whether it is good stress (eustress) or bad stress (distress). The same event can provoke eustress or distress, depending on the person experiencing the event; just as "one person's trash is another's treasure" (or so you know if you shop at secondhand stores), so one person's eustress may be another person's distress.

The primary difference between eustress and distress is in your body's response. It is impossible to exist in a totally stress-free environment; in fact, having some stress is important to your health and well-being. Only when the stress gets out of hand does your body become distressed. Some physical signs of distress are:

Headaches	Muscular tension and pain	Abdominal pain and diarrhea
Dry mouth	Hypertension and chest pain	Fatigue
Impotence	Heartburn and indigestion	Coughs
Menstrual disorders	Insomnia	Loss of appetite
Depression	Suicidal tendencies	

THREE TYPES OF STRESSORS IN YOUR LIFE

Type	Causes	Reduction
SITUATIONAL	Change in physical environment	Change your residence or environment to suit your needs.
	Change in social environment	Find a quiet place to relax and study.
		Arrange your classes to suit your needs.
PSYCHOLOGICAL	Unrealistic expectations	Surround yourself with positive people.
	Homesickness	Surround yourself with people who support you. Try to make new friends and develop a support group.
	Fear	Talk to professors, counselors, family, and friends.
BIOLOGICAL	Hormonal changes	Develop a healthy eating plan.
	Weight loss/gain	Develop an exercise plan.
	Change in physical activities	Increase your daily activity.

Take the following **Stress Assessment** to determine the level of distress you are experiencing in your life. Check the items that reflect your behavior at home, work, or school, or in a social setting.

☐   1. Your stomach tightens when you think about your schoolwork and all that you have to do.

☐   2. You are not able to sleep at night.

☐   3. You race from place to place trying to get everything done that is required of you.

☐   4. Small things make you angry.

☐   5. At the end of the day, you are frustrated that you did not accomplish all that you needed to do.

☐   6. You get tired throughout the day.

☐ 7. You need some type of drug, alcohol, or tobacco to get through the day.

☐ 8. You often find it hard to be around people.

☐ 9. You don't take care of yourself physically or mentally.

☐ 10. You tend to keep everything inside.

☐ 11. You overreact.

☐ 12. You fail to find the humor in many situations others see as funny.

☐ 13. You do not eat properly.

☐ 14. Everything upsets you.

☐ 15. You are impatient and get angry when you have to wait for things.

☐ 16. You don't trust others.

☐ 17. You feel that most people move too slowly for you.

☐ 18. You feel guilty when you take time for yourself or your friends.

☐ 19. You interrupt people so that you can tell them your side of the story.

☐ 20. You experience memory loss.

TOTAL NUMBER OF CHECK MARKS

0–5 = Low, manageable stress

6–10 = Moderate stress

11+ = High stress, could cause medical or emotional problems

open the door
Tips for Career Success

Consider the following strategies for dealing with stress in your life:

- Adjust your attitude—look at problems, and life in general, through different eyes.

- Maintain a positive attitude.

- Use relaxation techniques such as visualization, listening to music, and practicing yoga.

- Let minor hassles and annoyances go. Ask yourself, "Is this situation worth a heart attack, stroke, or high blood pressure?"

- Don't be afraid to take a break. Managing your time can help you take more relaxation breaks.

- Practice "seat aerobics" such as inhaling and exhaling, stretching, and neck rolls.

- Do whatever possible to get enough rest and sleep.

- Address ONE issue at a time and then move on to the next one. Don't try to face everything at once.

- Ask yourself, in 10 years will this really make a difference?

- Learn to say, "NO."

THINK ABOUT IT

Reflections for Success

Managing your time and reducing your levels of stress are two skills that you will need for the rest of your life. By learning to avoid procrastinating and taking the time to enhance the quality of your life, you are actually increasing your staying power as a college student. Further, as you enter the world of work, both of these skills will be necessary for your success. Technological advances, fewer people doing more work, and pressure to perform at unprecedented levels can put your life in a tailspin, but with the ability to plan your time and reduce your own stress level, you are contributing to your own success.

As you continue this term in college and work toward managing your time and stress level, consider the following ideas:

☐ Make a to-do list every evening to plan for the next day.

☐ Always include time for friends, joy, and adventure in your schedule.

☐ Avoid procrastination by practicing the "just do it" mentality.

"I wanted a perfect ending. Now I've learned, the hard way, that some poems don't rhyme, and some stories don't have a clear beginning, middle and end. Life is having to change; taking the moment and making the best of it without knowing what is going to happen next."

—Gilda Radner

☐ Work hard to lose the "superhuman" and perfectionist attitudes.
☐ Delegate everything that you can.
☐ Plan your day and week to avoid becoming too stressed.
☐ To reduce stress, take a few moments to relax in private.
☐ When stress is overwhelming, take time to decompress.

Good luck to you as you develop your plan for managing your time and stress management plan.

passages
An Activity for Critical Thinking and Career Development

On page 9 of Chapter 1, and inside the front cover, you read **The Ten Essential Cornerstones for Personal and Professional Success.** They are:

Passion	Motivation
Knowledge	Resourcefulness
Creativity	Adaptability
Open-mindedness	Communication
Accountability	Vision

The following chapter-end activity will ask you to use several of the *Essential Cornerstones* to help you manage your time more effectively and reduce stress in your life.

List five action steps that you plan to use to reduce the amount of time you spend procrastinating, thus increasing the amount of time you have for studying, family, and friends.

1. _____
2. _____
3. _____
4. _____
5. _____

List five action steps that you plan to use to reduce the amount of stress in your life so that you can better enjoy your time with peers, family, and friends.

1. _____
2. _____
3. _____
4. _____
5. _____

Using your plans above, how can **managing your time more effectively** and **reducing your level of stress** help develop and enhance the following *ESSENTIAL CORNERSTONES for Personal and Professional Success*?

Example
Relationships: *By managing my time more effectively, I can have more QUALITY time to meet people and learn from them. I can use this time to network, form a study group,*

- Insurance $_____
- Gas $_____
- Clothing $_____
- Food $_____
- Household items $_____
- Personal hygiene items $_____
- Health care and/or health insurance $_____
- Entertainment/fun $_____
- Other $_____
- Total expenditures $_____

If the amount of your total expenditures is smaller than your monthly income, you are on your way to controlling your finances. If your total expenditures figure is larger than your monthly income (as is the case for many students), you are heading for a financial crisis. Furthermore, you are establishing bad habits for money management that will carry over into your professional life.

The Latte Factor™

In his book *The Finish Rich Notebook*, Bach (2003) states, "How much you earn has no bearing on whether or not you will build wealth." As a rule, the more we make, the more we spend. Many people spend far more than they make and subject themselves to stress, exorbitant debt, fear, and an ultimate future of poverty.

Bach uses the Latte Factor™ to call people's attention to how much money we carelessly throw away when we should be saving and investing for the future. He uses the story of a young woman who said she could not invest because she had no money. Yet, almost every day she bought a large latte for $3.50 and a muffin for $1.50. If you add a candy bar here, a drink there, a shake at the gym, you could easily be spending $10 a day that could be invested.

If you take that $10 per day and invest it faithfully at 10 percent, in 34 years, you will have $1 million. This is the power of compound interest! If you are a relatively young person, you will probably work that many years and more, so you could retire with an extra $1 million in addition to any other savings you might accumulate.

The point is that most of us have the ability to become rich, but we either lack the knowledge or the discipline to do so. Remember the Latte Factor™ as you begin your college career and practice it, along with other sound financial strategies, if you want to become a millionaire.

Calculate your own Latte Factor™.   If you buy one McDonald's large Diet Coke each morning at $1.81, your Latte Factor™ is $685.84 per year ($1.81 × 7 days / week × 52 weeks / year).

My daily "have to have it" is _____

My Latte Factor™ is $ _____

How does this affect your overall financial picture? _____

_____

_____

LIVING ON BORROWED MONEY
Credit Cards—The WORST Kind of Debt

Credit card companies have been waiting for you to arrive on campus. They have your name and address on file, and they will start sending you credit card applications right away. They want you to begin the dangerous habit of living off borrowed money. Don't let them get their tentacles wrapped around you and your money! Getting yourself too deeply in debt by abusing credit cards can bring you many sleepless nights and years of debt with high interest rates.

Approximately 20 percent of all credit card holders have credit card debt in the $6,000 to $15,000 range, and 6 percent have credit card debt that exceeds $15,000 (DebtSteps.com, 2006). College students should try to keep their debt below 65 percent of the total limit to the credit card to avoid a bad reflection on credit scores ("College Credit Cards," 2006).

Most credit card companies charge a very high rate of interest—18 to 21 percent or higher. For every $1,000 you charge, you will pay from $180 to $210 each year, states Konowalow (2003). Don't be fooled by the ploy of "1.5 percent interest." This means 1.5 percent each month, which equates to 18 percent per year. If you make only the minimum required payment, you will begin paying interest on interest before the debt is paid off. If you have an extra $180, invest it. Years from now, it most likely will have doubled and even tripled. On the other hand, if you owe $1,000 and make only minimum payments, you will probably still owe $1,000 at the end of a year even if you don't continue to charge. Credit cards are a bad trap for people who use them unwisely. The best practice is to charge no more than you can pay off each month while avoiding high interest rates.

> "Most people are too busy earning a living to make any money."
>
> —Anonymous

According to statistics, the average college student is a better risk than the general adult population, with 67 percent of students sticking with one credit card. The bad news is that 33 percent have difficulty handling credit, according to Konowalow (2003). They fall into the instant gratification trap rather than saving until they can pay for something. Charging for extravagant items in the beginning, many people will begin charging for essentials because it seems like easy money. Nothing could be further from the truth!

SUCCESSFUL DECISIONS

Marietta is a single mother with two children and a full-time job. However, last month her car broke down and her utility bill was much higher than she expected. There simply was not enough money to pay the bills and get the car fixed.

She had to have her car to get to work, pick the kids up from school, and get to classes. Some hard decisions had to be made.

Marietta began to think of ways that she could make ends meet this month. She stopped by a payday loan center to borrow $300, but found out that she would have to repay much more than she could afford. "Wasted money," she thought.

She thought about a pawnshop but did not want to risk losing her possessions and setting a bad example for her children. Then, it came to her.

She called the utility company and asked if she could pay half of the utility bill. They said yes and helped her set up a payment schedule. Then, she called the garage and asked if they would consider a payment of $200 now and $100 next week. They agreed. It was not an easy thing to do, but ultimately . . .

Marietta made a *successful decision.*

Instead of using credit cards to pay for the expenditures that cause you to go over your budget, modify your expenditures. Almost every line on the expenditure chart can be modified. For example, adding a roommate or moving can lower your housing expense. You can change your car to a less expensive one or consider using public transportation or carpooling with colleagues. Gasoline is a very high-priced budget item today, and this is unlikely to change.

In the spaces below, list five ways you can modify your expenditures to avoid overwhelming credit card debt.

1. _____

2. _____

3. _____

4. _____

5. _____

HINTS FOR CUTTING YOUR EXPENSES

☐ Control impulse buying. Don't buy anything that costs more than $15 until you have waited 72 hours; it is amazing how often you decide you don't need the item that you thought you had to have.

> "I must say I hate money, but it's the lack of it that I hate most."
> —Katherine Mansfield

☐ If you think you simply *must* have an item and can't wait 72 hours, purchase it, take it home, don't open it for 72 hours, and see if you still need it. If not, return it.

☐ Carpool, take public transportation, or walk to classes.

☐ Don't eat out as often. Make your own meals. Make meals for several days on weekends to save time.

☐ Use coupons and buy during sales.

☐ Live more simply by getting rid of unnecessary items like cell phones, beepers, and cable television.

FACTS YOU NEED TO KNOW ABOUT CREDIT CARDS

What You Don't Know Can Wreck Your Credit Rating and Ruin Your Life

Here are some of the most important things you can learn about managing money:

> "The art is not in just making money, but in keeping it."
> —English proverb

☐ Understand that credit cards are nothing more than high-interest loans—in some cases, very high!

☐ Carry only one or two credit cards, so you can manage your debt and not get in over your head. Do not accept or sign up for cards that you don't need.

☐ When you accept a card, sign it right away and keep records of your credit card numbers and the phone number to contact in case they are lost or stolen. If you lose your card, report it immediately to avoid charges if it is used by someone else. Usually, you will not have to pay more than $50.

☐ Avoid credit cards that charge an annual fee. Most likely, you don't need a gold or platinum card. Does your card allow for a grace period before interest is charged?

ESSENTIAL CORNERSTONE

Creativity

How can being more creative with your finances help you avoid overwhelming credit card debt?

☐ Avoid the temptation to charge. You should use credit cards only when you absolutely must and only when you can pay the full amount before interest is added. "Buy now, pay later" is a dangerous game.

☐ Determine whether you can get cash advances from your card if you really need to in an emergency.

☐ When you pay off a card, celebrate and don't use that as a reason to charge again.

☐ If you have credit card debt, always pay more than the minimum.

☐ Pay your credit card payment early enough to avoid late charges, which now average $29.84. Send the payment at least five days in advance. Late fees now represent the third-largest revenue stream for banks. If you are assessed a late fee, call and complain. Tell the customer service representative that you are a good customer and have rarely been late, that you would like to have your lower interest rate restored if it was raised, and that you want the late charge removed. It helps if you have a good reason for being late. If you usually pay on time and don't max out your limit, you will probably get the charge removed. If you get more than two late fees in a year, you could be assessed a higher interest rate on your balance.

☐ Call the credit card company and negotiate a better rate. If it won't give you a better rate, state that you are going to transfer the debt to a different card.

☐ If you have several credit card debts, consolidate all the amounts to the card on which you have the lowest balance. Ask for a lower rate when you do. Destroy all the other cards so you don't accumulate debts again.

☐ If you pay off the full amount every month, some credit card companies allow you only 20 days from a purchase before they charge interest. If you carry a debt with them, however, they will allow you to have 25 days before your payment is due.

☐ Having a large number of credit cards with balances can seriously impact your credit rating. What you do today may inhibit your ability to buy a car, purchase a house, and even get some jobs!

☐ You only need one or two credit cards. Shred all applications that come to you in the mail.

☐ Do not leave any personal information (credit cards, Social Security numbers, checking accounts) in places where roommates or other students have access to them. Purchase a metal file box with a lock and keep it in a secure place. Your roommates and friends may be very trustworthy, but not everyone is!

☐ Use your credit card only for plane tickets, hotel rooms, and other travel necessities that you can pay for within 20 days.

☐ If you have already gotten into credit card trouble, get counseling. One of the best agencies is the National Foundation for Credit Counseling (NFCC). An ethical professional can help you reduce your interest rates, get control of your debt, and get relief from your creditors while you pay off the debt.

> "My money talks, but all it ever says is 'Goodbye.'"
>
> —American proverb

☐ Be very careful not to get involved with high-pressure credit card counseling agencies, which may cause you even more problems. Not all credit counselors are ethical or well trained.

☐ Be aware that using a credit card carelessly is similar to a drug addiction.

☐ Ask yourself these questions: "If I can't pay this credit card in full this month, what is going to change next month? Will I have extra income or will I reduce my spending enough to pay for this purchase?" If the answer is "no," you don't need to make the purchase.

☐ This may help you stop unnecessary spending: "How much do I have saved for fun, exciting plans for which I have a deadline?"

☐ Realize that you are building your future credit rating even though you are a student.

DACIE JACKSON PETERS
Student—Emergency Medical Paramedic
Delgado Community College and Southwest Tennessee
Community College   New Orleans, LA, and Memphis, TN

One minute your life is fine. You're in college studying in a field you love, your child is doing well in school, your husband is great, your home is secure, and life is good. The next moment, your home is gone, your school is underwater, your child is crying and terrified, and you're being airlifted from the roof of your home and taken to a state and city where you know no one. Yes, my family and I endured Hurricane Katrina. But we survived and even after all of this, I can say I am truly blessed.

I am a native of New Orleans. My family and I have lived in Louisiana all our lives until August of 2005, when the levees failed and washed our lives away. I was studying to work in the health care profession and was close to graduation when my life changed forever. After the rescue, my family and I were taken to a shelter in Arkansas and later moved to another in Memphis, Tennessee. I never thought that anything like this could happen to me and my family, but at 32 years old, the word "normal" disappeared from my dictionary.

We spent much of September through December just trying to survive, finding a place to live, looking for new jobs, and caring for our child. I found myself mad at everything and everybody. I was scared, I had watched everything disappear that I had worked for since high school, my child had to begin counselling to help her cope with the massive changes, and my life seemed out of control. Then it dawned on me.

I knew that I had to "get up" and start over. I had to find my footing again and get my family back on track. The first thing I did was to find a college in Memphis, transfer my credits, and begin to complete my degree. In January of 2006, I enrolled in classes and am now working toward the completion of my degree as an emergency medical paramedic.

I learned that when you are down, you have to look up. I learned that there are people who will help you and guide you. One of my past professors from Delgado Community College, Melanie Deffendall, will forever be a role model and guardian angel to me. She lost everything in Katrina, too. As I write this, she is living in a FEMA trailer. But through e-mail and later phone calls, she encouraged me, guided me, and is helping me complete my degree. She never put herself first, and I can only imagine the number of other students she helped during this time.

I plan to return to my home of New Orleans in the coming months, purchase a home, rebuild my life there, and help others in any way possible. I want to be the type of person and role model to my child that Ms. Deffendall and others were to me. I have learned that this is what life is all about—helping others rise up.

As you can tell by my story, my family and I have been through quite an ordeal, but as I wrote earlier, I am able to stand up today and say, *I am truly, truly blessed*.

Research and read two articles about credit card debt. Analyze your own credit card situation relative to the information you read in the articles. Predict where you will be in two years if you stay on the same course that you are on now.

_____

_____

_____

_____

_____

did you know?

Maya Angelou was born in St. Louis, Mo, in 1928. By the time she was in her 20s she had been a cook, streetcar conductor, cocktail waitress, dancer, madam, high school dropout, and an unwed mother. As a young girl, she was raped by her mother's boyfriend and did not speak again for four years.

Today, Dr. Angelou is a world-renowned poet, civil rights activist, historian, screen writer, and director. She is only the second poet _in history_ to write and deliver an original poem at a Presidential Inauguration (Clinton).

She won three Grammy Awards in the spoken word category and has been nominated twice for Broadway's prestigious Tony Award.

THE PITFALLS OF PAYDAY LOANS, CAR TITLE LOANS, AND RENT-TO-OWN CONTRACTS

There's Someone on Every Corner to Take Your Money

Many unsuspecting consumers have been duped into signing car title loans, payday loans, or rent-to-own contracts that resulted in very high monthly payments and penalties. Some were told by their title loan broker before they signed the contract that they could make a partial payment if they needed to and this would be OK. Unfortunately, the unsuspecting victims find out too late that their car is going to be repossessed due to one late or partial payment. Others realize too late that on a loan of $400, they must pay back over $500 that month. According to recent reports from consumer affairs groups, some institutions have been charging as much as 250 percent interest on an annualized basis (Coj.net, 2003). In some instances, interest rates as high as 900 percent have been charged due to poor government regulatory policies.

By using rent-to-own companies, you are paying double and sometimes triple the actual cost of the item. Try never to walk into a rent-to-own company.

The main point that you need to remember is that you should borrow money only from a reputable bank or credit union. NEVER get involved in a payday loan or car title loan. Not only could you lose your car, but you also could ruin your credit. There are indeed people on every corner who will take your money if you don't manage your affairs very carefully.

GLOSSARY OF FINANCIAL TERMS

Annual fee   amount charged by a lender to keep a credit card.

Annual percentage rate   the cost of credit at an annual rate.

Bankruptcy   Chapter 7 bankruptcy allows one's unprotected assets to be sold and disbursed to creditors. Chapter 13 allows the debtor time to pay debts.

Budget   A plan that takes into consideration one's income, expenses, and savings.

Car title loans   Loans made against one's car, usually at a very high rate of interest.

Collateral   Assets that may be used to secure a loan.

Credit   A promise to buy now and pay later.

Credit history   A record of one's history of loans and credit card debts and how one has repaid the debts.

Credit line   The amount of credit issued by a lender.

Credit report   Your credit history, compiled by several companies and made available to banks and other companies.

Debit card   Card that allows purchases to be charged directly to one's personal bank account.

Default   Failure to repay a debt.

Delinquency   Past-due payment on a loan.

Discretionary income   Amount of money one has left after all expenses have been paid.

Disposable income   Money left over after taxes have been deducted.

Fixed expenses   Expenses that remain the same every month.

Flexible expenses   Expenses that vary from month to month.

Grace period   Period one has in which to pay a debt before being assessed finance charges.

Identity fraud   Crime that occurs when someone assumes another person's identity.

Income taxes   A percentage of one's income that is assessed by the federal and some state governments and deducted from one's paycheck.

Installment loan   A debt in which the amount and number of payments are predetermined.

Interest   Cost of borrowing money.

Interest rate   Percentage of the principal charged by a lender.

Investment   Buying stock, real estate, art, bonds, and so forth with the idea that the investment will appreciate in value.

Late fee   Charges made to a delinquent account.

Payday loans   Loans made against one's next paycheck, usually at a very high rate of interest.

Principal   The outstanding balance of a loan exclusive of interest.

Repossession   Creditor legally takes back something purchased and not paid for.

> "If you can make a million by starting to invest after 45, how much more could you accumulate if you started at 25?"
>
> —Price Pritchett

PROTECT YOURSELF FROM IDENTITY THEFT

Living Large on Your Good Name

Every year thousands of people are victims of identity theft. In other words, someone uses their name and personal information and charges on their credit cards. Identity theft may also include filing fraudulent tax returns, accessing bank accounts, and committing other crimes. NEVER put any personal information in the garbage that has not been shredded. Buy an inexpensive shredder and use it! Many identity theft victims have spent over 175 hours and over $10,000 per incident to resolve their problems.

People who may steal your identity can be roommates, relatives, friends, estranged spouses, restaurant servers, household workers who have ready access to your papers, not to

open the door
Tips for Career Success

Consider the following strategies for minimizing your risk of identity theft:

- Carry only the ID and cards you need at any given time.
- Sign all new credit cards immediately with permanent ink and write across the back of them "CHECK ID" in bold red letters.
- Do not make Internet purchases from sites that are unsecured (check for a padlock icon to ensure safety).
- Do not write your PIN, Social Security number, or passcode on any paper that can be stolen or that you are discarding.
- Try to memorize your passwords instead of recording them on paper or in the computer.
- Get someone you trust to check your mail in your absence.
- Avoid providing your Social Security number to any organization until you have verified its legitimacy.
- Check your credit file periodically by requesting a copy of your report.

(Adapted from "Identifying Theft and Fraud," *Money Matters 101*, p. 9, 2005).

"A full purse is not as good as an empty purse is bad."

—Yiddish proverb

mention complete strangers. Or they may steal your wallet, go through your trash, or take your mail. They can even legally photocopy your vital information at the courthouse if, for example, you have been divorced. The Internet provides thieves many other opportunities to use official-looking e-mail messages designed to obtain your personal information.

It is very difficult, if not impossible, to catch identity thieves. While you may not be liable, you still have to spend your time filing expensive legal affidavits, writing letters, and making telephone calls to clear your good name.

Victims of identity theft can suffer staggering consequences:

- They must resolve unauthorized debts and delinquent accounts.
- Some have lost their jobs.
- Some have faced criminal investigation, arrest, or conviction.
- Victims may not even know their identity has been stolen until, after several months, a negative situation arises.
- Order a credit report once a year to be sure you have no major problems!

What to Do If Your Credit Card Is Stolen

- ☐ Contact your local police immediately.
- ☐ Notify your creditors immediately and request that your accounts be closed.
- ☐ Ask the card company to furnish copies of documents that show fraudulent transactions.
- ☐ Refuse to pay any bill or portion of any bill that is a result of identity theft.
- ☐ Report the theft or fraud to credit reporting agencies.

What to Do If You Lose Your Driver's License

- ☐ Notify the state Department of Motor Vehicles and place a fraud alert on your license number.
- ☐ Request a new driver's license.

THINK ABOUT IT

Reflections for Success

Although many people fail in the management of their personal finances, there is no reason that you cannot manage your financial business well. You should think about personal finance and the management of money and investments as basic survival skills that are very important to you now and will be for the rest of your life.

Because only 10 percent of students graduate from high school with any kind of instruction in personal finance, learning to budget your money, make wise investments, and avoid credit card debt are priority needs of all college students. As you move toward establishing yourself in a career, it is important to remember that to get what you want out of life, a significant part of your success will depend on your ability to make sound money decisions. En route to becoming a good money manager, you will benefit from the following tips:

☐ Don't get caught in the credit card trap.
☐ Know exactly how you are spending your money.
☐ Protect your credit rating by using wise money management strategies.
☐ Learn all you can about scholarships and grants.
☐ Understand the regulations about repaying student loans.
☐ Don't borrow any more money than you absolutely have to.
☐ Ask for your credit score at least once a year and be sure you have a good one.
☐ Use only one or two credit cards.
☐ Try to pay off your credit card each month before any interest is charged.
☐ Write down your credit card numbers and keep them in a safe place in case your cards are lost or stolen.
☐ If you get into credit card trouble, get counseling.

Learning to manage your money and protect your credit rating will be as important to you as getting your degree. It is never too early to learn about money management. If you can do it when you have just a little, it is easier when you have more.

> "Never work just for money or for power. They won't save your soul or help you sleep at night."
>
> —Marian Wright Edelman

passages
An Activity for Critical Thinking and Career Development

On page 9 of Chapter 1, and inside the front cover, you read **The Ten Essential Cornerstones for Personal and Professional Success.** They are:

Passion	Motivation
Knowledge	Resourcefulness
Creativity	Adaptability
Open-mindedness	Communication
Accountability	Vision

Using the following activity, look critically at your current financial situation and determine how you can best use the *Essential Cornerstones* listed below to help you manage your money and debts.

LIST YOUR **TOP FIVE** MONEY
MANAGEMENT STRATEGIES
(How do you best save money each month)

1._____
2._____
3._____
4._____
5._____

LIST YOUR **WORST FIVE** MONEY
MANAGEMENT MISTAKES
(How do you waste money each month)

1._____
2._____
3._____
4._____
5._____

Now, using the five **ESSENTIAL CORNERSTONES** listed below, write a brief statement as to how each Cornerstone can help you overcome your five worst money management mistakes:

By having personal **MOTIVATION**, I can overcome my worst money management mistakes by

_____

_____

_____

_____

_____

By using **CREATIVITY**, I can overcome my worst money management mistakes by

_____

_____

_____

_____

_____

By becoming more **ADAPTABLE**, I can overcome my worst money management mistakes by

_____

_____

_____

_____

_____

By becoming more **ACCOUNTABLE**, I can overcome my worst money management mistakes by

_____

_____

_____

_____

_____

By developing a **VISION** of my financial future, I can overcome my worst money management mistakes by

_____

_____

_____

_____

_____

ARE YOU ACTIVE OR PASSIVE?

Discovering Your Reading Style

Take a few moments and circle true or false for each of the following statements to determine if you are more of an active or passive reader.

DISCOVERING YOUR READING STYLE

1. I enjoy reading for pleasure.	TRUE	FALSE
2. College textbooks have little connection to my real life.	TRUE	FALSE
3. I look for the deeper meaning in words and phrases.	TRUE	FALSE
4. I seldom visualize what I am reading.	TRUE	FALSE
5. I look up words that I do not understand.	TRUE	FALSE
6. I read only what I have to read, and that is a stretch for me.	TRUE	FALSE
7. I stop reading to ponder what something means.	TRUE	FALSE
8. I never take notes when reading.	TRUE	FALSE
9. Reading brings me great joy.	TRUE	FALSE
10. My mind wanders constantly when I read.	TRUE	FALSE
11. I make time for reading even when I am not required to read.	TRUE	FALSE
12. Words are just words—they add no real meaning to my life or work.	TRUE	FALSE
13. I get excited about reading something new because I know I will learn something new and useful.	TRUE	FALSE
14. When reading, I just want to get it over with.	TRUE	FALSE
15. I usually have no trouble concentrating when reading.	TRUE	FALSE
16. I never look up words; I just read on.	TRUE	FALSE

Total of even TRUE responses _____

Total of odd TRUE responses _____

If you answered TRUE to more even numbers, you tend to be a more passive reader.
If you answered TRUE to more odd numbers, you tend to be a more active reader.

Active reading is really nothing more than a mind-set. It is the attitude you have as you begin the reading process. For the next few days, try approaching your reading assignments with a positive, open-minded approach and notice the difference in your own satisfaction, understanding, and overall comprehension.

Now that you have discovered if you are an active or passive reader, the following section will help you determine your reading speed.

I FEEL THE NEED . . . THE NEED FOR SPEED!

Determining Your Personal Reading Rate

You've heard the advertisements: "Breeze through a novel on your lunch hour," "Read an entire computer instruction book over dinner," or "Read the *New York Times* in ten minutes." Sure, there are people who have an incredible gift for speed reading and a photographic memory, but those people are not the norm. Speed is not everything. Most instructors agree that comprehension is *much* more important than speed. If you are a slow reader, does this mean that you are not intelligent? Absolutely not! Reading speeds will vary from person to person depending on training, frequency in reading, comprehension, and the complexity of the material.

> **ESSENTIAL CORNERSTONE**
>
> ### PASSION
>
> How can learning to read more effectively and reading more often increase your passion for learning?

This section is included in your text to give you some idea about how long it will take to read a chapter so that you can *plan your reading time* more effectively. There are an average of 450 words on a college textbook page. If you read at 150 words per minute, each page may take you an average of 3 minutes to read.

This is a *raw number* for just reading. It does not allow for marking, highlighting, taking notes, looking up words, or reflecting. When these necessary skills are coupled with basic reading, they can sometimes triple the amount of reading time required. So, that page that you estimated would take you 3 minutes to read may actually take you 9 to 10 minutes.

If your instructor has assigned a chapter that is 21 pages long and it takes you 9 minutes on average to read each page, you need to allow at least 189 minutes (or 3 hours and 9 minutes) to read and comprehend the chapter.

In the following activity, you will find a passage from a later chapter in this book. Read the section at your normal pace. Use a stopwatch or a watch with a second hand to accurately record your time, and then calculate your rate and comprehension level using the scales provided.

Calculating your Reading Rate

Start Time _____   _____   Minutes _____   Seconds_____

BINGE DRINKING

Binge drinking is classified as having more than five drinks at one time. Many people say, "I only drink once a week." However, if that one drinking spell includes drink after drink after drink, it can be extremely detrimental to your liver, your memory, your digestive system, and your overall health.

Most college students report that they do not mean to binge drink, but it is caused by the situation, such as a ballgame, a party, a campus event, or special occasions. Researchers at Michigan State University found that only 5 percent of students surveyed say they party to "get drunk" (Warner, 2002).

In their breakthrough work, *Dying to Drink,* Harvard researcher Henry Wechsler and science writer Bernice Wuethrich explore the problem of binge drinking. They suggest, "two out of every five college students regularly binge drink, resulting in approximately 1,400 student deaths, a distressing number of assaults and rapes, a shameful amount of vandalism, and countless cases of academic suicide" (Wechsler and Wuethrich, 2002).

(continued)

It is a situation reminiscent of the old saying, "Letting the fox guard the henhouse." After a few drinks, it is hard to "self-police," meaning that you may not be able to control your actions once the drinking starts.

Perhaps the greatest tragedy of drug and alcohol abuse is the residual damage of pregnancy, sexually transmitted diseases, traffic fatalities, verbal/physical abuse, and accidental death. You know that drugs and alcohol lower your resistance and can cause you to do things that you would not normally do, such as drive drunk or have unprotected sex. Surveys and research results suggest that students who participate in heavy episodic (HE) or binge drinking are more likely to participate in unprotected sex with multiple sex partners. One survey found that 61 percent of men who *do* binge drink participated in unprotected sex as compared to 23 percent of men who *do not* binge drink. The survey also found that 48 percent of women who *do* binge drink participated in unprotected sex as compared to only 8 percent of women who *do not* binge drink (Cooper, 2002).

These staggering statistics suggest one thing: alcohol consumption can cause people to act in ways in which they may never have acted without alcohol—and those actions can result in personal damage from which recovery may be impossible.

(387 words)

Finishing Time _____   _____ Minutes _____ Seconds

Reading time in SECONDS = _____

Words per MINUTE (use the following chart) = _____

Example: If you read this passage in 2 minutes and 38 seconds, your reading time in seconds would be 158. Using the Rate Calculator Chart, your reading rate would be about 146 words per minute.

RATE CALCULATOR FOR RELATIVELY EASY PASSAGES

Time in Seconds and Minutes	Words Per Minute
40	581
50	464
60 (1 minute)	387
120 (2 minutes)	194
130	179
140	165
150	155
160	145
170	137
180 (3 minutes)	129
190	122
200	116
210	110
220	106
230	101

Source: B. Smith, *Breaking Through,* 8th ed. (2007).

Test Your Comprehension Skills

Answer the following questions with T (true) or F (false) without looking back over the material.

_____ 1. Binge drinking has resulted in the deaths of students.

_____ 2. Men who binge drink have unprotected sex more often than men who do not binge drink.

_____ 3. Women who binge drink have unprotected sex no more often than women who do not binge drink.

(continued)

_____ 4. "Self-policing" means that you are able to look out for yourself.

_____ 5. Binge drinking is classified as having more than three drinks at one time.

Each question is worth 20 percent.   Comprehension = _____%

Example: If you answered two correctly, your comprehension rate would be 40% (2 × 20%). If you answered four correctly, your comprehension rate would be 80% (4 × 20%).

Test Your Comprehension Skills Answers: 1 = T, 2 = T, 3 = F, 4 = T, 5 = F

WHAT DOES IT ALL MEAN?

According to Brenda D. Smith (2007), professor and reading expert, "rate calculators vary according to the difficulty of the material. Research indicates, however, that on relatively easy material, the average adult reading speed is approximately 250 words per minute at 70% comprehension. For college students, the rate is sometimes estimated at closer to 300 words per minute." The passage that you just read would be classified as relatively easy.

If you are reading below the 250-word-per-minute rate, several factors could be contributing to this situation. They include:

- Not concentrating on the passage
- Vocabulary words with which you are not familiar
- Stopping too long on any given word (called fixations, which is discussed later)
- Not reading often enough to build your speed

The remainder of this chapter is intended to assist you with improving your reading speed and comprehension.

YOU DON'T HAVE TO BE A LOGODAEDALIAN TO ENJOY WORDS
The Power of a Dynamic Vocabulary

Thankfully, it is not every day you run across the word *logodaedalian*. (A logodaedalian is a person who has a great passion for unique, sly, and clever words and phrases.) Perhaps the best way to develop a dynamic vocabulary is by reading. By reading, you come across words that you may have never seen before. You are exposed to aspects of language that you may not have experienced in your family, neighborhood, or geographic location.

"The more that you read, the more things you will know. The more that you learn, the more places you'll go."

—Dr. Seuss

Of course, the words in a passage, section, or chapter with which you are unfamiliar will not become a part of your vernacular unless you STOP and look them up. This is the way to begin building a masterful vocabulary.

Let's start by looking up the word *vernacular.* Take a moment and jot down the definition.

Vernacular means: _____

_____

_____

_____

See how simple that was? Now, you have a new word in your vocabulary—actually, you have two new words in just a few paragraphs: vernacular and logodaedalian. You're on your way to becoming a logophile!

IT'S NOT JUST A DOORSTOP
Using Your Dictionary

Your dictionary will become a good friend to you in college. There will be many words and phrases that you will not understand when reading texts that are written on the thirteenth- and fourteenth-grade levels. There is nothing to be ashamed of because you resort to "looking up" a word. You'll be smarter because of it.

When you look up a word in the dictionary, you are given more than just a definition (see Figure 6.1). You are given the phonetic pronunciation, the spelling, the meaning, the parts of speech in which the word can be used, the origin of the word, and usually several definitions. You may have to choose the definition that best suits the context of the sentence.

Using the definition for *magnitude,* determine which definition would be best suited to this sentence:

The magnitude of the power she had over him was truly amazing.

FIGURE 6.1   Annotated Dictionary Entry

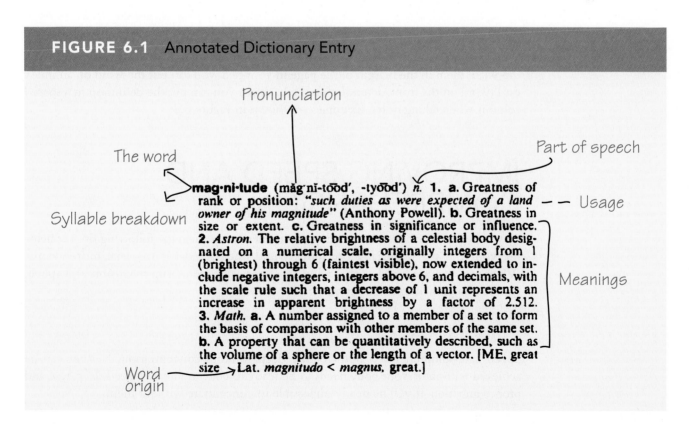

FIGURE 6.2   Define Unknown Words

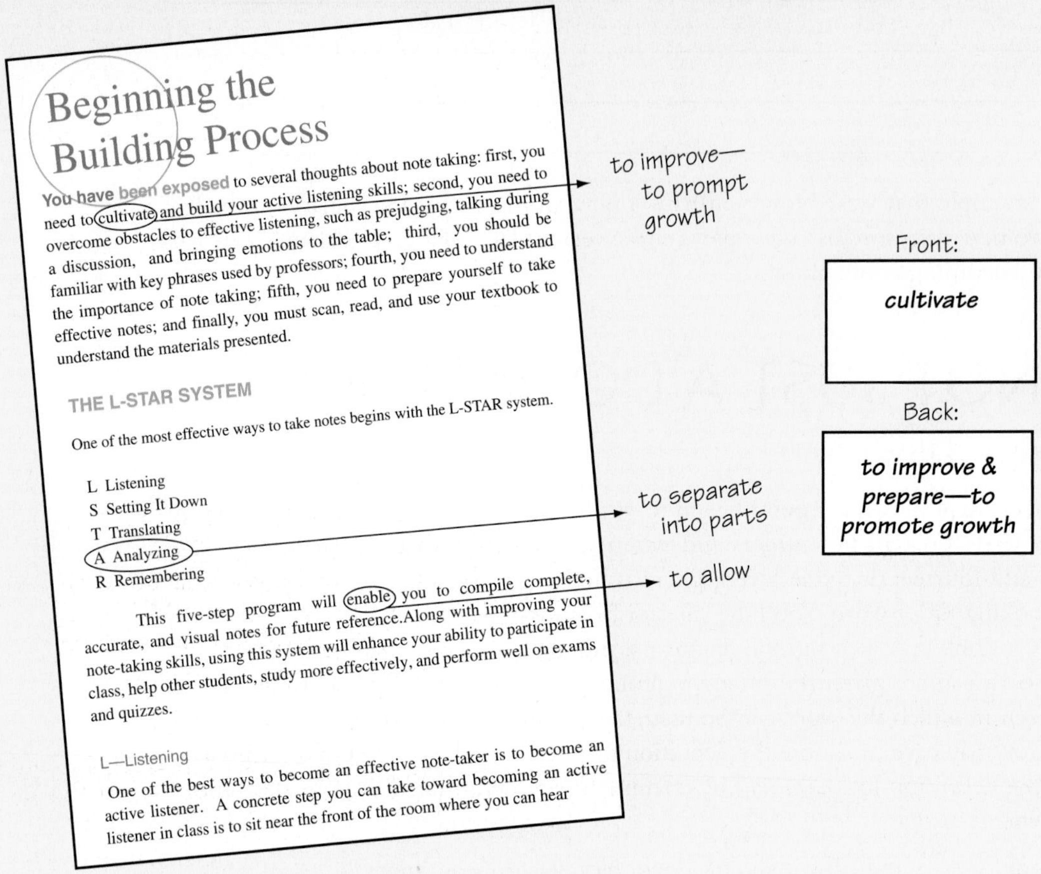

> ### Beginning the Building Process
>
> You have been exposed to several thoughts about note taking: first, you need to cultivate and build your active listening skills; second, you need to overcome obstacles to effective listening, such as prejudging, talking during a discussion, and bringing emotions to the table; third, you should be familiar with key phrases used by professors; fourth, you need to understand the importance of note taking; fifth, you need to prepare yourself to take effective notes; and finally, you must scan, read, and use your textbook to understand the materials presented.
>
> **THE L-STAR SYSTEM**
>
> One of the most effective ways to take notes begins with the L-STAR system.
>
> L Listening
> S Setting It Down
> T Translating
> A Analyzing
> R Remembering
>
> This five-step program will enable you to compile complete, accurate, and visual notes for future reference. Along with improving your note-taking skills, using this system will enhance your ability to participate in class, help other students, study more effectively, and perform well on exams and quizzes.
>
> **L—Listening**
>
> One of the best ways to become an effective note-taker is to become an active listener. A concrete step you can take toward becoming an active listener in class is to sit near the front of the room where you can hear

to improve—
to prompt growth

to separate into parts

to allow

Front:

cultivate

Back:

to improve & prepare—to promote growth

There are several ways to begin your collection of unfamiliar words as you read. You can write them in the margin of the page in your text, you can put the word on an index card (word on the front, definition on the back), or you can put the definition in a special column when taking notes. Examples are shown in Figure 6.2.

IMPROVING SPEED AND COMPREHENSION

As you begin to practice your reading comprehension, review the following tips for helping you read the material more quickly and understand the material more clearly. Whenever you are faced with having to choose between comprehension and speed, choose comprehension every time.

Concentration

Speed and comprehension both require deep, mindful concentration. Neither can be achieved without it. Your body needs to be ready to concentrate. You need sleep, rest, and proper nutrition. It will be nearly impossible to concentrate without them.

EXTRAORDINARY

DINO J. GONZALEZ, M.D.

Gonzalez Internal Medicine
Board-Certified Internal Medicine
AAHIVM Certified HIV Specialist

Can one person make a difference in your life? Can one person change the course of your destiny? The answer is yes! Most definitely, yes! The person who altered the course of my future was my third-grade teacher, Mrs. Allison. She was a strong African American lady who pushed us to do our best and would not let us fail. She was hard and demanded the best from us, but she was fair and an awesome teacher. She made us bring a toothbrush from home so that we could brush our teeth after lunch. She corrected our grammar and let us know that "street English" would not fly in her classroom. She even made us do Jazzercise after lunch to teach us how to take care of our bodies. I was lucky to be under her tutelage again in the fifth grade.

Why was she so dynamic? Why did she mean so much to my life? Well, I had always been a good student in school, earning mostly A's. However, my home life was another story, I was born in 1970 in a HUD housing project in Las Vegas, Nevada, in the gang-infested 28th Street area. My mother, two brothers, and I lived in poverty. By the time I was three, my mother was bedridden and on disability due to chronic obstructive pulmonary disease, caused by a three-pack-a-day smoking habit. We were on welfare, food stamps, and the free lunch program.

As it turned out, my father never married my mother or helped support us because he was already married to another woman with children of their own. My mother did not know this until after my birth. So basically, we were on our own. Often, I felt alone in my community because I looked different. My father was Hispanic, but my mother was a blond, light-skinned Norwegian. I was not brown. I was not white. I felt like I did not have a real place in my community or in school. Mrs. Allison helped change all of that.

Because of her and a few close friends, I began to see the positive aspect of school and getting an education. I managed to stay away from the heavy gang influence that had engulfed my brothers. By the time I began high school, one of my brothers was already in prison because of drugs and gang activity. Because of Mrs. Allison's influence, I began to surround myself with people who were positive and worked hard. I wanted to be around people who *wanted something*— who had a wider view of the world than I had.

The harder I worked and studied, the better I did. I excelled in junior high and high school and by the time I graduated, I did so with honors. I became the first person in my family to attend college. I was offered four scholarships and they paid for everything, even giving me some spare money to live on. I had been working anywhere from 20 to 30 hours per week since I was fourteen years old, but I continued to work full-time while attending college.

I had always loved science and the study of the human body, so I decided to major in chemistry and education. I began to develop a keen interest in infectious diseases and viruses. By the time I was a junior in college, I had decided to become a doctor, so I dropped my education major and focused on biology. After graduation, I applied to medical school and was accepted into the University of Nevada School of Medicine. I completed my studies, did a three-year residency, and decided to open my own practice. I became board certified in internal medicine and as an HIV specialist. Six years later, my practice is hugely successful and I enjoy days filled with helping people maintain or regain their health. My dream of doing something real and helping others is now an everyday occurrence in my life.

My advice to you as a first-year college student is this: You have the power to make your dreams come true. *YOU can CHANGE* your life if you truly know what you want and do the work that comes with making dreams come true. Surround yourself with upbeat, positive, smart, giving, open-minded people from whom you can learn and grow. Mrs. Allison was my inspiration. Yours is out there, too.

SCAN

The first step of SQ3R is to scan, or preread, an assigned chapter. You've been doing this since you began reading Chapter 1 of this text. You begin by reading the title of the chapter, the headings, and each subheading. Look carefully at the vocabulary, time lines, graphs, charts, pictures, and drawings included in each chapter. If there is a chapter summary, read it. Scanning also includes reading the first and last sentence in each paragraph. Scanning is not a substitute for reading a chapter. Reading is discussed later. Before going any further, scan Chapter 7 using the following eight questions.

CHAPTER SCAN

1. What is the title of the chapter? _____

2. What is the subheading of the chapter? _____

3. List the chapter major headings. _____

   _____

   _____

   _____

4. Who is introduced in the "Did You Know?" feature? List one thing you learned about him/her. _____

   _____

   _____

   _____

5. If the chapter contains quotations, which one means the most to you? Why?

   _____

   _____

   _____

6. What is the most important graph or chart in the chapter? Why?

   _____

   _____

   _____

7. Close your book and list five topics that this chapter will cover.

   _____

   _____

   _____

   _____

   _____

QUESTION

The second step is to question. There are five common questions you should ask yourself when you are reading a chapter: Who? When? What? Where? and Why? As you scan and read your chapter, turn the information into questions and see if you can answer them. If you do not know the answers, you should find them as you read along. You have been doing this for each chapter thus far.

Another way to approach the chapter is to turn the major headings of each section into questions (see an example in Figure 6.3). When you get to the end of the section, having carefully read the material, taken notes, and highlighted important information, answer the question that you posed at the beginning of the section.

READ

After you scan the chapter and develop some questions to be answered from the chapter, the next step is to read the chapter. Remember, scanning is not reading. There is no substitute for reading in your success plan. Read slowly and carefully. The SQ3R method

FIGURE 6.3   Forming Questions from Headings

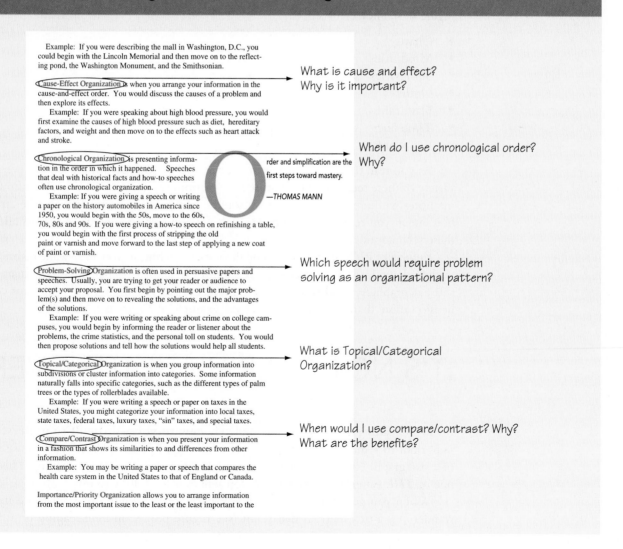

Example: If you were describing the mall in Washington, D.C., you could begin with the Lincoln Memorial and then move on to the reflecting pond, the Washington Monument, and the Smithsonian.

What is cause and effect?
Why is it important?

Cause-Effect Organization is when you arrange your information in the cause-and-effect order. You would discuss the causes of a problem and then explore its effects.

Example: If you were speaking about high blood pressure, you would first examine the causes of high blood pressure such as diet, hereditary factors, and weight and then move on to the effects such as heart attack and stroke.

When do I use chronological order? Why?

Chronological Organization is presenting information in the order in which it happened. Speeches that deal with historical facts and how-to speeches often use chronological organization.

Example: If you were giving a speech or writing a paper on the history automobiles in America since 1950, you would begin with the 50s, move to the 60s, 70s, 80s and 90s. If you were giving a how-to speech on refinishing a table, you would begin with the first process of stripping the old paint or varnish and move forward to the last step of applying a new coat of paint or varnish.

Order and simplification are the first steps toward mastery.
—THOMAS MANN

Which speech would require problem solving as an organizational pattern?

Problem-Solving Organization is often used in persuasive papers and speeches. Usually, you are trying to get your reader or audience to accept your proposal. You first begin by pointing out the major problem(s) and then move on to revealing the solutions, and the advantages of the solutions.

Example: If you were writing or speaking about crime on college campuses, you would begin by informing the reader or listener about the problems, the crime statistics, and the personal toll on students. You would then propose solutions and tell how the solutions would help all students.

What is Topical/Categorical Organization?

Topical/Categorical Organization is when you group information into subdivisions or cluster information into categories. Some information naturally falls into specific categories, such as the different types of palm trees or the types of rollerblades available.

Example: If you were writing a speech or paper on taxes in the United States, you might categorize your information into local taxes, state taxes, federal taxes, luxury taxes, "sin" taxes, and special taxes.

When would I use compare/contrast? Why? What are the benefits?

Compare/Contrast Organization is when you present your information in a fashion that shows its similarities to and differences from other information.

Example: You may be writing a paper or speech that compares the health care system in the United States to that of England or Canada.

Importance/Priority Organization allows you to arrange information from the most important issue to the least or the least important to the requires a substantial amount of time, but if you take each step slowly and completely, you will be amazed at how much you can learn and how much your grades will improve.

Read through each section. It is best not to jump around or move ahead if you do not understand the previous section. Paragraphs are usually built on each other, so you need to understand the first before you can move on to the next. You may have to read a chapter or section more than once, especially if the information is new, technical, or difficult.

Take notes, highlight, and make marginal notes in your textbook as you read along. You own your textbook and should personalize it as you would your lecture notes. Highlight areas that you feel are important, underline words and phrases that you did not understand or that you feel are important, and jot down notes in the margins.

As you begin to read your chapter, mark the text, and take notes, keep the following in mind:

- Read the entire paragraph before you mark anything.
- Identify the topic or thesis statement of each paragraph and highlight it.
- Highlight key phrases.
- Don't highlight too much; the text will lose its significance.
- Stop and look up words that you do not know or understand.

While reading, you will want to take notes that are more elaborate than your highlighting or marginal notes. Taking notes while reading the text will assist you in studying the material and committing it to memory. **This is a major part of LEARNING ACTIVELY**. There are several effective methods of taking notes while reading (see Figure 6.4). They include:

- Charts
- Mind maps
- Summaries
- Outlines
- Flash cards
- Time lines
- Key words

As you read through a chapter in your textbook, you may find that you have to use a variety of these techniques to capture information. Try them for one week. Although taking notes while reading a chapter thoroughly is time consuming, you will be amazed at how much you remember and how much you are able to contribute in class after using these techniques.

Especially if the material is difficult or very technical, you may want to break your reading down into smaller parts and *stop after each paragraph* to paraphrase the main idea of that paragraph. Again, this is time consuming, but few techniques will assist your comprehension more than this one. Consider the example in Figure 6.5.

IT'S NOT OVER UNTIL IT'S OVER
Reading Piece by Piece

If you are reading material that is completely **new to you—difficult to understand** yet important to remember—you may have to disregard paragraphs and paraphrase sections of a paragraph. This can be done with simple "tick marks" in your reading. This can be one of *THE most effective reading tools* you will ever learn how to use.

When you get to a point where you have "read enough," or your mind begins to wander, put a tick mark at that point (see Figure 6.6). Continue reading until you get

FIGURE 6.4   Sample Note-Taking Methods

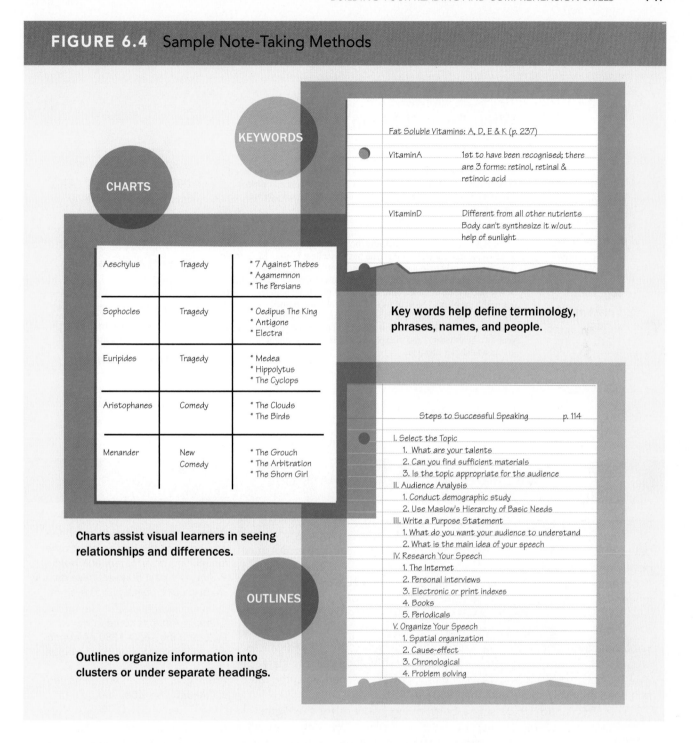

KEYWORDS

CHARTS

Aeschylus	Tragedy	* 7 Against Thebes * Agamemnon * The Persians
Sophocles	Tragedy	* Oedipus The King * Antigone * Electra
Euripides	Tragedy	* Medea * Hippolytus * The Cyclops
Aristophanes	Comedy	* The Clouds * The Birds
Menander	New Comedy	* The Grouch * The Arbitration * The Shorn Girl

Fat Soluble Vitamins: A, D, E & K (p. 237)

VitaminA — 1st to have been recognised; there are 3 forms: retinol, retinal & retinoic acid

VitaminD — Different from all other nutrients Body can't synthesize it w/out help of sunlight

Key words help define terminology, phrases, names, and people.

Charts assist visual learners in seeing relationships and differences.

OUTLINES

Steps to Successful Speaking   p. 114

I. Select the Topic
  1. What are your talents
  2. Can you find sufficient materials
  3. Is the topic appropriate for the audience
II. Audience Analysis
  1. Conduct demographic study
  2. Use Maslow's Hierarchy of Basic Needs
III. Write a Purpose Statement
  1. What do you want your audience to understand
  2. What is the main idea of your speech
IV. Research Your Speech
  1. The Internet
  2. Personal interviews
  3. Electronic or print indexes
  4. Books
  5. Periodicals
V. Organize Your Speech
  1. Spatial organization
  2. Cause-effect
  3. Chronological
  4. Problem solving

Outlines organize information into clusters or under separate headings.

to another section, putting tick marks in the places where you feel you have read a complete thought. You will not want to read an entire chapter at one time—simply sections. After you understand the section, move on to the next and then the next until the chapter is complete. (Figure 6.6 illustrates this technique using different colors.)

When you get to the end of the paragraph or section, reread the first section that you marked off. Out to the side, paraphrase that section. Then go to the next section. Consider Figure 6.6. Few techniques will assist your comprehension and retention more than this one because it requires you to be actively involved in the reading process. You are reading, paraphrasing, clarifying, and looking up words you do not know. This process is essential to you if your reading comprehension is not at the college level.

FIGURE 6.5   Breaking Down the Meaning

1. *Infirmity = the lack of power, a disability*

2. *Continuum = a whole where all parts work together.*

3. *Debilitating = to make weak.*

What Does It Mean to Be Healthy?

Most people consider themselves healthy. They believe that if they are not sick, they are healthy. However, the absence of illness does not mean that you are healthy; it simply means that you are currently without illness.

The World Health Organization defines health as "not merely the absence of disease or <u>infirmity</u>, but a state of complete physical, mental, and social well-being." Realistically, health is a <u>continuum</u>: on one end you have death, and on the other you have excellent health. Most students are somewhere in the middle of the continuum, experiencing neither excellent health nor <u>debilitating</u> diseases. Often students slip slowly into a state of unhealthiness, which if ignored, could lead to serious health problems. Most of us take our health for granted. We place undue stress on ourselves and assume that our bodies will continue to take this abuse. This chapter will afford you the opportunity to review your own health status and to explore some issues that might help you to lead a healthier lifestyle.

Just because you are not sick, this does not mean you are healthy

—Wellness = a state of complete physical, mental, and social health.

—Health is a whole part of life—one end is excellent health, the other end is death.

FIGURE 6.6   A Brief History of Crime in America

What we call criminal activity has undoubtedly been with us since the dawn of history, and crime control has long been a primary concern of politicians and government leaders world-wide. Still, the American experience with crime during the last half century has been especially influential in shaping the criminal justice system of today. /

In this country, crime waves have come and gone, including an 1850–1880 crime epidemic, which was apparently related to social upheaval caused by large-scale immigration, and the spurt of widespread organized criminal activity associated with the Prohibition years of the early twentieth century. / Following World War II, however, American crime rates remained relatively stable until the 1960's. /

The 1960's and 1970's saw a burgeoning concern for the rights of ethnic and racial minorities, women, the physically and mentally challenged, and many other groups. The civil rights movement of the period emphasized the equality of opportunity and respect for individuals, regardless of race, color, creed, or personal attributes. / As new laws were passed and suits filed, court involvement in the movement grew. Soon, a plethora of hard-won individual rights and prerogatives, based on the U.S. Constitution, the Bill of Rights, and the new federal and state legislation, were recognized and guaranteed. By the 1980's, the civil rights movement had profoundly affected all areas of social life – from education throughout employment to the activities of the criminal justice system. /

Although criminal activity has been around since the beginning of time influencing government and politics, in Am., the past 50 years have greatly shaped our criminal justice system.

Crime in Am. has come in waves including the 1850–1880 epidemic due to immigration and prohibition.

After WWII, crime in Am. remained stable until the '60's.

During the '60's and '70's, Am. saw the rise of individual rights regardless of race, creed, or attributes.

Due to laws based on the US Constitution, the C.R. Movement profoundly impacted all aspects of life in Am. including the C. J. system.

Source: (from Criminal Justice: A Brief Introduction, 6th edition. F. Schmalleger. Prentice Hall, 2006.)

Examine how breaking this down piece-by-piece can help you understand it more. It is shown with its original paragraph breaks. The tick marks or sections are shown here in color and marked with a "/" after each break. Once you've broken down the sections, come back and paraphrase each section in your own words. The paraphrasing is shown in corresponding colors.

RECITE

Recitation is simple, but crucial. Skipping this step may result in less than full mastery of the chapter. Once you have read a section using one or more of the techniques from above, ask yourself this simple question: *"What was that all about?"* Find a classmate, sit down together, and ask questions of each other. Discuss with each other the main points of the chapter. Try to explain the information to each other without looking at your notes. If you are at home, sit back in your chair, recite the information, and determine what it means. If you have trouble explaining the information to your friend or reciting it to yourself, you probably did not understand the section and you should reread it. If you can tell your classmate and yourself exactly what you just read and what it means, you are ready to move on to the next section.

Another way to practice reciting is to use the materials you produced as you READ the chapter. Hopefully, you took notes, highlighted passages, underlined phrases, and paraphrased sections. From these, you can create flash cards, outlines, mind maps, timelines, and keyword note cards. Using these materials is another way to "recite" the material.

open the door
Tips for Career Success

Consider the following strategies for making the most of your reading time:

- Reduce the distractions around you. Try to find an atmosphere that is comfortable and effective for you.
- Discover what time of day is best for you to read and concentrate on your material.
- Read with a healthy snack.
- Read in sections. Don't try to read an entire chapter in one sitting. Break it down and take breaks.
- Form questions about the material from headings as you are reading.
- Never just skip over words or phrases that you don't understand. Look them up in a dictionary.
- Allow yourself enough time to read the material effectively. Time management and reading comprehension go hand-in-hand.

REVIEW

After you have read the chapter, immediately go back and read it again. **"What?! I just read it!"** Yes, you did. And the best way to determine whether you have mastered the information is once again to survey the chapter; review marginal notes, highlighted areas, and vocabulary words; and determine whether you can answer the questions you posed during the "Question Step" of SQ3R. This step will help you retain this information in long-term memory.

THINK ABOUT IT

Reflections for Success

SQ3R can be a lifesaver when it comes to understanding material that is overwhelming. It is an efficient, comprehensive, and DOABLE practice that can dramatically assist you in your reading efforts. It may take more time than your old method, but you will begin to see the results almost immediately. Seriously considering and practicing the strategies outlined in this chapter will help increase your comprehension level, and it will also help your ability to recall the information when you need it later on.

It has been suggested that if you can effectively read, write, and speak the English language, there is nothing that you can't accomplish. The power of knowledge is monumental in your quest to become a productive and active citizen. Effective reading skills will help you acquire that knowledge.

As you continue to work to become an active, engaged learner, consider the following tips for reading comprehension and retention:

☐ Approach the text, chapter, or article with an *open mind*.
☐ *Free your mind* to focus on your reading.
☐ Always read with your *"six pack"* at your side.
    ☐ Underline and look up words you do not *understand*.
    ☐ Write down your *vocabulary words*, and review them often.
    ☐ Use *SQ3R* to increase and test your comprehension.
    ☐ If you're having trouble, *get a tutor* to help you.
    ☐ Understand that *the more you read*, the better you'll become at it.

"The knowledge of words is the gateway to learning."

—W. Wilson

passages
An Activity for Critical Thinking and Career Development

On page 9 of Chapter 1, and inside the front cover, you read **The Ten Essential Cornerstones for Personal and Professional Success.** They are:

Passion	Motivation
Knowledge	Resourcefulness
Creativity	Adaptability
Open-mindedness	Communication
Accountability	Vision

PROCESS: Read the following story carefully, looking up words that you do not understand, highlighting phrases that you think are important, and paraphrasing in the spaces provided. When reading the story, use the SQ3R method. We've done paragraph #1 for you as an example.

THE LIFE AND DEATH OF HARVEY MILK

Read This Section, Identify Unfamiliar Words, Highlight Important Words and Phrases	Look Up Words That Need to Be Defined	Paraphrase the Main Idea in Your Own Words
More *perplexing* things have happened, but a Twinkie caused the death of Harvey Milk. That's right. In 1978, defense lawyers using the "Twinkie Defense" explained an *inexplicable* murder away. This was the first mainstream trial to use the "I am not responsible for my actions" defense.	*Unfamiliar words and definitions* *Perplexing = confusing or puzzling* *Inexplicable = not easily explained, unreasonable*	*The main idea of this paragraph is:* In 1978, defense lawyers used a new strategy called "the Twinkie Defense" to explain why someone murdered Harvey Milk.

(continued)

Read This Section, Identify Unfamiliar Words, Highlight Important Words and Phrases	Look Up Words That Need to Be Defined	Paraphrase the Main Idea in Your Own Words
Harvey Milk was the first openly gay man elected to a significant office in America. In 1977, Milk was elected as a member of the San Francisco Board of Supervisors. This was quite arduous at this point in American history when most people, including many psychologists and religious leaders, still classified homosexuality as deviant and a mental illness.	*Unfamiliar words and definitions*	*The main idea of this paragraph is*
Harvey Milk is to the gay rights movement what Martin Luther King Jr. is to the civil rights movement. Before King, little was happening with the Civil Rights Movement, and before Milk, little was happening with the Gay Rights Movement. He changed the face of California politics and paved the way for countless other gays and lesbians to enter the world of politica.	*Unfamiliar words and definitions*	*The main idea of this paragraph is*
Dan White, a staunch antigay advocate, served on the board with Milk. They were constantly at odds with each other and often engaged in verbal confrontations.	*Unfamiliar words and definitions*	*The main idea of this paragraph is*
White had been a policeman and a fireman in San Francisco before running for office. While running for office, he vowed to restore "family values" to the city government. He vowed to "rid San Francisco of radicals, social deviants, and incorrigibles."	*Unfamiliar words and definitions*	*The main idea of this paragraph is*
Dan White was one of the most conservative members of the board, and many proposals brought to the board by Milk and the mayor of San Francisco, George Moscone, were defeated because of the heavily conservative vote led by White.	*Unfamiliar words and definitions*	*The main idea of this paragraph is*

(continued)

Read This Section, Identify Unfamiliar Words, Highlight Important Words and Phrases	Look Up Words That Need to Be Defined	Paraphrase the Main Idea in Your Own Words
At that time, the Board of Supervisors was made up of eleven members; six of them, including Dan White, were conservative and had the power to defeat most of the liberal measures brought before the board. This did not fare well with Harvey Milk and the other liberal members of the board.	*Unfamiliar words and definitions*	*The main idea of this paragraph is*
Because the job offered diminutive wages, Dan White soon realized that he could not support his family on $9,800 per year, and he submitted his resignation to Mayor Moscone. This did not set well with the people who elected him. They urged him to reconsider and when he tried to rescind his resignation, Mayor Moscone refused. This decision was made, in part, because Harvey Milk convinced Moscone to deny his reinstatement.	*Unfamiliar words and definitions*	*The main idea of this paragraph is*
In a fit of wrath over the decision, Dan White entered the San Francisco City Hall on the morning of November 27, 1978, through a basement window. He went to Mayor Moscone's office and shot him in the chest, and as he lay dying, shot him again in the head.	*Unfamiliar words and definitions*	*The main idea of this paragraph is*
He then walked calmly down the hall and asked to see Harvey Milk. Once inside the office, he slew Milk with two bullets to the brain. He then left City Hall, called his wife, spoke with her in person at St. Mary's Cathedral, and then turned himself in.	*Unfamiliar words and definitions*	*The main idea of this paragraph is*
It is reported that policemen representing the city of San Francisco shouted, cheered, and applauded when news of the murders reached the police department.	*Unfamiliar words and definitions*	*The main idea of this paragraph is*

(continued)

Read This Section, Identify Unfamiliar Words, Highlight Important Words and Phrases	Look Up Words That Need to Be Defined	Paraphrase the Main Idea in Your Own Words
Dan White's defense lawyers used a "diminished capacity" defense suggesting that he was led to his actions by too much sugar from junk food. The lawyers convinced a jury that he was not himself and his senses were off kilter. This became known as the "Twinkie Defense."	*Unfamiliar words and definitions*	*The main idea of this paragraph is*
Dan White was convicted of second-degree manslaughter and was sentenced to only seven years for two premeditated murders. After serving only five years, he was released. The "Twinkie Defense" had worked.	*Unfamiliar words and definitions*	*The main idea of this paragraph is*
In 1985, after being released from Soledad Prison, Dan White walked into his garage, took a rubber hose, connected it to his car's exhaust, and killed himself with carbon monoxide poisoning. He was 39 years old. His tomb reads, "*Daniel J. White (1946–October 21, 1985), Sgt. U. S. Army, Vietnam. Cause of death: Suicide.*"	*Unfamiliar words and definitions*	*The main idea of this paragraph is*

Sources: "He Got Away with Murder" at http://www.findagrave.com; "Dan White" at http://www.backdoor.com/castro/milk; "The Pioneer Harvey Milk" at http://www.time.com; "Remembering Harvey Milk" at http://www.lambda.net.

In 100 words or fewer, thoroughly summarize this entire article. Be certain to include dates, names, places, and circumstances. Pretend that you have to explain this entire story to an eight-year-old. This exercise will help you become more adept at the **ESSENTIAL CORNERSTONE** skill of **KNOWLEDGE.**

_____

_____

_____

_____

_____

_____

_____

_____

_____

_____

_____

Now, write a brief paragraph explaining how **The Essential Cornerstone of PASSION** could be enhanced by reading with more comprehension.

_____

_____

_____

_____

_____

_____

_____

Write a brief paragraph explaining how **The Essential Cornerstone of OPENMINDED-NESS** can be enhanced by reading with more comprehension.

_____

_____

_____

_____

_____

_____

_____

_____

_____

INTRAPERSONAL

- Study in a quiet area.
- Study by yourself.
- Allow time for reflection and meditation about the subject matter.
- Study in short time blocks and then spend some time absorbing the information.
- Work at your own pace.

NATURALISTIC

- Study outside whenever possible.
- Relate the information to the effect on the environment whenever possible.
- When given the opportunity to choose your own topics or research projects, choose something related to nature.
- Collect your own study data and resources.
- Organize and label your information.
- Keep separate notebooks on individual topics so that you can add new information to each topic as it becomes available.

UNDERSTANDING LEARNING STYLES THEORY

Rita Dunn (2000) defines learning styles as "the way in which each learner begins to concentrate on, process, and retain new and difficult information." We must note that there is a difference between a *learning style* and a **learning strategy.** A learning strategy is how you might choose to learn or study, such as by using note cards, flip charts, color slides, or cooperative learning groups. Flip charts and slides are strategies. Learning styles are more sensory. They involve seeing, hearing, and touching.

TAKE THE LEAD

The Learning Evaluation and Assessment Directory

© Robert M. Sherfield, Ph.D., 1999, 2002, 2005, 2008.

Directions: Read each statement carefully and thoroughly. After reading the statement, rate your response using the scale below. There are no right or wrong answers. This is not a timed survey. The LEAD is based, in part, on research conducted by Rita Dunn.

3 = Often Applies
2 = Sometimes Applies
1 = Never or Almost Never Applies

_____ 1. I remember information better if I write it down or draw a picture of it.

_____ 2. I remember things better when I hear them instead of just reading or seeing them.

_____ 3. When I get something that has to be assembled, I just start doing it. I don't read the directions.

_____ 4. If I am taking a test, I can "see" the page of the text or lecture notes where the answer is located.

_____ 5. I would rather the professor explain a graph, chart, or diagram than just show it to me.

_____ 6. When learning new things, I want to "do it" rather than hear about it.

_____ 7. I would rather the instructor write the information on the board or overhead instead of just lecturing.

_____ 8. I would rather listen to a book on tape than read it.

(continued)

_____　9.　I enjoy making things, putting things together, and working with my hands.

_____　10.　I am able to quickly conceptualize and visualize information.

_____　11.　I learn best by hearing words.

_____　12.　I have been called hyperactive by my parents, spouse, partner, or professor.

_____　13.　I have no trouble reading maps, charts, or diagrams.

_____　14.　I can usually pick up on small sounds like bells, crickets, or frogs, or distant sounds like train whistles.

_____　15.　I use my hands and gesture a lot when I speak to others.

Refer to your score on each individual question. Place that score beside the appropriate question number below. Then, tally each line at the side.

Score					Total Across	Code
1 _____	4 _____	7 _____	10 _____	13 _____	_____	Visual
2 _____	5 _____	8 _____	11 _____	14 _____	_____	Auditory
3 _____	6 _____	9 _____	12 _____	15 _____	_____	Tactile

LEAD SCORES

Learning Styles

Look at the scores on the LEAD. What is your top score?

Top Score _____　　　　Code _____

If you learn best by _seeing_ information, you have a more dominant _visual_ learning style. If you learn best by _hearing_ information, you have a more dominant _auditory_ learning style. If you learn best by _touching or doing,_ you have a more dominant _tactile_ learning style. You may also hear the tactile learning style referred to as kinesthetic or hands-on.

Some of the most successful students have learned to use all three styles. If you were learning how to skateboard, you might learn best by hearing someone talk about the different styles or techniques. Others might learn best by watching a video where someone demonstrates the techniques. Still others would learn best by actually getting on the board and trying it. However, the student who involved all of his or her senses might gain the most. She might listen to the instructor tell about skateboarding, watch the video, and then go do it. Therefore, she would have involved all of her learning styles: visual, auditory, and tactile. Here are brief descriptions of the three styles.

Visual (Eye Smart).　Thinks in pictures; enjoys visual instructions, demonstrations, and descriptions; would rather read a text than listen to a lecture; avid note taker; needs visual references; enjoys using charts, graphs, and pictures.

Auditory (Ear Smart).　Prefers oral instructions; would rather listen than read; often tapes lectures and listens to them in the car or at home; recites information out loud; enjoys talking, discussing issues, and verbal stimuli; talks out problems.

Tactile (Action Smart).　Prefers hands-on approaches to learning; likes to take notes and uses a great deal of scratch paper; learns best by doing something, by touching it, or manipulating it; learns best while moving or while in action; often does not concentrate well when sitting and reading.

SUCCESSFUL DECISIONS

Kristin knew that her most powerful learning style was visual. She knew that she had always learned best when she could "see" the information in pictures, charts, graphs, PowerPoints, videos, or other powerful visuals.

Kristin also knew that when she was able to get involved with the information, she seemed to retain it better. She did not know what this was called, but later learned that she was also a tactile or "hands-on" learner.

When she discovered that different people have different ways of learning and instructors have different ways of teaching, things began to make more sense to her. She wondered why she had also done poorly in classes that were all lecture—like her history class.

This semester, she was becoming increasingly worried about her Medical Terminology class. It, too, was all lecture—term after term after term. She decided to go to the Tutoring Center to find out what she could do to retain the information more effectively.

Her tutor showed her how to make the terms more "visual" by drawing pictures beside each term, using colors in her notes, creating small story boards, and creating a visual image of the definitions.

Things began to click for her and retention became easier because she learned to convert a "lecture" class into "visual" study time.

Kristin made a *successful decision*.

THE SIMILARITIES AND DIFFERENCES BETWEEN MULTIPLE INTELLIGENCES THEORY AND LEARNING STYLES THEORY

As you read over the components of multiple intelligences theory and learning styles theory, you begin to see several common elements. Both theories deal with the visual, auditory, and tactile (or kinaesthetic). Below the surface, there are also similarities. Simply stated, you can be a visual learner (this is a learning style) and yet not have visual/spatial (this is one of the multiple intelligences) be your dominant intelligence. How can this be possible? It may be that you learn best by watching someone paint a picture—watching their brush strokes, their method of mixing paints, and their spatial layout—but it may be that you will not be as engaged or as talented at painting as the person you watched. Your painting may lack feeling, depth, and expression. This is an example of how your visual learning style can be strong but your visual/spatial intelligence may not be your dominant intelligence.

On the other hand, your learning style may be visual and your dominant intelligence may be verbal/linguistic. If that is the case, you would learn how to paint by watching someone go through the process. Then, using your verbal/linguistic intelligence, you would be masterful at describing how to paint and talking about the process you observed.

In your own words, compare and contrast learning styles with multiple intelligences. ___

_____

_____

_____

_____

(continued)

_____

_____

_____

_____

_____

_____

_____

_____

TAKE THE PAP

The Personality Assessment Profile

© Robert M. Sherfield, Ph.D., 1999, 2002, 2005, 2008

Directions: Read each statement carefully and thoroughly. After reading the statement, rate your response using the scale below. There are no right or wrong answers. This is not a timed survey. The PAP is based, in part, on the Myers-Briggs Type Indicator (MBTI) by Katharine Briggs and Isabel Briggs-Myers.

3 = Often Applies
2 = Sometimes Applies
1 = Never or Almost Never Applies

_____   1a.   I am a very talkative person.

_____   1b.   I am a more reflective person than a verbal person.

_____   2a.   I am a very factual and literal person.

_____   2b.   I look to the future and I can see possibilities.

_____   3a.   I value truth and justice over tact and emotion.

_____   3b.   I find it easy to empathize with other people.

_____   4a.   I am very ordered and efficient.

_____   4b.   I enjoy having freedom from control.

_____   5a.   I am a very friendly and social person.

_____   5b.   I enjoy listening to others more than talking.

_____   6a.   I enjoy being around and working with people who have a great deal of common sense.

_____   6b.   I enjoy being around and working with people who are dreamers and have a great deal of imagination.

_____   7a.   One of my motivating forces is to do a job very well.

_____   7b.   I like to be recognized for, and I am motivated by, my accomplishments and awards.

_____   8a.   I like to plan out my day before I go to bed.

_____   8b.   When I get up on a nonschool or nonwork day, I just like to let the day "plan itself."

_____   9a.   I like to express my feelings and thoughts.

_____   9b.   I enjoy a great deal of tranquility and quiet time to myself.

_____   10a.   I am a very pragmatic and realistic person.

_____   10b.   I like to create new ideas, methods, or ways of doing things.

ACCOUNTABILITY

Challenges: I found that I . . . _____

_____

_____

_____

_____

   # PREPARING FOR SUCCESS

Refer to page 159 of this chapter and answer the questions you developed from headings. You should also be able to answer the following questions if they were not on your list:

1. Explain the difference between a learning style and your dominant intelligence.

2. How can your personality type affect your study time?

3. What is the difference between a visual learning style and a visual intelligence?

4. Briefly discuss each of the three learning styles.

5. Who is Howard Gardner and what did he do?

record

"To listen well is as powerful a means
of communication as to talk well."

Chinese proverb

record

Cultivating Your *Listening Skills* and Developing a *Note-Taking System* That Works for You

THE BIG WHY

WHY do I need to become a better listener? *WHY* will a chapter on listening and note-taking help me in college, at work, with my family, and beyond? *WHY* do instructors make such a big deal about note taking?

THE BIG WHY
from another perspective

Name:	Griffin Jones
Institution:	Park Point University, Pittsburgh, PA
Age:	19
Major:	Cinema

When you're making big decisions in your life you will always have people who are older and more experienced than you bursting at the seams to give you "life lessons" and other advice. There is no point in your life where this will be more prevalent than when you first begin college. You will be bombarded with advice on sex, classes, drinking games, relationships, and so on. A lot of it's just a rehash of all of the stuff you heard going into high school. However, many of the things we're asked to listen to can be helpful, and figuring out which ones are helpful is the hardest part. This is where listening comes in handy.

For most teens, listening to adults is a ludicrous concept. They want to try everything themselves. As someone who is quite stubborn, I completely understand, but over the past couple of years I've found that it's good to find a middle ground with these things. First, many adults do actually know what they are talking about because they have "lived it," and we're just better off listening to their hard-earned advice and taking their word on it. On the other hand, trying something new for yourself isn't always a bad idea either. There are those people who don't know what they're talking about either, because they're completely oblivious to the real world or they're trying to tell you stuff that doesn't necessarily apply to everyone. Again, this is where critical listening can come in very handy. Sometimes, you have to listen between the lines—for what is not said. Also, trying something for yourself and failing is a great way of learning. Trial and error shouldn't be a forbidden activity.

What I have discovered is this: Find people that you know to be level headed and in touch with the present day and listen to them. Really listen to them. And even if you determine that they're not level-headed, take in and consider what they have to say anyway . . . store it away for another time, you never know when you'll need their advice. They may still know what they're talking about and just don't know how to present it rationally. Just don't be afraid to step out of their boundaries and listen to others' viewpoints, listen to their lives, and use others' advice to live life for yourself. This chapter on listening and note taking can help you become a much more active listener.

> "Listening is a magnetic and strange thing, a creative force. When we are listened to, it creates us, makes us unfold and expand. Ideas actually begin to grow within us and come to life. When we listen to people there is an alternating current, and this recharges us so that we never get tired of each other."
> —Brenda Ueland

Listening is considered by many communication experts to be one of the, if not THE, most essential skills for building healthy relationships, solving problems, learning information, and getting along in life. Listening is certainly essential to your success as a college student. It will help you in terms of note taking, retaining information, and becoming actively involved in the learning process. The ability to listen in a variety of situations will also help you become a more efficient note taker. Notes create a history of your time in class, what you have read in your text and various articles, and what you might have studied with a group. *This chapter can help you:*

- Understand the difference between listening and hearing
- Understand and apply the Chinese definition of listening to everyday situations
- Overcome the obstacles to listening
- Identify key words in a lecture which indicate important information
- Learn and use the L-STAR note-taking system
- Identify and choose the best note-taking system for you
- Determine what to do if you get lost during a lecture

Some students have incredible memory and don't need to take many notes, but most of us are not so lucky. We need to write information so that we can refer to it later. This chapter will help you become a better listener and note taker.

SCAN AND QUESTION

Take a few moments and **scan this chapter**. As you scan, **list five questions** you can expect to learn the answers to while reading and studying Chapter 8.

Example
- What are the four components of the Chinese verb "to listen"? (from page 183)
- Why is it important to identify key words during a lecture? (from page 188)

My Questions

1. _____

_____ from page _____

2. _____

_____ from page _____

3. _____

_____ from page _____

4. _____

_____ from page _____

5. _____

_____ from page _____

Reminder: At the end of the chapter, come back to this page and answer these questions in your notebook, text margins, or online chapter notes.

College classes demand active critical listening skills.

THE IMPORTANCE OF LISTENING

Why It Matters in Classes, Relationships, and Avoiding Misunderstandings

Listening is a survival skill. Period! It is that simple! "I know listening is important," you might say, but few ever think of the paramount significance listening has on our everyday lives. It is necessary for:

- Establishing and improving relationships,
- Personal growth,
- Showing respect to others,
- Professional rapport,
- Showing empathy and compassion,
- Learning information,
- Understanding others' opinions and views,
- Basic survival,
- Entertainment, and
- Health.

How much time do you think you spend listening every day? Research suggests that we spend almost 70 percent of our waking time communicating, and **53 percent of that time is spent in listening situations** (Adler, Rosenfeld, and Towne, 2006). Effective listening skills can mean the difference between success or failure, As or Fs, relationships or loneliness, and in some cases and careers, life or death.

For students, good listening skills are critical. Over the next two to four years, you will be given a lot of information through lectures. Cultivating and improving your active listening skills will help you to understand the material, take accurate notes, participate in class discussions, communicate with your peers more effectively, and become more actively engaged in your learning process.

THE DIFFERENCE BETWEEN LISTENING AND HEARING

No doubt you've been in a communication situation where a misunderstanding took place. Either you hear something incorrectly or someone hears you incorrectly *or* it could be that someone hears your message but misinterprets it. These communication blunders arise because we tend to view listening (and communication in general) as an automatic response when in fact it is not.

"You can not truly listen to anyone and do anything else at the same time."

—M. Scott Peck

Listening is a learned, voluntary activity. You must choose to do it. It is a skill just as driving a car, painting a picture, or playing the piano is a skill. Becoming an active listener requires practice, time, mistakes, guidance, and active participation.

Hearing, however, is not learned; it is automatic and involuntary. If you are within range of a sound, you will probably hear it although you may not be listening to it.

Hearing a sound does not guarantee that you know what it is or what made it. Listening actively, though, means making a conscious effort to focus on the sound and determine what it is.

LISTENING DEFINED

According to Ronald Adler (Adler et al., 2006), the drawing of the Chinese verb "to listen" provides a comprehensive and practical definition of listening (see Figure 8.1).

To the Chinese, listening involves the ears, the eyes, undivided attention, and the heart. Do you make it a habit to listen with more than your ears? The Chinese view listening as a whole-body experience. People from Western cultures seem to have lost the ability to involve their whole body in the listening process. We tend to use only our ears, and sometimes we don't even use them very well.

At its core, listening is "the ability to hear, understand, analyze, respect, and appropriately respond to the meaning of another person's spoken and nonverbal messages" (Daly and Engleberg, 2006). Although this definition involves the word "hear," listening goes far beyond just the physical ability to catch sound waves.

The first step in listening *is* hearing, but true listening involves one's full attention and the ability to filter out distractions, emotional barriers, cultural differences, and religious biases. Listening means that you are making a conscious decision to understand and show respect for the other person's communication efforts.

Listening needs to be personalized and internalized. To understand listening as a whole-body experience, we can define it on three levels:

1. Listening with a **purpose**

2. Listening **objectively**

3. Listening **constructively**

FIGURE 8.1   Chinese Symbol for "To Listen"

SUCCESSFUL DECISIONS

Jennifer greatly disliked her Biology instructor. She could not put her finger on just WHY she disliked her, but she just knew that Dr. Lipmon rubbed her the wrong way. This had been the case since the first day of class.

Other students seemed to like Dr. Lipmon and were able to carry on conversations with her—but not Jennifer. "Why?" she thought. "Why do I dislike her so much? She's not a bad teacher. But I just can't stand to listen to her."

Jennifer decided to sit back for the next week and really try to figure out what the main problem was. As she sat in class and listened, she figured it out. She finally put her finger on the problem: She and Dr. Lipmon had completely different views on many things including evolution and woman's reproductive rights.

Every time Dr. Lipmon made a statement contrary to Jennifer's core beliefs, she cringed. She "shut down" and refused to listen any further. She transferred her dislike of Dr. Lipmon's lectures and opinions onto her as a person. She knew this was affecting her grade and her knowledge base in class, but she did not know how to manage or change the situation.

Jennifer decided to go to the Counseling Center's workshop on *Effective Listening Skills*, where she learned how to become a more open-minded listener. She learned that she did not have to agree with everything taught, but she also learned that everyone has something to teach. Because she made the decision to learn more about listening, her attitude toward Dr. Lipmon, Biology, and education in general changed.

Jennifer made a *successful decision*.

Objective listening can be a difficult skill to learn. Have you encountered people with views radically different from your own? How did you respond?

Listening with a purpose suggests a need to recognize different types of listening situations—for example, class, worship, entertainment, and relationships. People do not listen the same way in every situation.

Listening objectively means listening with an open mind. You will give yourself few greater gifts than the gift of knowing how to listen without bias and prejudice. This is perhaps the most difficult aspect of listening. If you have been cut off in midconversation or midsentence by someone who disagreed with you, or if someone has left the room while you were giving your opinion of a situation, you have had the experience of talking to people who do not know how to listen objectively.

Listening constructively means listening with the attitude: "How can this be helpful to my life, my education, my career, or my finances?" This type of listening involves evaluating the information you are hearing and determining whether it has meaning to your life. Sound easy? It is more difficult than it sounds because, again, we all tend to shut out information that we do not view as immediately helpful or useful. To listen constructively, you need to know how to listen and store information for later.

WHAT IS YOUR ORIENTATION?
Four Listening Styles Defined

According to Steven McCornack (2007), interpersonal communication expert, author, and educator, there are four listening styles. They are action oriented, time oriented, people oriented, and content oriented. Study Table 8.1 to determine which best describes you as a listener.

Table 8.1

Action-Oriented Listeners	Time-Oriented Listeners
Want to get their messages quickly and to the point	Want their information in brief, concise meetings
Do not like fluff and grow impatient when they perceive people to be "wasting their time"	Are consumed with how much time is taken to convey a message
Become frustrated when information is not orderly	Set time limits for listening (and communicating in general)
Are quick to dismiss people who "ramble" and falter when they speak	Will ask people to "move the message along" if they feel it is taking too long

People-Oriented Listeners	Content-Oriented Listeners
Are in contrast to time- and action-oriented listeners	Enjoy an intellectual challenge
View listening as a chance to connect with other people	Like to listen to technical information, facts, and evidence
Enjoy listening to people so that relationships can be built	Enjoy complex information that must be deciphered and filtered
Become emotionally involved with the person communicating	Carefully evaluate information and facts before forming an opinion
	Enjoy asking questions

Which style best describes you? _____

What are the "pros" of being this type of listener? _____

_____

_____

_____

What are the "cons" of being this type of listener? _____

_____

_____

_____

WHAT DID YOU SAY?

Overcoming the Obstacles to Listening

Several major obstacles stand in the way of becoming an effective listener. To begin building active listening skills, you first have to remove some barriers.

OBSTACLE ONE: PREJUDGING

Prejudging means that you automatically shut out what is being said; it is one of the biggest obstacles to active listening. You may prejudge because you don't like or agree with the information or the person communicating. You may also have prejudging problems because of your environment, culture, social status, or attitude.

Do You Prejudge Information or Its Source?

Answer yes or no to the following questions:

1.	I tune out when something is boring.	**YES**	**NO**
2.	I tune out when I do not agree with the information.	**YES**	**NO**
3.	I argue mentally with the speaker about information.	**YES**	**NO**
4.	I do not listen to people I do not like.	**YES**	**NO**
5.	I make decisions about information before I understand all of its implications or consequences.	**YES**	**NO**

If you answered yes to two or more of these questions, you tend to prejudge in a listening situation.

Tips for Overcoming Prejudging

☐ Listen for information that may be valuable to you as a student. Some material may not be pleasant to hear but may be useful to you later on.

☐ Listen to the message, not the messenger. If you do not like the speaker, try to go beyond personality and listen to what is being said, without regard to the person saying it. Conversely, you may like the speaker so much that you automatically accept the material or answers without listening objectively to what is being said.

☐ Try to remove cultural, racial, gender, social, and environmental barriers. Just because a person is different from you or holds a different point of view does not make that person wrong; and just because a person is like you and holds a similar point of view does not make that person right. Sometimes, you have to cross cultural and environmental barriers to learn new material and see with brighter eyes.

OBSTACLE TWO: TALKING

Not even the best listener in the world can listen while he or she is talking. The next time you are in a conversation with a friend, try speaking while your friend is speaking—then see if you know what your friend said. To become an effective listener, you need to learn the power of silence. Silence gives you the opportunity to think about what is being said before you respond.

Are you a Talker Rather Than a Listener?

Answer yes or no to the following questions:

1.	I often interrupt the speaker so that I can say what I want.	**YES**	**NO**
2.	I am thinking of my next statement while others are talking.	**YES**	**NO**
3.	My mind wanders when others talk.	**YES**	**NO**
4.	I answer my own questions.	**YES**	**NO**
5.	I answer questions that are asked of other people.	**YES**	**NO**

Listening to people from different cultures, backgrounds, and religions can open many doors.

If you answered yes to two or more questions, you tend to talk too much in a listening situation.

Tips for Overcoming the Urge to Talk Too Much

☐ Avoid interrupting the speaker. Force yourself to be silent at parties, family gatherings, and friendly get-togethers. We're not saying you should be unsociable, but force yourself to be silent for 10 minutes. You'll be surprised at what you hear. You may also be surprised how hard it is to do this. Test yourself.

☐ Ask someone a question and then allow that person to answer the question.

☐ Too often we ask questions and answer them ourselves. Force yourself to wait until the person has formulated a response. If you ask questions and wait for answers, you will force yourself to listen.

☐ Concentrate on what is being said at the moment, not what you want to say next.

OBSTACLE THREE: BECOMING TOO EMOTIONAL

Emotions can form a strong barrier to active listening. Worries, problems, fears, and anger can keep you from listening to the greatest advantage. Have you ever sat in a lecture, and before you knew what was happening your mind was a million miles away because you were angry or worried about something? If you have, you know what it's like to bring your emotions to the table.

Do You Bring Your Emotions to the Listening Situation?

Answer yes or no to the following questions:

1. I get angry before I hear the whole story.   **YES   NO**
2. I look for underlying or hidden messages in information.   **YES   NO**
3. Sometimes, I begin listening on a negative note.   **YES   NO**
4. I base my opinions of information on what others are saying or doing.   **YES   NO**
5. I readily accept information as correct from people whom I like or respect.   **YES   NO**

If you answered yes to two or more of these questions, you tend to bring your emotions to a listening situation.

Tips for Overcoming Emotions

☐ Know how you feel before you begin the listening experience. Take stock of your emotions and feelings ahead of time.

☐ Focus on the message; determine how to use the information.

☐ Create a positive image about the message you are hearing.

☐ Avoid overreacting and jumping to conclusions.

did you know?

Thomas Edison invented the light bulb, the phonograph, the battery, the forerunner to the movie camera, and 1,089 other creations. He was also kicked out of school at age 12. His teachers thought he was too dumb to remain in class because of his constant questioning. He was deaf in one ear and 80 percent deaf in the other. He also had what would today be called ADHD. At one point during his career, he had to borrow money from a friend to avoid starvation.
Edison read constantly, had an incredible memory, and sometimes worked 20 hours a day.
He was one of the most important scientists in history. His inventions led the world into modern society.

"FOR EXAMPLE, YOU SHOULD BE ABLE TO . . ."
Listening for Key Words, Phrases, and Hints

Learning how to listen for key words, phrases, and hints can help you become an active listener and an effective note taker. For example, if your English instructor begins a lecture by saying, "There are 10 basic elements to writing poetry," jot down the number 10 under the heading "Poetry" or number your notebook page 1 through 10, leaving space for notes. If at the end of class you listed six elements to writing poetry, you know that you missed a part of the lecture. At this point, you need to ask the instructor some questions.

Here are some key phrases and words to listen for:

- in addition
- most important
- you'll see this again
- for example
- in contrast
- the characteristics of
- on the other hand

- another way
- such as
- therefore
- to illustrate
- in comparison
- the main issue is
- as a result of

- above all
- specifically
- finally
- as stated earlier
- nevertheless
- moreover
- because

Picking up on *transition words* will help you filter out less important information and thus listen more carefully to what is most important. There are other indicators of important information, too. You will want to listen carefully when the instructor:

Writes something on the board

Uses an overhead

Uses computer-aided graphics

Speaks in a louder tone or changes vocal patterns

Uses gestures more than usual

Draws on a flip chart

LISTENING WHEN ENGLISH IS YOUR SECOND LANGUAGE
Suggestions for ESL Students

For students whose first language is not English, the college classroom can present some uniquely challenging situations. One of the most pressing and important challenges is the ability to listen, translate, understand, and capture the message on paper in a quick and continuous manner. According to Lynn Forkos, instructor and coordinator of the Conversation Center for International Students at the College of Southern Nevada, the following tips can be beneficial:

- Don't be afraid to stop the instructor to ask for clarification. Asking questions allows you to take an active part in the listening process. If the instructor doesn't answer your questions sufficiently, make an appointment to speak with him or her during office hours.

- If you are in a situation where the instructor can't stop or you're watching a movie or video in class, listen for words that you do understand and try to figure out unfamiliar words in the context of the sentence. Jot down questions you need to ask later.
- Enhance your vocabulary by watching and listening to TV programs such as *Dateline, 20/20, Primetime Live, 60 Minutes,* and the evening news. You might also try listening to radio stations such as National Public Radio as you walk or drive.
- Write down everything that the instructor puts on the board, overhead, or PowerPoint display. You may not need every piece of this information, but this technique gives you (and hopefully your study group) the ability to sift through the information outside of class. It gives you a visual history of what the instructor said.
- Finally, if there is a conversation group or club that meets on campus, take the opportunity to join. By practicing language, you become more attuned to common words and phrases. If a conversation group is not available, consider starting one of your own.

WHY TAKE NOTES?

Is It Just a Big, Crazy Chore?

Go to class, listen, and write it down. Read a text, take notes. Watch a film, take notes. Is it really that important? Actually, knowing how to take useful, accurate notes can dramatically improve your life as a student. If you are an effective listener and note taker, you have two of the most valuable skills any student could ever use. There are several reasons why it is important to take notes:

- You become an active part of the listening process.
- You create a history of your course content when you take notes.
- You have written criteria to follow when studying.
- You create a visual aid for your material.
- Studying becomes much easier.
- You retain information at a greater rate than non–note takers.
- Effective note takers average higher grades than non–note takers (Kiewra and Fletcher, 1984).

WRITING IT RIGHT

Tips for Effective Note Taking

You have already learned several skills you will need for taking notes, such as cultivating your active listening skills, overcoming obstacles to effective listening, and familiarizing yourself with key phrases used by instructors. Next, prepare yourself mentally and physically to take effective notes that are going to be helpful to you. Consider the following ideas as you think about expanding your note-taking abilities.

- ☐ **Attend class.** This may sound like stating the obvious, but it is surprising how many college students feel they do not need to come to class.
- ☐ Come to **class prepared.** Scan, read, and use your textbook to establish a basic understanding of the material before going to class. It is always easier

ESSENTIAL CORNERSTONE
KNOWLEDGE
How can learning to take more effective notes help you master knowledge and learn more?

Good note-taking skills help you do more than simply record what you learn in class or read in a book so that you can recall it. These skills can also help reinforce that information so that you actually know it.

to take notes when you have a preliminary understanding of what is being said. Coming to class prepared also means bringing the proper materials for taking notes: lab manuals, pens, a notebook, and a highlighter.

☐ **Bring your textbook** to class. Although many students think they do not need to bring their textbooks to class if they have read the homework, you will find that many instructors repeatedly refer to the text while lecturing. The instructor may ask you to highlight, underline, or refer to the text in class, and following along in the text as the instructor lectures may also help you organize your notes.

☐ **Ask questions** and participate in class. Two of the most critical actions you can perform in class are to ask questions and to participate in the class discussion. If you do not understand a concept or theory, ask questions. Don't leave class without understanding what has happened and assume you'll pick it up on your own.

YOU'LL BE SEEING STARS
The L-STAR System

One of the most effective ways to take notes begins with the **L-STAR system**. This system involves:

This five-step program will enable you to compile complete, accurate, and visual notes for future reference. Along with improving your note-taking skills, using this system will enhance your ability to participate in class, help other students, study more effectively, and perform well on exams and quizzes.

L—Listening

One of the best ways to become an effective note taker is to become an active listener. A concrete step you can take toward becoming an active listener in class is to sit near the front of the room where you can hear the instructor and see the board and overheads. Choose a spot that allows you to see the instructor's mouth and facial expressions. If you see that the instructor's face has become animated or expressive, you can bet that you are hearing important information. Write it down. If you sit in the back of the room, you may miss out on these important clues.

S—Setting It Down

The actual writing of notes can be a difficult task. Some instructors are organized in their delivery of information; others are not. Some stick to an easy-to-follow outline and

FIGURE 8.3   A Blank Cornell Frame

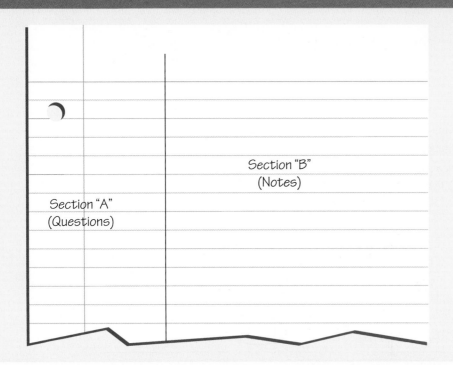

Section "B"
(Notes)

Section "A"
(Questions)

FIGURE 8.4   Outline Using a Cornell Frame

Study Skills 101   Oct. 19
Topic: Listening   Friday

What is the listening process? (ROAR)	*The Listening Process (ROAR)
	A= Receiving
	1. Within range of sound
	2. Hearing the information
	B = Organizing
	1. Choose to listen actively
	2. Observe origin
Definition of Listening (POC)	*Listening Defined
	A. Listening w/ a purpose
	B. Listening objectively
	C. Listening constructively
Obstacles (PET)	*What interferes w/ listening
	A. Prejudging
	B. Emotions
	C. Talking

The listening process involves Receiving, Organizing, Assigning &
Reacting - Talking, Prejudging & Emotions are obstacles.

FIGURE 8.5   Mapping Using a Cornell Frame

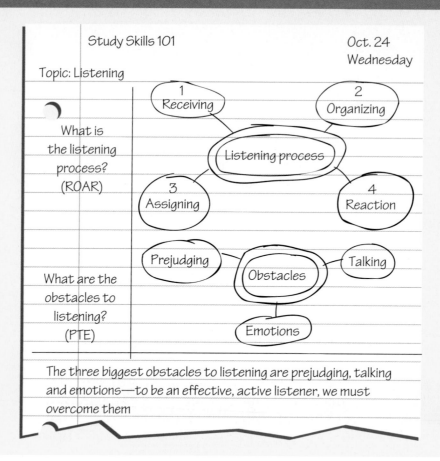

Study Skills 101   Oct. 24
                                                    Wednesday
Topic: Listening

What is
the listening
process?
(ROAR)

1 Receiving   2 Organizing

Listening process

3 Assigning   4 Reaction

What are the
obstacles to
listening?
(PTE)

Prejudging   Obstacles   Talking

Emotions

The three biggest obstacles to listening are prejudging, talking
and emotions—to be an effective, active listener, we must
overcome them

the technique that is most comfortable and beneficial for you; you might use mapping (discussed below) or outlining on a Cornell page. An example of outline notes using the Cornell system appears in Figure 8.4 and an example of mapping notes using the Cornell system appears in Figure 8.5.

GOING AROUND IN CIRCLES
The Mapping System

If you are a visual learner, the mapping system may be especially useful for you. The mapping system of note taking generates a picture of information (see Figures 8.5 and 8.6). The mapping system creates a map, or web, of information that allows you to see the relationships among facts or ideas. A mapping system might look something like the notes in Figure 8.6.

The most important thing to remember about each note-taking system is that ***it must work for you.*** Do not use a system because your friends use it or because you feel that you should use it. Experiment with each system or combination to determine which is best for you.

FIGURE 8.6 The Mapping System

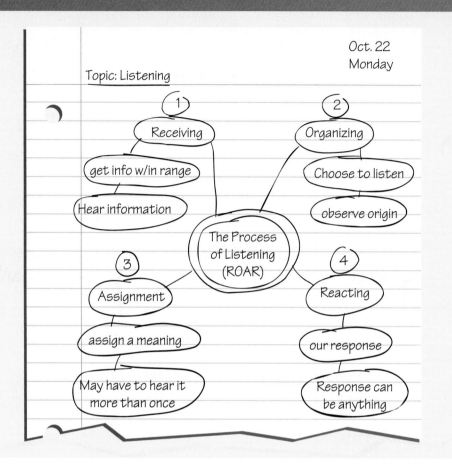

Always remember to keep your notes organized, dated, and neat. Notes that cannot be read are no good to you or to anyone else.

WHAT TO DO IF YOU GET LOST WHILE TAKING NOTES DURING THE LECTURE

Have you ever been in a classroom trying to take notes and the instructor is speaking so rapidly that you cannot possibly get all of the information? Just when you think you're caught up, you realize that he or she has made an important statement and you missed it. What do you do? How can you handle, or avoid, this difficult note-taking situation? Here are several hints:

☐ Raise your hand and ask the instructor to repeat the information.
☐ Ask your instructor to slow down.
☐ If he or she will do neither, leave a blank space with a question mark at the side margin (see Figure 8.7).

FIGURE 8.7   What to Do When You Get Lost

Public Speaking   Oct. 7
Lecture: Types of Research for Speeches

*Periodicals	- Magazines, trade & professional
*Newspapers	Local, state & national (some international as well)
*Reference materials	Specialized . . . (?)
*Government documents	- Maps, reports, federal proceedings

} If you missed it, leave it blank

You can get this information after class from your instructor, a classmate, or your study buddy. This can be a difficult task to master. The key is to focus on the information at hand. Focus on what is being said at the exact moment. Don't give up!

☐ Meet with your instructor immediately after class or at the earliest time convenient for both of you.

☐ Form a note-taking group that meets after each class. This serves two purposes: (1) You can discuss and review the lecture, and (2) you will be able to get the notes from one of your note-taking buddies.

☐ Never lean over and ask questions of other students during the lecture. This will cause them to lose the information as well. It will probably annoy your peers and the instructor as well.

☐ Rehearse your note-taking skills at home by taking notes from TV news magazines or channels like the History Channel.

☐ As a last resort, you can ask the instructor's permission to use a tape recorder during the lecture. Do not record a lecture without permission. We suggest that you try to use other avenues, such as the ones listed above, instead of taping your notes. It is a time-consuming task to listen to the lecture for a second time. However, if this system works for you, use it.

USING YOUR LAPTOP COMPUTER FOR NOTE TAKING

In this age of high technology, some students prefer to take notes or transfer their notes onto their computers. Some students bring laptops to class, while others immediately type and reorganize their notes after class. If you choose to use a computer for note taking, use the following tips:

IN CLASS

☐ Come to class early to set up your computer. Don't disturb others by arriving late.

☐ Try to sit where you can see the instructor and projection screen, but also be respectful of other students. Tapping on the keyboard can disturb others' concentration.

☐ Don't worry too much about spelling or grammar. You can run the spelling and grammar checker after class while cleaning up your notes.

☐ Set your tabs before you begin. You can set them to use an outline format or the Cornell format.

OUT OF CLASS

☐ If you are going to type your notes using a computer, do so as quickly after class as possible. The information obtained in class needs to be fresh in your mind. Try to reorganize your notes within 24 hours.

☐ Combine your textbook notes and lecture notes together. This will help you access the big picture of the information.

GENERAL HINTS

☐ Save your notes on both a disk and your hard drive.

☐ Always print your notes after each entry. It can be catastrophic if all of your notes are on one disk or one hard drive and the computer crashes or the disk is lost.

☐ After you have printed your notes, use a 3-hole punch and place your notes in a binder. Arrange computer notes with related handouts.

A last point about copying your notes by hand or into a computer: This technique, while valuable to some students, does not constitute studying. Dr. Walter Pauk (2007), creator of the Cornell note-taking system, suggests that "contrary to what most people think, almost no learning takes place during the keyboarding of scribbled notes." Finally, don't be threatened by those who decide to use the computer in class or those who come to class with typewritten, printed notes. They may not have retained as much as you have. *Cornerstone* in general, and this chapter specifically, is about choices. You have to find and use a system that is convenient, easy, and useful to you.

If you remember the concepts of the L-STAR system (listening, setting it down, translating, analyzing, and remembering) and use this system as a study pattern, and if you find a note-taking system that is comfortable and useful for you, then you will begin to see significant improvement in your ability as a note taker and in your performance as a student.

THINK ABOUT IT

Reflections for Success

Yes, listening is a learned skill, but it is more than that. It is a gift that you give to yourself. It is a gift that promotes knowledge, understanding, stronger relationships, and open-mindedness. Good listening skills can help you manage conflict, avoid misunderstandings, and establish trusting relationships. Perhaps most importantly at this point in your life, listening can help you become a more successful student. Once you learn how to listen with your whole body and mind, you will begin to see how your notes, your grades, your attitude, your relationships, and your learning process change. As you work toward improving your listening skills and developing your note-taking system, consider the following:

- ☐ When listening, evaluate the content before you judge the messenger.
- ☐ Keep your emotions and preconceived notions in check while listening.
- ☐ Sit where you can see and hear the instructor.
- ☐ Listen for "how" something is said.
- ☐ Listen to the "entire story" before making a judgment call.
- ☐ Listen for major ideas and key words.
- ☐ Use a separate notebook for every class.
- ☐ Use abbreviations whenever possible.
- ☐ Write down what the instructor puts on the board or PowerPoint.

Becoming adept at listening and developing your own note-taking system are two essential skills that can help you become a more active learner.

> "Listening is an attitude of the heart, a genuine desire to be with another person."
>
> —J. Isham

passages
An Activity for Critical Thinking and Career Development

On page 9 of Chapter 1, and inside the front cover, you read **The Ten Essential Cornerstones for Personal and Professional Success.** They are:

Passion	Motivation
Knowledge	Resourcefulness
Creativity	Adaptability
Open-mindedness	Communication
Accountability	Vision

Explanation: Seldom (if ever) would you pop in a CD, click your iPod, or tune your radio to a station to hear music that you strongly disliked. It just does not seem like a good use of time, and it is not something that you would probably enjoy. However, for this exercise, we are going to ask that you do precisely what we've described and then apply what you've experienced and learned to several questions and four **ESSENTIAL CORNERSTONES** from the list.

Process: Over the course of the next few days, find a song from your *least favorite* genre. If you are a huge fan of R&B, you might choose an old country song or a song from rap or bluegrass. If you enjoy listening to "easy love songs," try metal or swing. The only stipulation is that the **song must have lyrics.**

You will have to listen to the song several times to answer the questions below. However, it is important to read the following questions before you listen to the song—particularly question #2. The key to this exercise is to practice listening with an open mind, listening for content, and listening to words when barriers are in the way (the barrier would be the actual music, itself).

1. What is the song's title and artist? _____
    _____

2. What emotional and mental response did you have to the music the first time you listened to it? Why do you think you had this response? _____
    _____
    _____
    _____
    _____
    _____

3. While listening to the song, what happened to your appreciation level? Did it increase or decrease? Why?
    _____
    _____
    _____
    _____
    _____

4. In your opinion, what was the message (theme) of the song? _____
    _____
    _____
    _____
    _____

5. What were you most surprised about with the song? Was it the lyrics? The actual music? Your like or dislike of the song? The artist's voice? _____
    _____
    _____
    _____
    _____

6. If you had to say that you learned one positive thing from this song, what would it be? _____

_____

_____

7. From memory, list at least five statements, comments, or quotes from the song. __

_____

_____

_____

_____

_____

Now, using the following **ESSENTIAL CORNERSTONES,** consider how becoming a more effective listener can help you with each.

By enhancing my listening skills, I can become more **OPEN-MINDED** by _____

_____

_____

_____

_____

By enhancing my listening skills, I can become more **CREATIVE** by _____

_____

_____

_____

_____

By enhancing my listening skills, I can become more **KNOWLEDGABLE** by _____

_____

_____

_____

_____

By enhancing my listening skills, I can increase **RESOURCEFULNESS** level by ____

_____

_____

_____

_____

> "You live and you learn OR you don't live long."
> —Robert Heinlein

You've just learned that Whoopi Goldberg has dyslexia or that the Oedipus complex you read about in psychology class has its roots in a 2500-year-old Greek tragedy, or that the first copying machine was invented in 1778, or that Germany was the first foreign country to have a McDonald's, or that turtles can have upper respiratory tract disease diagnosed by dehydration and nasal discharge. ***Wow!*** How did you learn this? Through reading, listening, attending class, conversing with peers, and studying new material.

While these facts may not stun the world or cure cancer, studying for the sake of learning and understanding new material can be as exciting (or as dull) as you want it to be. It does not have to be the dreaded, "I'm in the library sitting in a hard chair in a wooden cubicle" routine that you may have been used to. The beauty of studying is that with a plan, you can learn almost anything that is *known to mankind. Anything!* That is what this chapter is all about—learning how to study, how to increase your memory capacity, and how to take assessments more effectively. *This chapter can help you:*

- Understand how your memory works and how to help it work better
- Identify the differences between short-term and long-term memory
- Learn to commit information to long-term memory
- Use mnemonics to help you remember information
- Develop strategies for studying math and science
- Identify the causes of your test anxiety and reduce your test anxiety

SCAN AND QUESTION

Take a few moments and **scan this chapter**. As you scan, **list five questions** you can expect to learn the answers to while reading and studying Chapter 9.

Example
- Discuss three strategies for studying math. (from page 221)
- Why are mnemonics important? (from page 216)

My Questions

1. _____
   _____ from page _____

2. _____
   _____ from page _____

3. _____
   _____ from page _____

4. _____
   _____ from page _____

5. _____
   _____ from page _____

Reminder: At the end of the chapter, come back to this page and answer these questions in your notebook, text margins, or online chapter notes.

- Learn how to predict test questions for upcoming assessments
- Maneuver the three types of testing responses
- Develop successful strategies for taking all types of tests

- Understand the internal and external ramifications of integrity

Learning how to study smart instead of studying hard will save you countless hours and more stress than you can imagine.

WHY STUDY?

I Can Fake It

Studying for college classes can be quite different from studying for high school classes. The types of questions asked may be different, and the depth of knowledge required of your response will almost certainly be different. In high school, you may have studied at the lower levels of Bloom's Taxonomy and learned simple facts, dates, places, and names. You'll need to know information at these levels in college, but you'll

"We can learn something new any time we believe we can."

—Virginia Satir

also be asked to analyze and evaluate information, too. You'll need to be able to defend your diagnosis of an upper respiratory tract disease in that turtle. And, you'll have to know how to compile a treatment plan to save his life. Those are examples of higher level learning skills required in college.

You may be saying to yourself, *"I didn't have to study very hard in high school; why should I do it now?"* Some students believe that they can glance at their notes for a moment and fake it. Quite truthfully, some students are able to do this because their learning style, instructors, type of test given, and memory lend themselves to this type of studying technique. More than you may imagine, however, this is not the case. College instructors are notorious for thorough exams, lengthy essay questions, tricky true–false statements, and multiple choices that would confuse Einstein. If you want to succeed in your classes in college, you will need to make studying at a higher level a way of life.

Effective studying requires a great deal of commitment, but learning how to get organized, taking effective notes, reading a textbook, listening in class, developing personalized study skills, and building memory techniques will serve you well in becoming a successful graduate. Faking it is now a thing of the past.

The Importance of Your Study Environment

You may wonder why your study place is important. The study environment can determine how constructively you are using your study time. If the location is too hot, too noisy, too dark, or too crowded, your study time may not be productive. In a room that is too hot and dimly lit, you may have a tendency to fall asleep. In a room that is too cold, you may spend time trying to warm yourself. Choose a location that is comfortable for you.

Different students need different study environments. You may need a degree of noise in the background, or you may need complete quiet. You have to make this decision. If you always have music in the background while you study, try studying in a quiet place one time to see if there is a difference. If you always try to study where it is quiet, try putting soft music in the background to see if it helps you. You may have to try several environments before you find the one that is right for you.

You may choose a nontraditional study environment, but be sure that you are able to study effectively in it.

I FORGOT TO REMEMBER!

Understanding How Your Memory Functions

"My brain is full." MYTH

"I can't remember another thing." MYTH

"I can't retain any information." MYTH

Several studies suggest that it is impossible to fill our brains full. One study in the 1970s concluded that if our brains were fed 10 new items of information every second for the rest of our lives, we would never fill even half of our memory's capacity (Texas A&M University, 2008).

At times, you may feel like if you study or read or learn any more, you'll forget everything. Some researchers suggest that we never forget anything—that the material is simply "covered up" by other material, but it is still in our brain. The reason we can't recall that information is that it was not important enough, not stored properly, or not used enough to keep it from being covered up. According to a German philosopher, Friedrich Nietzsche (1844–1900), "The ***existence of forgetting has never been proved;*** we only know that some things don't come to mind when we want them."

So, why is it so hard to remember the dates of the Civil War or who flew with Amelia Earhart or how to calculate the liquidation value of stocks or the six factors in the communication process? The primary problem is that we never properly filed or stored this information.

What would happen if you typed your English research paper into the computer and did not give it a file name? When you needed to retrieve that paper, you would not know how to find it. You would have to search through every file until you came across the information you needed. Memory works in much the same way. We have to store it properly if we are to retrieve it easily at a later time.

This section will detail how memory works and why it is important to your studying efforts. Here are some basic facts about memory:

- Everyone remembers some information and forgets other information.
- Your senses help you take in information.
- With very little effort, you can remember some information.
- With rehearsal (study), you can remember a great deal of information.
- Without rehearsal or use, information is forgotten.
- Incoming information needs to be filed in the brain if you are to retain it.
- Information stored, or filed, in the brain must have a retrieval method.
- Mnemonic devices, repetition, association, and rehearsal can help you store and retrieve information.

Psychologists have determined that there are three types of memory: sensory memory; short-term or working memory; and long-term memory.

Choosing the best study environment can be challenging. The best study place may depend on the different accommodations available to you and may vary with the kinds of studying required. What kind of study environment has worked best for you?

ESSENTIAL CORNERSTONE

MOTIVATION

How can your personal motivation help you increase your memory capacity?

Sensory memory stores information gathered from the five senses: taste, touch, smell, hearing, and sight. Sensory memory is usually temporary, lasting one to three seconds, unless you decide that the information is of ultimate importance to you and make an effort to transfer it to long-term memory.

Short-term, or working memory holds information for a short amount of time. Consider the following letters:

jmplngtoplntstsevng

Now, cover them with your hand and try to recite them.

It is almost impossible for the average person to do so. Why? Because your working memory bank can hold a limited amount of information, usually about five to nine separate new facts or pieces of information at once (Woolfolk, 2006). However, consider this exercise. If you break the letters down into smaller pieces and add MEANING to them, you are more likely to retain them. Example:

jum　lng　to　plnts　ts　evng

This may still not mean very much to you, but you can probably remember at least the first two sets of information—jum lng.

Now, if you were to say to yourself, this sentence means "Jump long to planets this evening," you are much more likely to begin to remember this information. Just as your memory can play tricks on you, you can play tricks on your memory.

Although it is sometimes frustrating to forget information, it is also useful and necessary to do so. If you never forgot anything, you would not be able to function. As a student, you would never be able to remember all that your instructor said during a 50-minute lecture. You have to take steps to help you to remember information. Taking notes, making associations, drawing pictures, and visualizing information are techniques that can help you move information from your short-term memory to your long-term memory bank.

Long-term memory stores a lot of information. It is almost like a computer disk. You have to make an effort to put something in your long-term memory, but with effort and memory techniques, such as rehearsal and practice, you can store anything you want to remember there. Long-term memory consists of information that you have heard often, information that you use often, information that you might see often, and information that you have determined necessary or important to you. Just as you name a file on a computer disk, you name the files in your long-term memory. Sometimes, you have to wait a moment for the information to come to you. While you are waiting, your brain disk is spinning; if the information you seek is in long-term memory, your brain will eventually find it. You may have to assist your brain in locating the information by using mnemonics and other memory devices.

THIS ISN'T YOUR DADDY'S VCR

Using VCR3 to Increase Memory Power

Countless pieces of information are stored in your long-term memory. Some of it is triggered by necessity, some may be triggered by the five senses, and some may be triggered by experiences. The best way to commit information to long-term memory and retrieve it when needed can be expressed by:

V Visualizing

C Concentrating

R Relating

R Repeating

R Reviewing

Consider the following story.

> As Katherine walked back to the dorm room after her evening class, she heard someone behind her. She turned to see two students holding hands walking about 20 feet behind her. She was relieved. This was the first night that she had walked back to the residence hall alone.
>
> Katherine pulled her book bag closer to her as she increased her pace along the dimly lit sidewalk between the Salk Biology Building and the Horn Center for the Arts. "I can't believe that Shana didn't call me," she thought to herself. "She knows I hate to leave class alone."
>
> As Katherine turned the corner onto Suddith Street, she heard someone else behind her. She turned but did not see anyone. As she continued to walk toward the residence hall, she heard the sound again. Turning to see if anyone was there, she saw a shadow disappear into the grove of hedges along the sidewalk.
>
> Startled and frightened, Katherine crossed the street to walk beneath the streetlights and sped up to get closer to a group of students about 30 feet in front of her. She turned once more to see if anyone was behind her. Thankfully, she did not see anyone.
>
> By this time, she was only one block from her residence hall. The lighting was better and other students were around. She felt better, but vowed never again to leave class alone at night.

To visualize information, try to create word pictures in your mind as you hear the information. If you are being told about a Revolutionary War battle in Camden, SC, try to see the soldiers and the battlefield, or try to paint a mind picture that will help you to remember the information. You may also want to create visual aids as you read or study information.

As you read Katherine's story, were you able to visualize her journey? Could you see her walking along the sidewalk? Did you see the two buildings? What did they look like? Could you see the darkness of her path? Could you see that shadow disappearing into the bushes? Could you see her increasing her pace to catch up to the other students? What was she wearing? If you did this, then you are using your visual skills—your mind's eye. This is one of the most effective ways to commit information to long-term memory. See it, live it, feel it, and touch it as you read it and study it, and it will become yours. Consider the following tips:

Concentrating on the information given will help you commit it to long-term memory. Don't let your mind wander. Stay focused. If you find yourself having trouble concentrating, take a small break (two to five minutes).

> "If a man is given a fish, he eats for a day. If a man learns to fish, he eats forever."
>
> —Chinese proverb

Relating the information to something that you already know or understand will assist you in filing or storing the information for easy retrieval. Relating the appearance of the African zebra to the American horse can help you remember what the zebra looks like. You may not know what the building in Katherine's story looked like, but try to see her in front of a building on *your campus*. All of these relationships increase retention.

Repeating the information out loud to yourself or to a study partner facilitates its transfer to long-term memory. Some people have to hear information many times before they can commit it to long-term memory. Memory experts agree that repetition is one of the STRONGEST tools for increasing the retention of material.

Reviewing the information is another means of repetition. The more you see and use the information, the easier it will be to remember it when the time comes. As you review, try to remember the main points of the information.

Walter Pauk (2007), educator and inventor of the Cornell note-taking method, found in a study that people reading a textbook chapter forgot 81 percent of what they had read after 28 days. With this in mind, it may behoove you to review Katherine's story (and other material in your texts) regularly. Reviewing is a method of repetition and of keeping information fresh.

Remembering Katherine

Without looking back, answer the following questions about Katherine. Use your visualization and concentration skills to recall the information.

1. What was the name of the biology building? _____

2. Did she see the shadow before or after she saw the two people behind her? _____

3. What were the two people behind her doing? _____

4. What was the name of the arts building? _____

5. Why did she cross the street? _____

6. How far ahead of her was the group of students? _____

7. When she saw the group of students in front of her, how far was she from her residence? _____

8. What was Katherine's friend's name? _____

WHAT HELPS? WHAT HURTS?

Attending to Your Memory

For any part of the body, there are things that help you and hurt you. Your memory is no different. Just as your body will begin to fail you without proper attention, exercise, and nutrition, if neglected or mistreated, your memory will do the same. Consider the following things that can help or hinder your memory:

MEMORY HELPERS

- ☐ Proper sleep
- ☐ Proper nutrition/diet
- ☐ Exercise
- ☐ Mental exercises such as crossword puzzles, brain teasers, name games
- ☐ A positive mind-set
- ☐ The proper environment
- ☐ Scheduled study breaks
- ☐ Repetition and visualization

MEMORY HINDRANCES

- ☐ Internal and external distractions
- ☐ Alcohol
- ☐ Drugs
- ☐ Stress
- ☐ Closed-mindedness (tuning out things you don't like)
- ☐ Inability to distinguish important facts from unimportant facts

KNOWING VERSUS MEMORIZING

Why don't you forget your name? Why don't you forget your address? The answer is that you KNOW that information. You OWN it. It belongs to you. You've used it often enough and repeated it so frequently that it is highly unlikely that you will ever forget it. Conversely, why can't you remember the details of Erickson's Stages of Development or Maslow's Hierarchy of Basic Needs or Darwin's Theory of Evolution? Most likely because you memorized it and never "owned" it.

If you think back to what you can and can't remember, memorization plays a great role. Rote memory is when you literally memorize something and days later it is gone. You memorized it because you needed it for something like a test or a discussion, but it was not important enough to you to know it for life.

Knowing something means that you have made a personal commitment to make this information a part of your life. For example, if you needed to remember the name *Stephen* and his phone number of 925–6813, the likelihood of your remembering this depends on *attitude.* Do you need to recall this information because he is in your study group and you might need to call him, or because he is the care giver for your infant daughter while you are in class? How badly you need that name and number will determine the commitment level that you make to just *memorizing* it (and maybe forgetting it) or *knowing* it (and making it a part of your life).

Think about your study habits for a moment. When you are reading your chapter, listening in class, or studying at home, what is your commitment level? How much energy, brainpower, zeal, and fervor do you put into it? Again, it will depend on how you perceive the value of that information.

To OWN knowledge, you have to work from many angles, and Bloom's Taxonomy can help you do that. After you have read a chapter, visualized the information, related it to something you already know, and reviewed it for accuracy, ask yourself a few questions. These questions can help you KNOW the information, thus helping you transfer it to long-term memory and *life-long ownership.*

Questions such as these can help you move from simple memorization to ownership of the material:

- Can I relate *x* to *y?*
- Can I illustrate how *x* does *y?*
- Can I compare and contrast *x* to *y?*
- Can I apply *x* to *y* in the real world?
- Can I distinguish *x* from *y?*
- Can I define, identify, name, and describe *x?*
- Can I solve the problem of *x?*
- Can I modify or rearrange *x* to make it work with *y?*
- Can I support the theory of *x* and *y?*
- Can I defend my knowledge of *x* or *y?*

(continued)

Freshman of the Year. In 1984, he was drafted by the Chicago Bulls of the National Basketball Association. He led the NBA in scoring for 10 seasons, he holds the top career and playoff scoring averages, and is today considered by many to be THE most accomplished basketball player ever to hit the court.

Consider the picture of the children playing. Study it carefully and completely. Look at everything in the picture from top to bottom, left to right.

Now, look at the picture with the areas marked.

Notice the number of people on the trampoline   **Notice the storage building**

Notice the color of the protective padding

Notice the green foliage

Notice the utility meter

Cover the picture and answer the following questions:

1. How many people are on the trampoline? _____

2. What color is the protective padding on the edge? _____

3. What is the season of the year, based on the foliage color? _____

4. What colors are used on the storage building? _____

5. Is there one utility meter or two? _____

6. How many children are in the air? _____

7. Are the children all male, female, or mixed? _____

8. How many people are wearing striped shirts? _____

9. What type of fence surrounds the house? _____

10. What colors are used on the house? _____

11. Is the house made of one material or more? _____

12. What color are the flowers on the bush? _____

Could you answer them all without looking? The purpose of this exercise is to help you understand the real difference between casually looking at something and REALLY looking at something. To truly know something, you have to go beyond what is given. You have to look and examine more than you are told or more than what is pointed out for you. In order to own information, you have to be totally committed to examining every detail, every inch, and every angle of it. You will need to practice and master the technique of "going beyond."

READY, SET, GO!
Memory and Studying

All it takes is a positive attitude and an open mind. Next, you'll learn about three methods of studying that you can use to put yourself in charge of the material. The box provides a summary of these methods.

THREE STUDYING STRATEGIES

SQ3R Method	Mnemonics	Cooperative Learning
Best used for scanning and reading textbooks	Can be used when studying lecture or text notes	Can be used when studying in groups for tests, projects, note sharing, and analysis
Scan	Jingles/Rhymes	Questioning
Question	Sentences	Comparing
Read	Words	Drilling
Recite	Story lines	Brainstorming
Review	Acronyms	Sharing
	Pegs	Mapping

THE SQ3R METHOD

You were introduced to this method in Chapter 5. This method can help you commit material to memory. As a quick review, to use SQ3R, you would:

☐ Scan the chapter: Note the headings, photos, quotes, indentions, bolded words, and so on.
☐ Write questions from headings: Use *who, what, when, where, why,* and *how.*
☐ Read the chapter: Look up unfamiliar words, highlight important sections, take notes while reading, paraphrase the information.
☐ Recite the information: Close the text and determine if you can "tell the story" of the chapter.
☐ Review the chapter: Return to the chapter often and look over the information.

"The illiterate of the 21st century will not be those who cannot read and write, but those who cannot learn, unlearn, and relearn."

—Alvin Toffler

Using SQ3R as a study method can help you increase your understanding of the material and commit the information to long-term memory.

MNEMONIC DEVICES

Mnemonic (pronounced ni-mon-ik) devices are memory tricks or techniques that assist you in putting information into your long-term memory and pulling it out when you need it. Research has shown that mnemonics create a phenomenon known as the *bizarreness effect*. This effect causes us to remember information that is "bizarre" or unusual more rapidly than "normal," everyday facts. "The bizarreness effect occurs because unusual information and events trigger heightened levels of our attention and require us to work harder to make sense of them; thus we remember the information and its associated interaction better" (McCornack, 2007). Consider the following example:

I recently gave a test on the basic principles of public speaking. A student asked if she had to know the parts of the communication process in order. When I replied that she should be able to recall them in order, she became nervous and said that she had not learned them in order. Another student overheard the conversation and said, "*Some monkeys can read backward fast.*" The first student asked, "*What do you mean by that?*" I laughed and said that the mnemonic was great! The student had created a sentence to remember *source*, *message*, *channel*, *receiver*, *barriers*, and *feedback*. The relationship worked like this:

Some	= Source
Monkeys	= Message
Can	= Channel
Read	= Receiver
Backward	= Barriers
Fast	= Feedback

This is a perfect example of how using memory tricks can help you invoke the bizarreness effect and then retrieve information easily.

The following types of mnemonic devices may help you with your long-term memory.

Jingles/Rhymes.   You can make up rhymes, songs, poems, or sayings to assist you in remembering information; for example, "Columbus sailed the ocean blue in fourteen hundred and ninety-two."

As a child, you learned many things through jingles and rhymes. You probably learned your ABCs, as well as your numbers, through a song pattern. If you think about it, you can still sing your ABCs, and maybe your numbers through the "Ten Little Indians" song. You could probably sing every word to the opening songs of *The Brady Bunch* or *Gilligan's Island* because of the continual reruns on TV. Jingles and rhymes have a strong and lasting impact on our memory—especially when repetition is involved.

Sentences.   You can make up sentences such as "Some men can read backward fast" to help you remember information. Another example is "Please excuse my dear Aunt Sally," which corresponds to the mathematical operations: parentheses, exponents, multiplication, division, addition, and subtraction. Other sentences in academic areas include:

1. **M**y **V**ery **E**lderly **M**other **J**ust **S**aved **U**s **N**icely. This is a sentence mnemonic for the eight planets **in order from the sun**: Mercury, Venus, Earth, Mars, Jupiter, Saturn, Uranus, Neptune.

2. **E**very **G**ood **B**ird **D**oes **F**ly is a sentence mnemonic for the line notes in the treble clef in music.

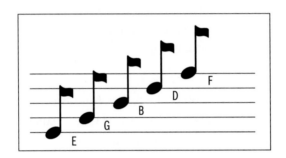

3. **S**ome **M**en **H**elp **E**ach **O**ther is a sentence mnemonic for the Great Lakes from **west to east:** Superior, Michigan, Huron, Erie, Ontario.

Words.   You can create words. For example, **Roy G. Biv** may help you remember the colors of the rainbow: **r**ed, **o**range, **y**ellow, **g**reen, **b**lue, **i**ndigo, and **v**iolet.

Other word mnemonics include:

1. **HOMES** is a word for the Great Lakes in no particular order: **H**uron, **O**ntario, **M**ichigan, **E**rie, **S**uperior.
2. **FACE** is a word mnemonic for the space notes in the treble clef.

Story lines.   If you find it easier to remember stories than raw information, you may want to process the information into a story that you can easily tell. Weave the data and facts into a creative story that can be easily retrieved from your long-term memory. This technique can be especially beneficial if your instructor gives essay exams, because the "story" that you remember can be what was actually told in class.

Acronyms.   An acronym is a word that is formed from the first letters of other words. You may see reruns for the famed TV show $M^{\star}A^{\star}S^{\star}H$. This is an acronym for Mobile Army Surgical Hospital. If you scuba dive, you know that *SCUBA* is an acronym for Self-Contained Underwater Breathing Apparatus. Other common acronyms are:

NASA (**N**ational **A**eronatics and **S**pace **A**dministration)

NASCAR (**N**ational **A**ssociation of **S**tock **C**ar **A**uto **R**acing)

NASDAQ (**N**ational **A**ssociation of **S**ecurities **D**ealers **A**utomated **Q**uotation)

NATO (**N**orth **A**tlantic **T**reaty **O**rganization)

BART (**B**ay **A**rea **R**apid **T**ransit)

Pegging.   The peg system uses association, visualization, and attachment for remembering. With this system, you "attach" what you want to remember to something that is already familiar to you. This is a visual means to remember lists, sequences, and even categories of information.

Most peg systems use numbers and rhyming words to correspond such as:

1 = sun	6 = sticks
2 = shoe	7 = heaven
3 = bee	8 = gate
4 = shore	9 = fine
5 = alive	10 = pen

To attach information to the number, you visually attach a word (such as sun, shoe, bee, shore) to the word you want to remember. For example, if you wanted to remember a shopping list that included ice cream, rice, Ajax, milk, water, and cookies, this might be your plan:

You see ice cream melting in the **sun.**

You see rice filling a **shoe.**

You see Ajax sprinkled on a **bee.**

Study at School.   Your schedule may have you running from work to school directly to home. Try to squeeze in even as little as half an hour at school for studying, perhaps immediately before or after class. A half hour of pure study time can prove more valuable than five hours at home with constant interruptions.

Create Crafts and Hobbies.   Your children need to be occupied while you study. It may help if you have crafts and hobbies that they can do while you are studying. Choose projects your children can do by themselves. Depending on their ages, children could make masks from paper plates, color, do pipe cleaner art or papier-mâché, use modeling clay or dough, or build a block city. Explain to your children that you are studying and that they can use this time to be creative; when everyone is finished, you'll share what you've done with each other.

Study with Your Children.   One of the best ways to instill the value of education in your children is to let them see you participating in your own education. Set aside one or two hours per night when you and your children study. You may be able to study in one place, or you may have separate study areas. If your children know that you are studying and you have explained to them how you value your education, you are killing two birds with one stone: You are able to study, and you are providing a positive role model as your children study with you and watch you.

If you view your studying responsibilities positively, your children will too. Try to separate the time you spend with your family from the time you need to spend on your school work.

"Don't just learn *something* from every experience, learn *something positive.*"
—Al Neuharth

Rent Movies or Let Your Children Watch TV.   Research has shown that viewing a limited amount of educational television, such as *Sesame Street, Reading Rainbow,* or *Barney and Friends,* can be beneficial for children. If you do not like what is on television, you might consider renting or purchasing age-appropriate educational videos for your children. This could keep them busy while you study, and it could help them learn as well.

Invite Your Children's Friends Over.   What?! That's right. A child who has a friend to play or study with may create less of a distraction for you. Chances are your children would rather be occupied with someone their own age, and you will gain valuable study time.

Hire a Sitter or Exchange Sitting Services with Another Student.   Arrange to have a sitter come to your house a couple of times a week if you can afford it. If you have a classmate who also has children at home, you might take turns watching the children for each other. You could each take the children for one day a week, or devise any schedule that suits you both best. Or you could study together, and let your children play together while you study, alternating homes.

Ask if Your College has an On-Site Day Care Center such as the Boys and Girls Club.   Some colleges provide day care facilities at a reduced cost, and some provide day care at no charge. It is certainly worth checking out.

Talk to the Financial Aid Office on Your Campus.   In some instances, there will be grants or aid to assist you in finding affordable day care for your child.

Studying at any time is hard work. It is even harder when you have to attend to a partner, children, family responsibilities, work, and a social life as well. You will have to be creative in order to complete your degree. You are going to have to do things and make sacrifices that you never thought possible. But if you explore the options, plan ahead, and ask questions of other students with children and with responsibilities outside the classroom, you can and will succeed.

WHAT DO YOU MEAN, THE TEST IS TOMORROW?

Studying in a Crunch

Let's be straight upfront. No study skills textbook will ever advise you to cram. It is simply a dangerous and often futile exercise in desperation. You'll never read the words, "Don't waste your party time studying. CRAM the night before." Cramming is just the opposite of what this whole chapter is about—knowing versus memorizing. Cramming will never help you know; it can only help you memorize a few things for storage in short-term memory. You may spend several hours cramming, and shortly after the test, the information is gone, evaporated, vanished!

Let's also be straight about something else. We know that you may have obligations that take enormous hours from your week. This is simply a matter of fact in the 21st century. So, there may be times when time runs out and the only option is to cram. If you find yourself in this spot, consider the following tips and suggestions for cramming. These probably won't get you an "A," but they may help you with a few questions.

ESSENTIAL CORNERSTONE

KNOWLEDGE

How can procrastinating and not studying effectively affect your knowledge base negatively?

Depressurize.   Just tell yourself up front what you are doing. Don't pretend that cramming is going to save you. Let yourself realize that you are memorizing material for short-term gain and that you won't be able to keep it all. With this admission, your stress will diminish.

Ditch the Blame Game.   You know you're at fault, so accept that and move on. Sitting around bemoaning your fate will not help. Just tell yourself, "I messed up this time; I won't let it happen again."

Know What.   When cramming, it is important to know what you're cramming for. If you're cramming for a multiple-choice test, you'll need different types of information than for an essay test. Know what type of test it is for which you are studying.

Read it Quick.   Think about H2 FLIB. This is a mnemonic for read the *headings*, *highlight* the important words, read the *first* sentence of every paragraph, read the *last*

SUCCESSFUL DECISIONS

After the second week of classes, José was devastated over his first test score. The instructor put the range of grades on the board, and he was even more shocked to see that many people passed the test and that his score was in the bottom 10 percent.

He began asking classmates if they did well or not and found some that had made A's and others that had made D's. When he spoke with one classmate, Letty, she told him that he should just chill and take a "cheat sheet" to class. "The instructor never looks, man, and she left the classroom twice. She'll never know. That's how I got my A."

"Cheat," José thought, "I don't think I can do that." He knew that others had made better grades than him over the years, but he also knew that he had never once cheated on an exam. Ever.

José went to the Tutoring Center and worked with a tutor on content and on how to take a test more effectively. On the next test, José scored a C. "It may not be the best grade in the class," he thought, "but it is all mine. I did it."

José made a *successful decision*.

sentence of every paragraph, read the *indented* and *boxed* material. This can help you get through the chapter when pinched for time.

Make Connections.   As you are reading, quickly determine if any of the information has a connection with something else you know. Is there a comparison or contrast? Is there a relationship of any kind? Is there a cause and effect in motion? Can you pinpoint an example to clarify the information? Is there a mnemonic that can help me with this information? These questions can help you with retention and long-term memory commitment.

Use Your Syllabus or Study Guide.   If your instructor lists questions that you should know (mastery questions) in the syllabus, or if he or she gave you a study sheet, this is the place to start. Answer those questions. If you don't have either, look to see if the text gives study questions at the end of the chapter. Try to answer the questions using the text *and* your lecture notes.

See it.   Visualizing the information through mapping, diagrams, photos, drawings, and outlines can help you commit this information to short-term memory.

Repeat!   Repeat! Repeat! Repetition is the key to committing information to memory. After you read information from the text or lecture notes, repeat it time and time again. When you think you've got it, write it down, then repeat it again.

Choose Wisely.   If you're cramming, you can't do it all. Make wise choices about which material you plan to study. This can be driven by your study sheet, your lecture notes, or questions in your syllabus (if they are listed).

One of the most important things about cramming is that this information is going to leave you. Don't rely on it for the next test or the final. You will need to go back and relearn (truly understand) this information to commit it to long-term memory. Good luck!

THINKING ABOUT TESTING
Your Attitude Makes All the Difference

A student jokes with her instructor, "*I have five thousand dollars in my savings account and it is yours if you don't make us take the test!*" Well, this may be a bit extreme, but many students would do almost anything to get out of taking exams. Some students, however, proudly walk into the classroom on test day relaxed, poised, and optimistic. Others have physical reactions to testing, including nausea, headaches, and blackouts. Those negative reactions may be a result of being under prepared or not knowing how to take an exam.

If you asked the relaxed and poised student why he or she feels so optimistic, his or her response may be:

- I studied over the past week and feel great about the material.
- I'm ready and I know I'm going to do a great job.
- I used some helpful study techniques to help me remember information.
- I tested myself at home using the techniques of Bloom's Taxonomy.
- I've learned so much in this class.

Conversely, if you asked the student who is pale and about to throw up, his or her response may be:

- I didn't know what to study.
- I just know I'm going to fail this miserable test.
- I crammed all night and I can't remember half of what I studied.

Studying, predicting questions, reviewing, and relaxing can reduce most test anxiety.

- I hate this class and the instructor. I should have dropped it weeks ago.
- When am I ever going to have to use this stuff?

A positive or negative attitude can truly mean the difference between success and failure. Yet, with an attitude adjustment from negative to positive and some basic preparation, you can overcome a good deal of your anxiety about tests and do well. You can reduce anxiety when you are in control of the situation, and you can gain control by convincing yourself that you can and will be successful. If you think positively and can honestly say that you have done everything possible to prepare for a test, then the results will most likely be positive.

> "Optimism is the faith that leads to achievement. Nothing can be done without hope and confidence."
>
> —Helen Keller

No test is an indication of who you are as a person or a mark of your worth as a human being. Not everyone can be good at all things. You will have areas of strength and of weakness. You will spare yourself a great deal of anxiety and frustration if you understand from the start that you may not score 100 on every test. If you expect absolute perfection on everything, you are setting yourself up for great disappointment. Think positively, prepare well, and do your best. No one can ask for more.

I KNOW I CAN, I KNOW I CAN, I KNOW I CAN . . .
Reducing Test Anxiety

As you learned in Chapter 5, "Prioritize," some stress is a good thing. It is the bad stress (distress) that can cause problems at many physical, emotional, and mental levels. Test anxiety can be described as distress. A little bit of nervousness and good stress (eustress) can help you focus, increase your energy level, and keep you sharp. The most powerful stress-reduction strategy that you can use is to **silence your negative self-talk** about the exam or change your self-talk to a positive tone. Consider the following tips for reducing test anxiety during your next test. You will not be able to employ them all, but if you learn and use a few new ones each time, you'll turn into a testing pro!

- ☐ Find out about the test before it is given; ask the instructor what types of questions will be on the test.
- ☐ Do you know anyone who has had this professor and might be able to tell you what kinds of questions to expect?
- ☐ Find out exactly what the test will cover ahead of time.
- ☐ Ask the instructor for a study sheet; you may not get one, but it does not hurt to ask!
- ☐ Know the rules of the test and of the instructor.
- ☐ Know what grade value the test holds.
- ☐ Ask whether there will be extra credit or bonus questions on the test.
- ☐ Attend the review session if one is offered.
- ☐ Come to the test with everything you need: pencils, calculator, and other supplies.
- ☐ Approach the test with an "I can" attitude.
- ☐ Prepare yourself emotionally for the test, control your self-talk, and be positive.
- ☐ Remind yourself that you studied and that you know the material.
- ☐ Overlearn the material—you can't study too much.
- ☐ Go to bed early. Do not pull an all-nighter before the test.
- ☐ Eat a healthy meal before the test.
- ☐ Chew gum or eat hard candy during the test if allowed; it may help you relax.

- ☐ Arrive early for the test (at least 15 minutes early).
- ☐ Listen to the instructor before the test begins.
- ☐ Read over the entire test first; read all the directions; highlight the directions.
- ☐ If you become nervous, sit back, relax, breathe, and clear your mind.
- ☐ When you get the test, jot down your mnemonics on the back or at the top of a page.
- ☐ Answer what you know first, the questions that are easiest for you.
- ☐ Keep an eye on the clock so that you can finish on time. However, don't let time cause undue stress or anxiety.
- ☐ Check your answers, but remember that your first response is usually correct.
- ☐ Never look at another student's test or let anyone see your test.

QUIZZING YOUR INSTRUCTOR AND PREDICTING EXAM QUESTIONS

Several classes before the test is scheduled, **quiz your instructor** about the logistics and specifics of the test. This information can help you study more effectively and eliminate the anxiety that comes with uncertainty. If you don't know whether the test is going to be true–false or essay or both, it is much more difficult to study. Some questions to ask are:

1. What type of questions will be on the test?
2. How long is the test? How many questions will be on the test?
3. Is there a time limit on the test?
4. Will there be any special instructions, such as use pen only or use a number 2 pencil?
5. Is there a study sheet?
6. Will there be a review session?
7. What is the grade value of the test?
8. What chapters or sections will the test cover?

> "If you can't change your fate, change your attitude."
>
> —Amy Tan

Asking these simple questions will help you know what type of test will be administered, how you should prepare for it, and what supplies you will need.

Predicting exam questions should come easily to you at this point as you have been doing this in the "*Scan and Question*" section of this text since Chapter 1. Instructors frequently give clues about what they will be asking and what types of questions will be given.

ESSENTIAL CORNERSTONE

ADAPTABILITY

How can learning how to predict exam questions help you become more adaptable in the workplace?

You will want to begin predicting questions early in the semester. Listen to the instructor carefully. Instructors use cue phrases, such as, "*You will see this again*" and "*If I were to ask you this question on the test. . . .*" Pay close attention to what is written on the board or PowerPoint, what questions are asked in class, and what areas the instructor seems to be concentrating on more than others. You will begin to get a feel for what types of questions to expect or at least the important areas to study.

It may also be beneficial for you to keep a running page of test questions that you have predicted. As you read through a chapter, ask yourself many questions at the end of each section or chapter as you have done in this text. When it is time to study for the test, you may have already predicted many of the questions your instructor will ask. Save all quizzes and exams that your instructor lets you keep (some instructors take the exams back after students have had a chance to review them). These are a wonderful resource for studying for the next exam or for predicting questions for the course final.

Take a moment and predict two essay test questions from Chapter 10, "Think."

Question 1._____

_____

_____

Why do you think this question will be asked? _____

_____

_____

Question 2. _____

_____

_____

Why do you think this question will be asked? _____

_____

_____

THREE TYPES OF RESPONSES TO TEST QUESTIONS

Almost every test question will elicit one of three types of responses from you as the test taker:

*Quick-time response   *Lag-time response   *No response

Your response is a **quick-time response** when you read a question and know the answer immediately. You may need to read only one key word in the test question to know the correct response. Even if you have a quick-time response, however, always read the entire question before answering. The question may be worded in such a way that the correct response is not what you originally expected. By reading the entire question before answering, you can avoid losing points to careless error.

You have a **lag-time response** when you read a question and the answer does not come to you immediately. You may have to read the question several times or even move on to another question before you think of the correct response. Information in another question will sometimes trigger the response you need. Don't get nervous if you have a lag-time response. Once you've begun to answer other questions, you usually begin to remember more, and the response may come to you. You do not have to answer questions in order on most tests.

No response is the least desirable situation. You may read a question two or three times and still have no response. At this point, you should move on to another question to try to find some related information. When this happens, you have some options:

1. Leave this question until the very end of the test.
2. Make an intelligent guess.
3. Try to eliminate all unreasonable answers by association.
4. Watch for modifiers within the question.

What's Sleep Got to Do with It?

You've heard the old saying, "You are what you eat." This may be true, but many sleep experts would say, "You are how you sleep." Sleep deprivation is one of the leading causes of poor productivity and academic performance, workplace and auto accidents, lack of concentration, diminished immune systems, decreased metabolism, cardiovascular problems, and even poor communication efforts.

The National Traffic Safety Administration estimates that 100,000 crashes each year are the result of sleepy drivers. These crashes cause nearly 1,600 deaths, 71,000 injuries, and $12.5 billion in property loss and diminished activity ("Hidden Menace," 2003).

Mark Rosekind, Ph.D., an expert on fatigue and performance issues and a member of the board of directors for the National Sleep Foundation, states, "Without sufficient sleep it is more difficult to concentrate, make careful decisions, and follow instructions; we are more likely to make mistakes or errors, and are more prone to being impatient and lethargic. Our attention, memory, and reaction time are all affected" (Cardinal, 2003).

According to the National Sleep Foundation, the following symptoms can signal inadequate sleep:

- Dozing off while engaged in an activity such as reading, watching TV, sitting in meetings, or sitting in traffic
- Slowed thinking and reacting
- Difficulty listening to what is said or understanding directions
- Difficulty remembering or retaining information
- Frequent errors or mistakes
- Narrowing of attention, missing important changes in a situation
- Depression or negative mood
- Impatience or being quick to anger
- Frequent blinking, difficulty focusing eyes, or heavy eyelids

Indeed, lack of sleep can decrease your ability to study, recall information, and perform well on tests and assignments. This can be especially true during midterm and final exam periods. Those late or all-night cram sessions can actually be more detrimental to your academic success than helpful. By including your study sessions in your time-management plan, you can avoid having to spend your sleep time studying.

Different people need different amounts of sleep within a 24-hour period. Some people absolutely need 8–10 hours of sleep, while others can function well on 4–6 hours. If you are not sleeping enough to rest and revive your body, you will experience sleep deprivation.

Researchers suggest that missing as little as 2 hours of sleep for *one* night can take as long as 6 days to recover—if it is recovered at all (Mass, 1990). It is generally estimated that 8–9 hours of *good, solid, restful* sleep per night can decrease your chances of sleep deprivation.

Here are some helpful hints for getting a good night's rest:

- Avoid alcohol and caffeine (yes, alcohol is a depressant, but it interrupts both REM and slow-wave sleep, and caffeine can stay in your system for as long as 12 hours).
- Exercise during the day (but not within four hours of your sleep time).
- Regulate the temperature in your bedroom to a comfortable setting for you.
- Wind down before trying to sleep. Complete all tasks at least one hour prior to your bedtime. This gives you time to relax and prepare for rest.
- Avoid taking naps during the day.

(continued)

- Have a set bedtime and try to stick to it.
- Take a warm bath before bedtime.
- Go to bed only when you are tired. If you are not asleep within 15–30 minutes, get up and do something restful like reading or listening to soft music.
- Use relaxation techniques such as visualization and mind travel.
- Avoid taking sleeping aids. This can cause more long-term problems than sleep deprivation.

It is very difficult to use intelligent guessing with essay or fill-in-the-blank questions. Remember these important tips about the three types of responses:

1. Don't be overly anxious if your *response is quick;* read the entire question and be careful so that you don't make a mistake.
2. Don't get nervous if you have a *lag-time response;* the answer may come to you later, so just relax and move on.
3. Don't put down just anything if you have *no response;* take the remaining time and use intelligent guessing.

TEST-TAKING STRATEGIES AND HINTS FOR SUCCESS

Wouldn't it be just great if every instructor gave the same type of test? Then, you would have to worry about content only, and not about the test itself. Unfortunately, this is not going to happen. Instructors will continue to test differently and to have their own style of writing tests. Successful students have to know the differences among testing techniques and know what to look for when dealing with each type of test question. You may have a preference for one type of question over another. You may prefer multiple-choice to essay questions, whereas someone else may prefer essay to true–false questions. Whatever your preference, you are going to encounter all types of questions. To be successful, you will need to know the techniques for answering each type.

The most common types of questions are:

- Matching
- True–false
- Multiple-choice
- Short answer
- Essay

Before you read about the strategies for answering these different types of questions, think about this: There is no substitute for studying! You can know all the tips, ways to reduce anxiety, mnemonics, and strategies on earth, but if you have not studied, they will be of little help to you.

Strategies for Matching Questions

Matching questions frequently involve knowledge of people, dates, places, or vocabulary. When answering matching questions, you should:

- Read the directions carefully.
- Read each column before you answer.
- Determine whether there is an equal number of items in each column.
- Match what you know first.
- Cross off information as it is used.

Using proper study techniques and remembering testing tips can increase your chances of success on most tests.

- Use the process of elimination for answers you might not know.
- Look for logical clues.
- Use the longer statement as a question; use the shorter statement as an answer.

SAMPLE TEST #1

Directions: Match the information in column A with the correct information in column B. Use uppercase letters.

GOALS, MOTIVATION, & SELF-ESTEEM

A	B
_____ They can be long or short, social, academic, religious, or financial	A. Child within
_____ They bring out the worst in you	B. Objectivity
_____ I CAN'T Syndrome	C. Contaminated people
_____ Your "true self"	D. Negative thoughts
_____ Listening with an open mind	E. Goals

Strategies for True–False Questions

True–false tests ask if a statement is true or not. True–false questions can be some of the trickiest questions ever developed. Some students like them; some hate them. There is a 50/50 chance of answering correctly, but you can use the following strategies to increase your odds on true–false tests:

- Read each statement carefully.
- Watch for key words in each statement, for example, negatives.
- Read each statement for double negatives, such as "not untruthful."
- Pay attention to words that may indicate that a statement is true, such as "some," "few," "many," and "often."
- Pay attention to words that may indicate that a statement is false, such as "never," "all," "every," and "only."
- Remember that if any part of a statement is false, the entire statement is false.
- Answer every question unless there is a penalty for guessing.

SAMPLE TEST #2

Place "T" for true or "F" for false beside each statement.

NOTE-TAKING SKILLS

_____ 1. Note taking creates a history of your course content.

_____ 2. "Most importantly" is not a key phrase.

_____ 3. You should always write down everything the instructor says.

_____ 4. You should never ask questions in class.

_____ 5. The L-STAR system is a way of studying.

_____ 6. W/O is not a piece of shorthand.

_____ 7. You should use 4-by-6-inch paper to take classroom notes.

_____ 8. The outline technique is best used with lecture notes.

_____ 9. The Cornell method should never be used with textbook notes.

_____ 10. The mapping system is done with a series of circles.

Strategies for Multiple-Choice Questions

Many college instructors give multiple-choice tests because they are easy to grade and provide quick, precise responses. A multiple-choice question asks you to choose from among usually two to five answers to complete a sentence. Some strategies for increasing your success in answering multiple-choice questions are the following:

- Read the question and try to answer it before you read the answers provided.
- Look for similar answers; one of them is usually the correct response.
- Recognize that answers containing extreme modifiers, such as *always, every,* and *never,* are usually wrong.
- Cross off answers that you know are incorrect.
- Read all the options before selecting your answer. Even if you believe that A is the correct response, read them all.
- Recognize that when the answers are all numbers, the highest and lowest numbers are usually incorrect.
- Recognize that a joke is usually wrong.
- Understand that the most inclusive answer is often correct.
- Understand that the longest answer is often correct.
- If you cannot answer a question, move on to the next one and continue through the test; another question may trigger the answer you missed.
- Make an educated guess if you must.
- Answer every question unless there is a penalty for guessing.

SAMPLE TEST #3

Directions: Read each statement and select the best response from the answers given below.

STUDY SKILLS

1. Which statement is true, according to the 2006 Labor Statistics, Bureau of Census?
   A. Men earn more than women.
   B. Women earn more than men.
   C. People with a bachelor's degree earn the most money of any education level.
   D. Males and females earn just about the same amount of money.

2. To calculate a GPA, you would:
   A. Divide quality points by the number of semester hours.
   B. Multiply total points by quality points.
   C. Divide total points by the number of semester hours.
   D. Multiply the quality points by the total points.

3. To be an effective priority manager, you have to:
   A. Be very structured and organized.
   B. Be very unstructured and disorganized.
   C. Be mildly structured and organized.
   D. Know what type of person you are and work from that point.

4. Objective listening is:
   A. Judging the speaker and not the message.
   B. Listening with an open mind.
   C. Mentally arguing with the speaker so you can formulate questions.
   D. Listening using the elements of the Korean verb "to listen."

COLUMN A (ANSWER)	COLUMN B (EXPLANATION)
_____	_____
_____	_____
_____	_____
_____	_____
_____	_____
_____	_____
_____	_____

This method can also be used to formulate new information on a subject. If you read a chapter or an article, hear a conversation, or are faced with a problem, you can analyze it by creating questions that need to be answered in Column A and providing the answer in Column B. You may have to use more than one source of information to answer the questions you posed in Column A.

Step Four: Asking Questions

You've asked questions all of your life. As a child, you asked your parents, "What's that?" a million times. You probably asked them, "Why do I have to do this?" In later years, you've asked questions of your friends, teachers, strangers, store clerks, and significant others. Questioning is not new to you, but it may be a new technique for exploring, developing, and acquiring new knowledge. Curiosity may have killed the cat, but it was a smart cat when it died! Your curiosity is one of the most important traits you possess. It helps you grow and learn, and it may sometimes cause you to be uncomfortable. That's OK. This section is provided to assist you in learning how to ask questions to promote knowledge, solve problems, foster strong relationships, and critically analyze difficult situations.

Sometimes you want to ask questions of experts whose opinions you value to aid your own thinking. Are there questions you have for any of these people?

Let's start with a simple questioning exercise. If you could meet anyone on earth and ask five questions, who would you meet, why would you meet that person, and what questions would you ask?

I'd like to meet _____

because _____

_____

_____

I'd ask the person:

1. _____

2. _____

3. _____

4. _____

5. _____

Asking questions can be fun in many situations. They help us gain insight in areas where we may have limited knowledge. They can also challenge us to look at issues from many different angles. Answering properly posed questions can help us expand our knowledge base.

SUCCESSFUL DECISIONS

Carson's class was assigned an activity asking them to determine whom they would like to meet if they could meet anyone and which questions they would like to ask them. Some of the class members thought it was a stupid assignment—and Carson was not so sure that she wanted to spend any time on this "weird" activity either.

That evening, she began to think about the question seriously. "Who has been important to the world," she thought? "Who had done something powerful and extraordinary? Who has been awful and caused needless pain?"

She decided that if she could ask anyone anything, she would choose Hitler. She decided that she would ask him these questions: 1) If you had to do it all over again, would you? 2) From where did your hatred come? 3) Why did you have everyone killed who could have revealed your own past? 4) You did not look like the master race you chose to promote. Why did you choose to promote it? 5) Why did you become such a coward in the end and kill yourself?

This interesting project led Carson to use World War II, Hitler, and the German Occupation as the basis for her presentation in speech class. She did not just brush off what seemed to be a "crazy" assignment and in the end . . .
Carson made a *successful decision*.

If you were assigned to write a paper or give a speech on the topic of creationism versus evolution, what five questions would you definitely want that paper or speech to answer? Take some time to think about the issue. Write down at least five questions.

My five questions are:

1. _____

_____

2. _____

_____

3. _____

_____

4. _____

_____

5. _____

_____

Questioning also involves going beyond the obvious. Examine the vehicle advertisement. The car dealership has provided some information, but it is not enough to make an educated decision. What other questions would you ask to make sure that you are getting a good deal?

1. _____

2. _____

3. _____

4. _____

5. _____

Step Five: Solving Problems

You face problems every day; some are larger and more difficult than others. You may have transportation problems. You may have child care problems. You may have academic problems or interpersonal problems. Many people don't know how to solve problems at school, home, or work. They simply let the problem go unaddressed until it is too late to reach an amiable solution. There are many ways to address and solve problems. In this section, we will discuss how to identify and narrow the problem, research and develop alternatives, evaluate the alternatives, and solve the problem.

It is important to remember that every problem does have a solution, but the solution may not be what we wanted. It is also imperative to remember the words of Mary Hatwood Futrell, president of the National Education Association: "Finding the right answer is important, of course. But more important is developing the ability to see that problems have multiple solutions, that getting from X to Y demands basic skills and mental agility, imagination, persistence, patience."

Identify and narrow the problem. Put your problem in writing. When doing this, be sure to jot down all aspects of the problem, such as why it is a problem, whom it affects, and what type of problem it is. Examine the following situation: You have just failed two tests this week and you are dreadfully behind on an English paper. Now, that's a problem . . . or is it? If you examine and reflect on the problem, you begin to realize that because of your nighttime job, you always get to class late, you are tired and irritable when you get there, and you never have time to study. So, the real problem is not that you can't do the work; the problem is that your job is interfering with your study time. Now that you have identified and narrowed the problem, you can begin to work toward a solution.

> "When I'm getting ready to reason with a man, I spend one-third of my time thinking about myself and what I am going to say – and two-thirds thinking about him and what he is going to say."
>
> —Abraham Lincoln

Research and develop alternatives. A valuable method of gathering ideas, formulating questions, and solving problems is brainstorming. To brainstorm, gather a group of people and ask them to let ideas flow. A brainstorming session allows all thoughts to be heard without any

from ordinary to EXTRAORDINARY

LEO G. BORGES
Co-founder and Former CEO, Borges and Mahoney, Inc.
San Francisco, CA

Tulare, California, is still a farming community today, but in 1928, when I was born, it was totally agricultural and an exceptionally rural, detached part of the world. My parents had immigrated to California from the Azore Islands years earlier in search of a better life—*the American dream*. My father died when I was 3 years old and when I was 11, my mother passed away. Even though I lived with and was raised by my sisters, the feelings of aloneness and isolation were the two primary feelings I had growing up. We were orphans. We were poor. We were farm kids. We were Portuguese—not Americans. Every day, someone reminded us of these realities. One positive thing remained, however. My mother always told us that we could *be anything* or *have anything* if we believed in it and worked hard for it.

I left home at 17 to attend a program in advertising in San Francisco. Later that year, I moved to Los Angeles and began working for a major advertising firm. From there I enlisted in the Coast Guard, and when my duty was over, I worked for an oil company and then a major leasing firm. In each position, I worked my way up the ladder, strove to do my very best, and proved that I was capable of doing anything regardless of my background.

When I was in my early forties, my best friend, Cliff, and I decided to start our own business. We were tired of working in "middle management" and knew that we could be successful if we worked hard. After much research and consulting with companies across the country, we determined that we would start a company in the water treatment business.

You may be asking yourself, "What experience did an advertising agency, an oil company, and a leasing firm give me to start a business in water treatment?" The answer is *none*. However, Cliff was an excellent accountant and I was an excellent salesman. We found a third partner who was one of the leading water treatment experts in the world and we were off. It was not easy and we had to eat beans for many meals, but Borges and Mahoney, Inc. was born.

Our first office was a small storefront in San Francisco. Through the development of our superior products, expert advice to clients, and outstanding customer service, we grew and grew, finally moving to our largest location in San Rafael, California. By the time we sold our business some 20 years later, we had 15 full-time employees and annual revenues in the millions of dollars.

To this day, I attribute my success to the fact that I was determined to show everyone—my sisters, cousins, aunts and uncles, former co-workers, friends, and foes—that I would never let my past, my heritage, my economic background, or my history hold me back. I knew that I could be a success. Through hard work, determination, and surrounding myself with supportive, brilliant people, I proved that the American dream my parents sought years earlier is truly possible for anyone who works hard, believes in him- or herself, and doesn't give up. It is possible for you, too.

254

fear of ridicule. You can brainstorm any matter, almost anywhere. You may want to set some guidelines for your sessions to make them more productive.

☐ Identify the topic, problem, or statement to be discussed.
☐ Set a time limit for the entire brainstorming session.
☐ Write all ideas on a board or flip chart.
☐ Let everyone speak.
☐ Don't criticize people for their remarks.
☐ Concentrate on the issue; let all of your ideas flow.
☐ Suspend judgment until all ideas are produced or the time is up.
☐ If you're using the session to generate questions rather than solutions, each participant should pose questions rather than make statements.

When solving a problem, it is helpful to look at all possible alternatives and decide on the best one. Sometimes there is one right answer, but often you'll have to settle for the best answer.

Using the problem identified on page 253 (my nighttime job is causing me to not have enough time for sleep or study), jot down the first few alternatives that come to mind. Don't worry about content, clarity, or quality. Just let your mind flow. Express these ideas when the class brainstorms this problem.

Ideas _____

_____

_____

_____

Evaluate the alternatives. Some of your ideas or your classmates' ideas may not be logical in solving the problem. After careful study and deliberation, without emotional interference, analyze the ideas and determine if they are appropriate or inappropriate for the solution. To analyze, create Columns A and B. Write the idea in Column A and a comment in Column B.

Example

A (IDEA)	B (COMMENTS)
Quit the job.	Very hard to do. I need the money for tuition and car.
Cut my hours at work.	Will ask my boss.
Find a new job.	Hard to do because of the job market—but will look into it.
Get a student loan.	Visit financial aid office tomorrow.
Quit school.	No—it is my only chance for a promotion.

With your comments in Column B, you can now begin to eliminate some of the alternatives that are inappropriate at this time.

Solve the problem. Now that you have a few strong alternatives, you have some work to do. You will need to talk to your boss, go to the financial aid office, and possibly begin to search for a new job with flexible hours. After you have researched each alternative, you will be able to make a decision based on solid information and facts.

Your Turn

Pretend that your best friend, Nathan, has just come to you with a problem. He tells you that his parents are really coming down hard on him for going to college. It is a strange problem. They believe that Nathan should be working full time and that he is just wasting his time and money, because he did not do well in high school. They have threatened to take away his car and kick him out of the house if he does not find a full-time job. Nathan is doing well and does not want to leave college.

In the space provided below, formulate a plan with multiple alternatives to help Nathan solve this problem.

A (IDEA)   **B (COMMENTS)**

_____   _____
_____   _____
_____   _____
_____   _____
_____   _____
_____   _____
_____   _____
_____   _____

Step Six: Distinguishing Fact from Opinion

One of the most important aspects of critical thinking is the ability to distinguish fact from opinion. In most situations—real life, TV, radio, friendly conversations, and the professional arena—opinions surface more often than facts. *Reread the previous sentence.* This is an example of an opinion cloaked as a fact. There is no research supporting this opinion. It sounds as if it could be true, but without evidence and proof, it is just an opinion.

> "Everyone is entitled to their own opinion, but not their own facts."
>
> —Senator Daniel Patrick Moynihan

A fact is something that can be proven, something that can be objectively verified. An opinion is a statement that is held to be true, but one that has no objective proof. *Statements that cannot be proved should always be treated as opinion.* Statements that offer valid proof and verification from credible, reliable sources can be treated as factual.

When trying to distinguish between fact and opinion, you should take the following guidelines into consideration:

- ☐ If you are in doubt, ask questions and listen for solid proof and documentation to support the statement.
- ☐ Listen for what is not said in a statement.
- ☐ Don't be led astray by those you assume are trustworthy and loyal.
- ☐ Don't be turned off by those you fear or consider untruthful.
- ☐ Do your own homework on the issue. Read, research, and question.
- ☐ If you are unsure about the credibility of the source or information, treat the statement as opinion.

Examine the following statements. Before you glance at the answer below, try to determine if you think the statement is a fact or an opinion. **Circle one.**

Gone with the Wind is a movie.	Fact	Opinion
Gone with the Wind is a movie made in 1939.	Fact	Opinion
Gone with the Wind is the best movie ever made.	Fact	Opinion
Tom Hanks is an actor.	Fact	Opinion
There are a heaven and a hell.	Fact	Opinion
Some people believe in a heaven and a hell.	Fact	Opinion
Lincoln was the best president to ever lead the United States.	Fact	Opinion

Statement	Answer	Evidence
Gone with the Wind is a movie.	Fact	This can be proved by watching the movie and by reading movie reviews.
Gone with the Wind is a movie made in 1939.	Fact	This can be verified by many movie sources and by the Motion Picture Association of America.
Gone with the Wind is the best movie ever made.	Opinion	This is only the opinion of some critics and could never be proved.
Tom Hanks is an actor.	Fact	This can be proved by viewing his movies and verifying his two Academy Awards for acting.
There are a heaven and a hell.	Opinion	As controversial as this answer is, the existence of heaven and hell has never been scientifically proven. Both are opinions of various religions.
Some people believe in a heaven and a hell.	Fact	This can be verified by many books and articles and by simply taking a poll of people you know.
Lincoln was the best president to ever lead the United States.	Opinion	This is only an opinion that can be disputed by many people. This cannot be proved.

Step Seven: Seeking Truth in Arguments and Persuasion

Whether or not you realize it, arguments and persuasive efforts are around you daily—hourly, for that matter. They are in newspaper and TV ads, editorials, news commentaries, talk shows, TV magazine shows, political statements, and religious services. It seems at times that almost everyone is trying to persuade us through argument or advice. This section is included to assist you in recognizing faulty arguments and implausible or deceptive persuasion.

First, let's start with a list of terms used to describe faulty arguments and deceptive persuasion. As you read through the list, try to identify situations in which you have heard arguments that fit these descriptions.

> "There is nothing so powerful as truth, and often, nothing so strange."
>
> —Daniel Webster

TERMINOLOGY FOR FALLACIOUS ARGUMENTS

Ad baculum	Ad baculum is an argument that tries to persuade based on force. Threats of alienation, disapproval, or even violence may accompany this type of argument.
Ad hominem	Ad hominem is when someone initiates a personal attack on a person rather than listening to and rationally debating his or her ideas. This is also referred to as slander.
Ad populum	An ad populum argument is based on the opinions of the majority of people. It assumes that because the majority says X is right, then Y is not. It uses little logic.
Ad verecundiam	This argument uses quotes and phrases from people in authority or popular people to support one's own views.
Bandwagon	The bandwagon approach tries to convince you to do something just because everyone else is doing it. It is also referred to as "peer pressure."
Scare tactic	A scare tactic is used as a desperate measure to put fear in your life. If you don't do X, then Y is going to happen to you.
Straw argument	The straw argument attacks the opponent's argument to make one's own argument stronger. It does not necessarily make argument A stronger; it simply discounts argument B.
Appeal to tradition	This argument looks only at the past and suggests that we have always done it "this way" and we should continue to do it "this way."
Plain folks	This type of persuasion is used to make you feel that the people making the argument are just like you. Usually, they are not; they are only using this appeal to connect with your sense of space and time.
Patriotism	This form of persuasion asks you to ignore reason and logic and support what is right for state A or city B or nation C.
Glittering generalities	This type of persuasion or argumentation is an appeal to generalities (Bosak, 1976). It suggests that a person or candidate or professional is for all the "right" things: justice, low taxes, no inflation, rebates, full employment, low crime, free tuition, progress, privacy, and truth.

IDENTIFYING FALLACIOUS ARGUMENTS

Here are statements intended to persuade you or argue for a cause. Beside each statement, identify which type of faulty persuasion is used.

AB	Ad baculum		SA	Straw argument
AH	Ad hominem		AT	Appeal to tradition
AP	Ad populum		PF	Plain folks
AV	Ad verecundiam		PM	Patriotism
BW	Bandwagon		GG	Glittering generalities
ST	Scare tactic			

_____ 1. This country has never faltered in the face of adversity. Our strong, united military has seen us through many troubled times, and it will see us through our current situation. This is your country; support your military.

_____ 2. If I am elected to office, I will personally lobby for lower taxes, a new comprehensive crime bill, a $2,500 tax cut on every new home, and better education, and I will personally work to lower the unemployment rate.

_____ 3. This is the best college in the region. All of your friends will be attending this fall. You don't want to be left out; you should join us, too.

_____ 4. If you really listen to Governor Wise's proposal on health care, you will see that there is no way that we can have a national system. You will not be able to select your doctor, you will not be able to go to the hospital of your choice, and you will not be able to get immediate attention. His proposal is not as comprehensive as our proposal.

_____ 5. My father went to Honors College, I went to Honors College, and you will go to Honors College. It is the way things have been for the people in this family. There is no need to break with tradition now.

_____ 6. The witness's testimony is useless. He is an alcoholic; he is dishonest and corrupt. To make matters worse, he was a member of the Leftist Party.

_____ 7. The gentleman on the witness stand is your neighbor, he is your friend, he is just like you. Sure, he may have more money and drive a Mercedes, but his heart never left the Elm Community.

_____ 8. John F. Kennedy once said, "Ask not what your country can do for you; ask what you can do for your country." This is the time to act, my fellow citizens. You can give $200 to our cause and you will be fulfilling the wish of President Kennedy.

_____ 9. Of the 7,000 people polled, 72 percent believed that there is life beyond our planet. Therefore, there must be life beyond Earth.

_____ 10. Without this new medication, you will die.

_____ 11. I don't care what anyone says. If you don't come around to our way of thinking, you'd better start watching your back.

As you develop your critical-thinking skills, you will begin to recognize the illogical nature of thoughts, the falsehoods of statements, the deception in some advertisements, and the irrational fears used to persuade. You will also begin to understand the depths to which you should delve to achieve objectivity, the thought and care that should be given to your own decisions and statements, and the methods by which you can build logical, truthful arguments.

CREATIVE THINKING

From Ridiculous to Possible

Creative thinking is much like critical thinking in that you are producing something that is uniquely yours. You are introducing something to the world that is new, innovative, and useful. Creative thinking does not mean that you have to be an artist, a musician, or a writer. Creative thinking means that you have examined a situation and developed a new way of explaining information, delivering a product, or using an item. It can be as simple as discovering that you can use a small rolling suitcase to carry your books around campus instead of the traditional backpack. Creative thinking means that you have opened your mind to possibilities!

Creative thinking involves everyday activities at home, at work, with friends, and at play.

open the door
Tips for Career Success

Consider the following strategies for creative thinking:

- Understand that the creative process is not an organized process. It can be chaotic and disorderly—downright crazy at times.
- Never be afraid to ask ANY question, even those you think may be silly.
- Jot your weirdest and funkiest ideas down; you may need them later.
- Take risks! Greatness has never been achieved by playing it safe. Dream, and dream big.
- Hone your sense of adventure and exploration by playing and thinking like a child.
- Force yourself to develop at least five creative solutions to any problem you face.
- Force yourself to do something old in a new way.

Creative thinking and critical thinking both require that you "loosen up" your brain and be more flexible in your approaches and tactics. In her book *The Artist's Way: A Spiritual Path to Higher Creativity* (1992), Julia Cameron suggests that there are basic principles of creativity, including the following:

- Creativity is the natural order of life.
- There is an underlying, indwelling creative force infusing all of life.
- We are, ourselves, creations. And we, in turn, are meant to create ourselves.
- The refusal to be creative is counter to our true nature.

So, how do you become more creative in your thought process? It may be easier than you think. Your individual creativity can be revealed if you make a daily effort to hone and use your creative skills. Consider the tips in the box at left.

As you explore your own creativity, you may find yourself struggling and even at odds with your own opinions. That is perfectly OK. Remember, if everything is easy and smooth, it only means that you are not challenging and stretching yourself. Thinking creatively and critically is NOT easy for everyone, but can benefit you greatly.

To begin the creative process, consider the items in the "Creative Thinking Involves . . . " chart. These are some of the characteristics that creative thinkers have in common.

CREATIVE THINKING INVOLVES . . .

Compassion	Creative thinkers have a zest for life and genuinely care for the spirit of others.	**Example:** More than 40 years ago, community members who wanted to feed the elderly created Meals on Wheels, now a national organization feeding the elderly.
Courage	Creative thinkers are unafraid to try new things, to implement new thoughts and actions.	**Example:** Barack Obama, a relatively new Democratic senator from Illinois, decides that America needs a change. He does not let his fears or the fact that he has little experience stop him. He became the first African American president of the United States of America.
Truth	Creative thinkers search for the true meaning of things.	**Example:** Astronomer and scientist Copernicus sought to prove that Earth was *not* the center of the universe—an unpopular view at the time.
Dreams	Creative thinkers allow themselves time to dream and ponder the unknown. They can see what is possible, not just what is actual.	**Example:** John F. Kennedy dreamed that space exploration was possible. His dream became reality.

Risk Taking	Creative thinkers take positive risks every day. They are not afraid to go against popular opinion.	**Example:** WWF wrestler Jesse "The Body" Ventura took a risk and ran for mayor in a Minnesota town, never having had any experience in politics. Later, he became governor of the state.
Innovation	Creative thinkers find new ways to do old things.	**Example:** Instead of continuing to fill the earth with waste such as aluminum, plastic, metal, and old cars, means were developed to recycle these materials for future productive use.
Competition	Creative thinkers strive to be better, to think bolder thoughts, to do what is good and to be the best at any task.	**Example:** Andre Agassi had a several-year slump in tennis. Most people thought he was a has-been. He came back to win tournament after tournament because he knew that he could.
Individuality	Creative thinkers are not carbon copies of other people. They strive to be true to themselves.	**Example:** A young man decides to take tap dancing instead of playing baseball. He excels and wins a fine arts dancing scholarship to college.
Thinking	Creative thinkers are always thinking about the world, people, and new ideas.	**Example:** A scientist is not afraid to take time to sit alone with his or her data to study and ponder the results, make connections, and develop ways to use the information.
Curiosity	Creative thinkers are interested in all things; they want to know much about many things.	**Example:** A 65-year-old retired college professor goes back to college to learn more about music appreciation and computer programming to expand her possibilities.
Perseverance	Creative thinkers do not give up. They stick to a project to its logical and reasonable end.	**Example:** Dr. Martin Luther King Jr. did not give up on his dream in the face of adversity, danger, and death threats.

Using your imaginative and innovative juices, think about how you would *creatively* solve the following problem. Write down at least five possibilities. Come on, make it count!

> "Why should we use our creative power? Because there is nothing that makes people so generous, joyful, lively, bold and compassionate."
>
> —Brenda Ueland

The Problem

Jennifer is a first-year student who does not have enough money to pay her tuition, buy her books, and purchase a few new outfits and shoes to wear to class and to her work–study job on campus. What should she do? Should she pay her tuition and purchase her books, or pay her tuition and buy new clothes and shoes to wear to class and work? What creative ideas (solutions) can you give Jennifer?

MY CREATIVE SOLUTIONS:

1. _____

2. _____

3. _____

4. _____

5. _____

THINK ABOUT IT

Reflecting for Success

Both critical and creative thinking require a great deal of commitment on your part. Critical and creative thinking are not easy for everyone, but with practice, dedication, and an understanding of the need, everyone can achieve both.

Critical and creative thinking can affect the way you live, from relationships to purchasing a new car, from solving family problems to investing money, from taking the appropriate classes for graduation to getting a promotion at work.

As you continue on in the semester and work toward personal and professional motivation, consider the following ideas:

☐ Use only *credible* and *reliable* sources.
☐ Distinguish *fact* from *opinion*.
☐ Be *flexible* in your thinking.
☐ Use emotional *restraint*.
☐ *Avoid* generalizations.
☐ Avoid *stereotyping* and prejudging.
☐ Strive for *objectivity* in all of your thinking.
☐ *Reserve* judgment until you have looked at very side.
☐ Do *not* assume—do the research.
☐ *Ask* questions—and strive to ask the proper questions.
☐ Seek *truth*.

"The significant problems we face cannot be solved at the same level of thinking we were at when we created them."

—Albert Einstein

Creative and critical thinking are truly the hallmarks of an educated person. They are hallmarks of character and integrity, and they are hallmarks of successful students. Let them be yours.

passages
An Activity for Critical Thinking and Career Development

On page 9 of Chapter 1, and inside the front cover, you read **The Ten Essential Cornerstones for Personal and Professional Success.** They are:

Passion	Motivation
Knowledge	Resourcefulness
Creativity	Adaptability
Open-mindedness	Relationships
Accountability	Vision

Explanation: Thousands of articles are printed every day in magazines, newspapers, online journals, and other media. Depending on the article or where it is published, it can have a slant. You may have heard this called bias (as in liberal or conservative bias). One of journalism's objectives should be to present the facts of what has happened in an incident or the facts of what is being discussed. Bias should not enter the argument unless it is an editorial.

Process: For this activity, you are to find an article (not an editorial) in a mainstream newspaper or magazine (*USA Today, Newsweek, Time, New York Times, Washington Post,* etc.), read the article, and determine if the article has bias, unsubstantiated opinions, or research that is weak. After you complete this, you will be asked to think about several **ESSENTIAL CORNERSTONES** and assess how critical and creative thinking applies to each.

You will find a list of questions below to help you evaluate and assess your article.

Name of the article: _____

Writer of the article: _____

His/her affiliation: _____

Publication in which the article was found: _____

Date of publication: _____

What is the author's main reason for writing the article? _____

_____

_____

_____

What is the most important fact(s) or information in the article? _____

_____

_____

_____

By writing this article, what is the author implying? _____

_____

_____

_____

By writing this article, what is the author proving? _____

_____

_____

_____

In writing this article, what assumptions were made? _____

_____

_____

_____

What sources does the writer cite to prove his/her point? _____

_____

_____

_____

Is the article fairly presented? In other words, does the author examine both sides of the issue or just one side? _____

_____

_____

_____

Do you believe and trust the article? Why or why not? Justify your answer. _____

_____

_____

_____

_____

_____

_____

If this article is accurate (or inaccurate, depending on your judgment), what are the implications for society? _____

_____

_____

_____

Source: (This project is adapted from the work of Richard Paul and Linda Elder).

Now, consider the following **ESSENTIAL CORNERSTONES** and how each can be enhanced by critical thinking.

By expanding my critical and creative thinking skills, I can become more **OPEN-MINDED** by

_____

_____

_____

By expanding my critical and creative thinking skills, I can improve my **COMMUNICATION** skills by _____

_____

_____

_____

IT CAN BE SHAKY GROUND, BUT YOU WILL MAKE IT

Defining and Refining Yourself in Today's "Workquake"

People holding degrees and certificates are a dime a dozen. This does not mean, however, that *you* are a dime a dozen. Herein lies the challenge. How do you distinguish yourself from the countless job seekers out there? What are you going to do that sets you apart from your competition? What do you have to offer that no one else can possibly offer to an employer? Below, we will discuss some of the talents and qualities that are becoming increasingly rare, yet constantly sought after, in today's "workquake." By understanding more about these qualities, you can put yourself miles ahead of the competition.

Writing, Speaking, and Listening Skills

As you have read this book, you may have thought that we were beating a dead horse. Over and over again, in almost every chapter, we have offered some type of advice, suggestion, or tip for becoming a more effective communicator in written, oral, and nonverbal forms. We emphasize these skills because they are constantly listed as top requirements needed for success—in ANY profession. We do so because so few people actually possess these qualities. If you want to put yourself ahead of the competition, then attend every class, every seminar, every meeting, and every function where you can learn more about effective writing, speaking, and listening skills.

A Strong Work Ethic

Your work ethic is how you perform at work without a job description, constant supervision, or someone threatening you. Your work ethic is not tied to what you do to get a raise or a promotion, but rather what you do because it is the right thing to do. Pride, ownership, and honor all play a role in one's work ethic. In today's work environment, employers want to make sure that you are dedicated to your job, your company, and your colleagues. Our suggestion is to develop a strong work ethic that is healthy for you and your employer.

Loyalty and Trustworthiness

Loyalty to your employer is a highly valued trait. However, one's loyalty cannot be measured by a resume or determined by a simple interview. Proving that you have the characteristics of loyalty and trustworthiness comes over time. It may take years to establish these characteristics with your company and within your industry. But be forewarned: It only takes seconds to destroy what took years to create.

Teamwork

Employers are looking for people who not only understand the details of teamwork, but who also excel as team members. There is a humorous cartoon figure who says, "Teamwork is a bunch of people doing what I say!" Unfortunately, many people think this *is* teamwork. A true team has shared responsibilities, shared purposes, shared goals, shared visions, and most important, shared accountability.

Employers are looking for people who excel as team members.

did you know?

César Chávez, was born in 1927 near Yuma, Arizona. He was raised during the Great Depression in unspeakable poverty. His parents owned a small store but lost everything during the

(continued)

(continued)
Depression. The entire family became migrant workers just to survive. He spent his youth working in the fields of Arizona and California. From the first to eighth grades (when he left school), he attended over 30 schools.

Often his family did not have even the basic necessities of water and toilets to survive. They faced not only poverty, but extreme prejudice and injustice.

Later, Chávez joined the Navy and then later founded the United Farm Workers which was responsible for increasing public awareness of the plight of the migrant workers in America. He is considered to be one of the greatest civil rights activists in American history.

Professionalism

The meaning of the term *professionalism* varies from workplace to workplace. What is professional in one office or setting may be totally inappropriate in another. This includes everything from language usage to dress to personal grooming to conduct to your overall demeanor. Unlike loyalty and trustworthiness, professionalism *can* be judged before a potential employer actually meets you. Most interviewers can establish the level of your professionalism by the quality of your resume and cover letter. Some will even judge the quality of paper on which your resume is printed. We have never actually met a person who lost a job over a watermark being turned the wrong way on a cover letter, but it certainly says something about your professionalism to many who will interview you. You can be assured that you can actually lose a chance for a job interview by submitting a sloppy resume filled with typing errors and other obvious and careless mistakes.

Confidence and Decision-Making Abilities

There is a difference between having confidence in your work and your ability to make decisions and being "cocky." Confidence comes from experience, calculated risk taking, and previous successes. Employers are looking for confident people who are not afraid to make hard decisions and for individuals who have confidence in their abilities. When you meet with the person interviewing you, avoid emphasizing (and believing) "I'm a nurse," or "I'm an accountant," or "I'm a computer networking engineer." Instead, find ways to discuss your overall qualities. Steer the conversation to your general and specific abilities and characteristics.

Priority Management Skills

Today, maybe more than any other time in mankind's history, we are faced with more and more to do and what seems like less and less time in which to do it. Your success depends on how well you manage your priorities both personally and professionally. Priority management not only involves getting today's work accomplished, but it also involves the ability to plan for your personal and professional future.

The Ability to Change and Grow

A decade ago, few people could have predicted that there would be full-time college instructors teaching classes and holding office hours online. Now, this is commonplace in many institutions. This is a perfect example of how changes in technology drive changes in many professions. Even if you are unable or unwilling to change and grow, thousands of your peers can, and will. Our advice is to keep abreast of trends and technology pertaining to your field. Attend conferences, read professional literature, take classes, and have open discussions with colleagues and mentors regarding the issues surrounding your company and industry.

ESSENTIAL CORNERSTONE

ADAPTABILITY

How can being a person who knows how to adapt and change help you in YOUR chosen field?

Critical-Thinking Skills

Not only do employers want associates who can make decisions and proceed with confidence, but they also demand that you be able to think your way through problems and challenges. Employers are looking for people who can distinguish fact from opinion; identify fallacies; analyze, synthesize, and determine the value of a piece of information; think beyond the obvious and see things from varying angles; and arrive at sound solutions.

Multitasking

A recent newspaper cartoon suggested that you are too busy if you are multitasking in the shower. This may be true, but in keeping pace with today's workforce, this is another essential task: the ability to do more than one thing at a time—and the ability to do them all very well. If you have not had much experience in multitasking, we suggest that you begin slowly. Don't take on too many things at one time. As you understand more about working on and completing several tasks at a time, you can expand your abilities. An example of multitasking at home is to have a casserole baking while clothes are washing at the same time you are researching a project on the Internet. To be successful in our fast-paced world, you must be able to manage several tasks at once.

Human Relations Skills

We saved this one for last, certainly not because it is least important, but because this quality is an overriding characteristic of everything listed previously. Employers are looking for individuals who have "people skills." This concept goes so much further than being a team player; it goes to the heart of many workplaces. It touches on your most basic nature, and it draws from your most inner self.

The ability to get along with grouchy, cranky, mean, disagreeable, burned-out colleagues is, indeed, a rare quality. But don't be mistaken, there are those who do this, and do it well. Peak performers, or those at the top of their game, have learned that this world is made up of many types of people and there is never going to be a time when one of those cranky, grumpy people is not in our midst. More about this topic is discussed later in this chapter.

> "The four great questions: Why are you here? Where have you been? Where are you going? What difference will you make?"
>
> —Hal Simon

CONNECTING WITH YOUR CAREER

The Job Search Plan

You've got it all together—education, experience, and a strong sense of your moral and value system. What do you do now? Where do you go to put all of this to work? How do you find the job of your dreams?

The first thing you need to know about searching for a job is this: Getting a job—the right job—is hard work! Regardless of your status in school, now is the time to begin your job search. If you are in the last quarter or module of your program, your job search should be a top priority.

Selling Yourself

Remember the old saying, "You are what you eat?" When searching for a professional position, you could change that to read, "You are what you write." Most likely, the people conducting the job search have never met you and know nothing about you except what you provide to them. A carefully crafted resume communicates your history (skills and experience) that makes you the ideal candidate for their position. Your resume is the first marketing piece and in many cases must stand alone when a recruiter is determining whether or not to interview you. Just as a well-designed

Always present yourself with confidence and poise. If you don't promote your strengths and talents, no one will.

from ordinary to EXTRAORDINARY

MATTHEW L. KARRES
Motivational speaker/Team leader
Weight Watchers International

"FATSO!" The words still ring in my years 40 years after she yelled them. When I was four years old in preschool, I rode a bus to school and I was the second person to be picked up. One student was already on the bus and when I climbed the steps and took my seat that first day, she yelled the words that began the years of verbal and emotional abuse.

I had always been big for my age. I had to have a larger desk than "normal" from kindergarten onward. By my eighth birthday, I weighed about 120 pounds and stood 5 feet 9 inches tall. By the time I was in the sixth grade, I was 6 feet 2 inches tall and even heavier. So there I was, tall, overweight, shy, and introverted. In junior high school, when we had to weigh in for gym class, my classmates would run over to see how much I weighed. The scale read 225 pounds. In the ninth grade, my weight had soared to 280 pounds and I wore a size 48 pants. This is when my mother took me to Overeaters Anonymous.

In the period between the ninth and tenth grade, I lost 100 pounds by going on a very restricted diet called "The Gray Sheet" from OA. By the time I began the tenth grade, I was thin, people noticed me for something other than my weight, and I looked good for the first time that I could remember. I was happy—or so I thought. My happiness was short-lived as my weight soon began rising again.

For the next eight years, I began to gain massive amounts of weight, and the depression that followed was just as massive. My parents moved 3,000 miles away; college was not going well for me; and I was lonely, fat, depressed, and, to be truthful, suicidal. Food became my only friend—my best friend. In 10 years, I gained over 250 pounds, reaching nearly 500 pounds and wearing a size 62 pant. I developed sleep apnea, heart problems, and limb numbness.

I had to try something drastic, so I applied to become one of the first candidates for weight loss surgery. I had the surgery, but was given very inadequate warnings about the side effects: throwing up, gas, withdrawal, and that it was not a miracle cure. However, over three years, I lost 300 pounds and had two reconstructive surgeries. Things were good. Again, this was short lived.

The problem with weight-loss surgery is that it is *not* a miracle cure and you can still gain weight. I started gaining weight again and before I knew it, I was up almost 100 pounds. I was in horrible despair. Hopelessness was all I felt. My mother suggested that I join Weight Watchers. I told her that I had tried that before and then she said the words that changed my life forever.

"Matt," she stated. "You have not tried Weight Watchers. You tried their program *your* way. You did not try their program *their* way." I decided to rejoin. I remember eating three Hostess Fruit Pies on the way to the meeting.

This time, I surrendered. I gave in to *their* program. I did the mental and the physical work. Soon, I was losing weight again in a healthy and lasting fashion. I dropped down to 190 pounds. By learning to eat properly, exercise, and think about everything that I put into my mouth, I have kept my weight steady for eight years, and now I hold my "dream job" as a motivational leader for Weight Watchers.

It has not been easy and I fight every day, but I write this to say that if I can do this, you can too. There is no bigger food addict than me, but I learned that there is hope. Motivation and mental preparation can take you further than you ever imagined.

and -written resume can be a wonderful first step, a poorly designed and written resume can doom you before you ever leave your house. A good thing to remember is this: A resume gets you the interview; the interview gets you the job. Although there is no single way to develop your career resume and formats may vary from discipline to discipline, this chapter will outline the key components of resumes and discusses how to develop a resume that will represent your best efforts.

Your second "advertising tool" is your cover letter. A cover letter is basically an expansion of your resume. A cover letter gives you the chance to link your resume, skills, and experience together with your interest in *a specific company's* position. You will need to write many cover letters to make this link work properly; in other words, you most likely need to write a cover letter designed for each job for which you apply. Your cover letter will often be the stepping-stone to get an employer to even look at your resume. Consider it "a teaser," if you will, to all of your talents and experience. Just as you would never send someone a greeting card and not sign it, you would never send a resume and not tell the person or committee *why* you sent it. Your cover letter tells why.

WRITE A POWERFUL AND CONCISE COVER LETTER

The most important part of the job search process is the preparation that must be done *prior to starting* the interview process. Two key elements of this preparation are your cover letter and resume. Both are key components in your career search.

Whenever you send your resume to a company, whether it is in response to a posted advertisement or requested, you must send a cover letter with it. Cover letters are extremely important; in fact, most recruiters say that they read four times as many cover letters as they do resumes because if the cover letter does not strike a chord then they never look past it to the resume.

Carol Robbins (2006), career development expert, author, and speaker states, "*During my 25 plus years that I've been involved in career development, I have found that of all the paperwork associated with job searching, cover letters give job searchers the most difficulty.*" The following information will help you overcome any anxiety associated with writing your cover letter or resume.

As you begin your cover letter and resume process, consider the following

"GOTTA DO IT, CAN'T SKIP IT, NO EXCUSE FOR MISSING IT" GENERAL TIPS

- ☐ Both your resume and cover letter MUST be typed. There are no exceptions to this rule. Ever! Seriously, EVER!
- ☐ Your cover letter and resume must be printed on the same type and color of fine-quality paper. Cheap paper sends the message that you don't care. This is not the place or time to pinch pennies; buy excellent quality, 100% cotton stock paper.
- ☐ Check your printer and be sure that the print quality is impeccable. Never send a cover letter or resume with smudges, ink smears, or poor print quality.
- ☐ When you print your cover letter and resume, be certain that the watermark on the paper is turned in the correct direction. Hold it up to the light to see the watermark embedded in the paper. This may sound silly and picky, but people notice attention to detail.
- ☐ Do not fold your cover letter or resume. Purchase a packet of 9 × 13 envelopes—white, if possible—to use for mailing your materials.
- ☐ Do not handwrite the address on the envelope. Use a label or type the address directly on the envelope. Remember, first impressions are important.
- ☐ Never send a generic photocopy of a cover letter or resume, even on the finest paper.

☐ Layout, design, font, spacing, and color must be considered in the building of your cover letter and resume.

☐ Unless you are specifically asked to do so, *never* discuss money or salary history in either your cover letter or resume. This could work against you. When asked for a salary history, use ranges. If asked for a salary requirement, specify "negotiable."

☐ Your resume and cover letter MUST be error-free. That's right, not one single error is acceptable, including grammar, spelling, punctuation, layout/spacing, dates, and content.

Simply put, the cover letter's purpose is to get the interviewer to read your resume. It sets the tone for who you are, what you have to offer, and what you want. *"It screams— ever so politely—that you have the intelligence, experience, and soft skills to be the answer to an employer's staffing problem"* (Britton-Whitcomb, 2003). The cover letter should say to the reader, "You have an opening, you have a detailed description of what you need done, and I can fill your opening and be the person who gets the job done—and done well."

Consider the following **FOUR STEPS to SUCCESS** when writing your cover letter:

Step 1: A effective cover letter will be *personally addressed and job specific.* If at all possible (and, yes, it is possible with just a little research), address your letter to a specific person. Avoid at all cost the dreaded "Dear Sir or Madam" or "To Whom It May Concern." In most cases, a phone call to the company will provide the name of the person, their title, and their address. Always verify spelling, even with common names. This single step can set you apart from lazy job-seekers. Also, make SURE you spell the company's name correctly.

Step 2: Once your letter is correctly addressed, your first paragraph should be an "attention grabber" and it should answer the question "Why am I writing?" Susan Britton-Whitcomb, author of *Resume Magic* (2003), calls this "the carrot." This simply means that your first paragraph has an interesting fact, an appeal, or maybe even a quote—something that makes the reader (hopefully, your future employer) read further. Your first paragraph should also have a transition statement that makes the reader want to read on. For example, your last sentence might read, *"With a degree in Medical Assisting and four years' experience at Desert Medical Center, I know that I can make a valued contribution to Grace Care Center."*

Step 3: Your second (and maybe third) paragraph(s) should clearly state why you are qualified for the position you are seeking. Use your cover letter to highlight those areas of your experience that specifically qualify you for the job. Your cover letter should not list all of your qualifications, instead it should indicate the two or three components that most qualify you for the position and closely match the position announcement. You may also include specific attributes that may not be on your resume. The key word to consider here is your "value." Relate your education, experience, and talents to the company's need. Mention facts and statistics of how you've been successful in the past. Remember, *"Employers are not interested in you for your sake, but rather because of what you can bring to the organization. This might sound harsh, but businesspeople have an obligation to improve the success of their organization. If you consistently show how you can help them do this . . . they will be much more motivated to talk to you."* (Farr and Kursmark, 2005).

Step 4: Your final paragraph should address the question of "Where do we go from here?" Do not be ambiguous by saying something trite like "I hope to hear from you in the near future," or "If you have any questions please do not hesitate to call me." Remember, YOUR job search is none of their business, nor is it their responsibility. Be proactive by stating that *you will be following up* with a phone call to discuss your resume and experience(s) in more detail. Make sure that once you have told them that you are going to call that you actually do call.

Your final paragraph should also continue to express what you can do for the company. End your letter with a statement about your qualities and their needs: *"Mr. Thompson, I will call you on Monday, January 24 at 11:30 a.m. to discuss how my experiences can help streamline operations and continue superior patient care at Grace Care Center."*

Don't forget to **sign your letter**. Figures 11.1 and 11.2 provide sample cover letters.

UNDERSTAND THE DO'S AND DON'TS OF MEMORABLE RESUMES

*"**Eight seconds**."* That is all you have to gain the attention of your potential employer, according to Susan Ireland (2003), author and consultant. *"In eight seconds, an employer scans your resume and decides whether she will invest more time to consider you as a job candidate. The secret to passing the eight-second test is to make your resume look inviting and quick to read"* (p. 14).

A resume is the blueprint that details what you have accomplished with regards to education, experience, skills acquisition, workplace successes, and progressive responsibility and/or leadership. It is a painting (that YOU are able to "paint") of how your professional life looks. It is the ultimate advertisement of YOU! Your resume must create **interest** and a **desire** to find out more about you!

When choosing your resume format, take into careful consideration the field in which you wish to be employed as well as the company with which you hope to interview. The one-size-fits-all ideology does not work with resumes. Personalizing your resume can set you apart from all of the other job seekers wanting that position.

As you begin to develop your resume, allow plenty of time. Plan to enlist several qualified proofreaders to check your work. We cannot stress strongly enough the need for your resume to be perfect. A simple typo or misuse of grammar can disqualify you from the job of your dreams. Don't allow a lack of attention to detail you need stand between you and your future career.

Further, your resume must be 100 percent completely accurate and truthful. Do not fabricate information or fudge dates to make yourself look better. It will only come back to haunt you in the long run. Dennis Reina, organizational psychologist and author of *Trust and Betrayal in the Workplace,* states, *"I think that what you put in a resume absolutely has to be rock-solid, concrete, and verifiable. If there are any questions, it will immediately throw both your application and your credibility into question"* (Dresang, 2007). People have been fired after they were hired because they misrepresented themselves in their resume, cover letter, or application.

FIGURE 11.1   Sample Cover Letter

Your name and address on high-quality paper. Your name should be larger and/or in a different font to call attention.

The date (then double space) →

The specific person, title, and address to whom you are writing (then double space) →

The formal salutation followed by a colon (then double space) →

Paragraph 1 (then double space) →

Paragraph 2 (then double space) →

Paragraph 3 (then double space) →

Final paragraph or closing (then double space) →

The complementary close (then four spaces) →
Your handwritten signature in black or blue ink →
Your typed name →
Enclosure contents →

BENJAMIN SHAW

1234 Lake Shadow Drive,
Maple City, PA 12345

(123) 555–1234
ben@bl.com

January 3, 2009

Mr. James Pixler, RN, CAN
Director of Placement and Advancement
Grace Care Center
123 Sizemore Street, Suite 444
Philadelphia, PA 1234

Dear Mr. Pixler:

Seven years ago, my mother was under the treatment of two incredible nurses at Grace Care Center in Philadelphia. My family and I agree that the care she was given was extraordinary. When I saw your ad in today's *Philadelphia Carrier*, I was extremely pleased to know that I now have the qualifications to be a part of the Grace Care Team as a Medical Assistant.

Next month, I will graduate with an Occupational Associate's Degree from Victory College of Health and Technology as a certified Medical Assistant. My resume indicates that I was fortunate to do my internship at Mercy Family Care Practice in Harrisburg. During this time, I was directly involved in patient care, records documentation, and family outreach.

As a part of my degree from Victory, I received a 4.0 in the following classes:

✓ Management Communications
✓ Microsoft Office (Word, Excel, Outlook, PowerPoint)
✓ Business Communications I, II, III
✓ Anatomy and Physiology I, II, III
✓ Medical Coding I, II
✓ Principles of Pharmacology
✓ Immunology I, II, III, IV
✓ Urinalysis and Body Fluids
✓ Clinical Practicum I, II, III

This, along with my past certificate in Medical Transcription and my immense respect for Grace Care Center, makes me the perfect candidate for your position.

I have detailed all of my experience on the enclosed resume. I will call you on Monday, January 24 at 11:30 a.m. to discuss how my education and experiences can help streamline operations and continue superior patient care at Grace. In the meantime, please feel free to contact me at the number above.

Sincerely,

Benjamin Shaw

Benjamin Shaw

Enclosure: Resume

FIGURE 11.2 Sample Cover Letter

Rosetta M. Alverez

August 18, 2009

Ms. Marilyn McAllen, President
TinyTot Day Care Center
125-A Adobe Falls Road
Crystal City, NJ 45678

Dear President McAllen:

After reading your ad in *Education Today*, reviewing your Web site, and giving serious consideration to your specific needs, I have determined that my experience in directing day care activities and my degree in Early Childhood Education make me the perfect candidate for your open position as Director of Infant Care.

My earliest recollection of a career field was that of a preschool teacher. I have loved children all of my life, and this led me to seek early employment and a college degree in caring for infants and preschoolers. As my resume will indicate, I have spent the past 14 years directly involved in almost every aspect of child care, preschool education, and infant development. In my current position as Assistant Director of Education for ChildPlay, my responsibilities involve:

✓ direct supervision of 12 child-care specialists,
✓ development of weekly nutritious meal and snack plans,
✓ development of educational curriculum, activities and lessons,
✓ toddler and infant artistic development, and
✓ oversight of office management, personnel, and budget matters.

I am certain that once you review my resume and we have an opportunity to speak in person, you will agree that my attitude, values, and work ethic are in complete alignment with those you promote at TinyTot. I will call you on Monday of next week to establish an appropriate time to stop by.

Thank you for your consideration,

Rosie Alverez

Rosetta M. Alverez, CCCS

Enclosures: Resume, Specialist Certificate

3456 Red Tip Boulevard	Atlanta, GA 12345	345.123.4567
rma@online.net	www.rosiema.com	

As you build your resume, remember to "call in the **DOCTOR**." (Sherfield and Moody, 2009):

D = Give attention to **D**esign and format.

O = Write an effective, clear, and specific **O**bjective.

C = Check for **C**larity and concreteness.

T = Tell the **T**ruth.

O = Use an **O**rganized format to sell yourself (chronological, functional, or accomplishment).

R = **R**eview for mistakes in content, grammar, and spelling.

D Visual **design** and format are imperative to a successful resume. Think about the font that you plan to use; whether color is appropriate; whether you will use bullets, lines, or shading; and where you are going to put information. You also need to pay attention to the text balance on the page (centered left/right, top/bottom). The visual aspect of your resume will make the first impression. "Make it pretty" (Britton–Whitcomb, 2003).

O Writing a clear and specific **objective** can help get your foot in the door. The reader, usually your potential employer, needs to be able to scan your resume and gather as much detail as possible as quickly as possible. A job-specific objective can help. Consider the following two objectives:

Before   **Objective:** To get a job as an elementary teacher in the Dallas Independent School District

After   **Objective:** Seeking an elementary teaching position that will use my 14 years of creative teaching experience, curriculum development abilities, supervisory skills, and commitment to superior instruction.

C **Clarity** is of paramount importance, especially when including your past responsibilities, education, and job growth. Be certain that you let the reader know exactly what you have done, what specific education you have gained, and what progress you have made. Being vague and unclear can cost you an interview.

T When writing your resume, you may be tempted to fudge here and there to make your resume look better. Perhaps you were out of work for a few months, and you think it looks bad to have this gap in your chronological history. Avoid the urge to fudge. Telling the absolute **truth** on a resume is essential. A lie, even a small one, can (and usually will) come back to haunt you.

O Before you begin your resume, think about the **organizational** pattern you will need to use. For some jobs, chronological might be best. For others, you may want to use an accomplishment format. It might serve you well to construct one of each so that you will have them if you need them. Plus, this gives you experience in writing each type of resume.

R **Reviewing** your resume and cover letter is important, but having someone else review them for clarity, accuracy, spelling, grammar, placement, and overall content can be one of the best things you can do for your job search.

The following basic tips will help you as you begin building a dynamic resume.

- General topics that you **must** include, **should** include, should **consider** including, or **should not** include on your resume are:

Contact information (name, complete mailing address, phone and cell numbers, fax number, e-mail address, Web-page URL)	Must include
Education, degrees, certificates, advanced training (to include dates and names of degrees)	Must include
Current and past work history, experience and responsibilities	Must include
Accomplishments (this is NOT the same things as work history or responsibilities)	Must include

Specific licensures	Must include
Specific career objective	Should include
Summary or list of qualifications, strengths, specializations	Should include
Special skills (including special technical skills or multiple language skills)	Should include
Volunteer work, public service, and/or community involvement	Should include
Internships, externships, and/or extracurricular activities	Should include
Awards, honors, certificates of achievement, special recognitions (at work or in the community)	Should include
Military experience	Consider including
Professional/Preprofessional memberships, affiliations and/or associations	Consider including
Publications and presentations	Consider including
Current *business* phone number and/or address (where you are working at the moment)	Do not include
"Availability" date/time to begin work	Do not include
Geographic limitations	Do not include
Personal hobbies or interests	Do not include
Personal information such as age, sex, health status, marital status, parental status, ethnicity, or religious affiliations	Do not include
Photos	Do not include
Salary requirements or money issues	Do not include (unless specifically asked to provide a salary history)
References	Do not include, but have the information ready on a separate sheet of paper that matches your resume

- Do not date stamp or record the preparation date of your resume in any place.
- Limit your resume (and cover letter) to one page each (a two-page resume is appropriate if you have more than ten years' experience).
- Use standard resume paper colors such as white, cream, gray, or beige.
- Use bullets (such as these) to help profile lists.
- Avoid fancy or hard-to-read fonts such as curlz or borg.
- Use a standard font size between 10 and 14 points.
- Do not staple anything to your resume or cover letter.
- Avoid the use of "I" or "me" or "my" in your resume.
- Avoid contractions such as "don't," and do not use abbreviations.

- Keep your resume formal and professional.
- Use action-oriented verbs such as "designed," "managed," "created," "recruited," "simplified," and "built."
- Avoid the use of full sentences; fragments are fine on a resume.
- Use the correct verb tense. Use past tense (such as "recruited") except for your current job.
- Remember that when phrasing your information, less is more.
- Do not include information that does not pertain to this particular job search.
- Choose a format that puts your "best foot" or greatest assets forward.

Build a Timely Chronological Resume

There are different types of resumes, but primarily they can be classified as chronological resumes, functional resumes, accomplishment resumes, or a combination of each.

- A **chronological resume** organizes education and work experience in reverse chronological order (your last or present job is listed first).
- A **functional resume** organizes your work and experience around specific skills and duties.
- An **accomplishment** resume allows you to place your past accomplishments into categories that are not necessarily associated with an employer but that show your track record of "getting the job done."
- A **combination resume** generally combines elements of one or more of the above.

A **chronological resume** is the most common type of resume. It can easily highlight your career and education progression. It is relatively easy to construct because of its straightforward nature. However, it *may not* be the most effective type of resume if you have had gaps in your employment or if you wish to show off your skills and talents more than your past positions or educational degrees.

You must determine which type of resume best profiles your education, skills, and experience. This may be based on the wording of the job advertisement. An example of a chronological resume is shown in Figure 11.3.

A **functional resume** will emphasize (highlight) the skills and talents that you have gained. This is a fine resume format if you want to show what you know rather than emphasize where you've worked or from where you gained your training. This type of resume can be effective when you are trying to get a potential employer to look at what you have to offer the company in terms of usable, transferable skills. The functional resume allows the reader to quickly identify emphasized skills and downplays past employers or education.

One problem with the functional resume is that it does not show how or from where you gained or learned the skills mentioned, whether work experiences or educational training. Some employers do not like functional resumes because they assume you are trying to "hide" something. However, a well-constructed functional resume can highlight your skills, talents, work experience, and training.

An example of a functional resume is shown in Figure 11.4.

An **accomplishment resume** gives the same basic information as the chronological or functional resume, but it showcases what you accomplished in your past positions rather than your skills, your work history, or your training. Susan Britton-Whitcomb, author of *Resume Magic* (2003), refers to this type of resume as showing your "trophies." Often, an accomplishment resume will downplay or omit previous job descriptions, dates, and experiences. A powerful accomplishment resume, however, will show your accomplishments *and* job descriptions, dates, and experiences.

An example of an accomplishment resume is shown in Figure 11.5.

FIGURE 11.3 Chronological Resume

BENJAMIN SHAW

1234 Lake Shadow Drive, Maple City, PA 12345   (123) 555–1234   ben@online.com

OBJECTIVE: To work as a medical assistant in an atmosphere that uses my organizational skills, compassion for people, desire to make a difference, and impeccable work ethic.

PROFESSIONAL EXPERIENCE:

January 2007–Present

Medical Assistant Intern
Mercy Family Care Practice, Harrisburg, PA

- Responsible for completing patient charts
- Took patient's vitals
- Assisted with medical coding

February 2003–December 2006

Medical Transcriptionist
The Office of Brenda Wilson, MD, Lancaster, PA

- Interpreted and typed medical reports
- Worked with insurance documentation
- Assisted with medical coding
- Served as Office Manager (1/05–12/06)

March 1998–February 2003

Ward Orderly
Wallace Hospital, Lancaster, PA

- Assisted nurses with patient care
- Cleaned patient rooms
- Served patient meals

August 1995–March 1998

Administrative Assistant
Ellen Abbot Nursing Care Facility

- Typed office reports
- Organized patient files

EDUCATION:

Occupational Associate's Degree—Medical Assistant
Victory Health Institute, Harrisburg, PA
May 2008 (with honors)

Certificate of Completion—Medical Transcription
Philadelphia Technical Institute
December 2002

Vocational High School Diploma—Health Sciences
Philadelphia Vocational High School
August 1995

FIGURE 11.4   The Functional Resume

BENJAMIN SHAW

1234 Lake Shadow Drive, Maple City, PA 12345   (123) 555–1234   ben@online.com

OBJECTIVE: To work as a medical assistant in an atmosphere that uses my organization abilities, people skills, compassion for patients, desire to make a difference, and impeccable work ethic.

SKILLS:

Bilingual (English/Spanish)	Data Protection
Claims Reimbursement	Client Relations
Highly Organized	Problem-Solving Skills
Motivated, Self-starter	Team Player
Priority Management Skills	Delegating Ability
Strategic Planning	Budget Management

PROFESSIONAL PREPARATION:

Occupational Associate's Degree—Medical Assistant
Victory Health Institute, Harrisburg, PA
May 2008 (with honors)

Certificate of Completion—Medical Transcription
Philadelphia Technical Institute
December 2002

Vocational High School Diploma—Health Sciences
Philadelphia Vocational High School
August 1995

PROFESSIONAL EXPERIENCE:

January 2007–Present   **Medical Assistant Intern**
                              Mercy Family Care Practice, Harrisburg, PA

February 2003–December 2006   **Medical Transcriptionist**
                              The Office of Brenda Wilson, MD, Lancaster, PA

March 1998–February 2003   **Ward Orderly**
                              Wallace Hospital, Lancaster, PA

August 1995–March 1998   **Administrative Assistant**
                              Ellen Abbot Nursing Care Facility

References: Provided upon request

FIGURE 11.5   Accomplishment Resume

BENJAMIN SHAW

1234 Lake Shadow Drive
Maple City, PA 12345
(123) 555–1234

ben@online.com
www.bjs@netconnect.com

Career Target:

MEDICAL ASSISTANT

A highly qualified medical professional with eight years' experience in patient care, client relations, and medical coding seeking a challenging career that uses my strong problem-solving skills, deep compassion for the people, and medical training.

PROFESSIONAL ACCOMPLISHMENTS

Mercy Family Care Practice
✓ Revised and updated medical coding procedures
✓ Increased insurance payments by 11%
✓ Revised and streamlined new patient intake process
✓ Assisted Lead MA with ethics plan revision
✓ Revamped treatment procedure guidelines

Office of Brenda Wilson, MD
✓ Developed new medication administration checklist
✓ Implemented new guidelines for lab specimen collection
✓ Assisted with compliance of OSHA regulations

SKILLS / STRENGTHS
✓ Highly organized
✓ Team player
✓ Impeccable work ethic
✓ Bilingual (English and Spanish)
✓ Budget minded
✓ Motivated, self-starter
✓ Excellent client relations
✓ Superior time management skills

PROFESSIONAL PREPARATION

Occupational Associate's Degree—Medical Assistant
Victory Health Institute, Harrisburg, PA
May 2008 (with high honors)

Certificate of Completion—Medical Transcription
Philadelphia Technical Institute
December 2002 (with honors)

Vocational High School Diploma—Health Sciences
Philadelphia Vocational High School
August 1995

PROFESSIONAL EXPERIENCE

January 2007–Present	**Medical Assistant Intern** Mercy Family Care Practice
February 2003–December 2006	**Medical Transcriptionist** The Office of Brenda Wilson, MD
March 1998–February 2003	**Ward Orderly** Wallace Hospital
August 1995–March 1998	**Administrative Assistant** Ellen Abbot Nursing Care Facility

CHOOSE APPROPRIATE REFERENCES

If an employer is interested in you, he or she will most likely ask that you provide three to five references: people who can attest to your professional skills, work ethic, and workplace knowledge. There are five steps for successfully soliciting letters of reference.

Step 1:   Select three to five people with whom you have had professional contact. As you determine the best ones to select, choose people who are very familiar with your work ability. Current and former employers with whom you have experienced a good working relationship are excellent sources of references. Your instructors are also excellent sources. If you do not have anyone who falls into these two categories, consider asking friends of your family who are respected members of the community. As you consider possible reference sources, be sure to choose individuals who are responsible and timely in their reply to your request. Typically, you should not use your minister, rabbi, or other religious figures as references.

References are a reflection of you, and reference sources who do not respond in the appropriate manner will cast a shadow on your credibility. Your references should have excellent written communication skills. A poorly written recommendation letter reflects badly on you.

Step 2:   Request permission from your reference sources. Always ask people before you list them as a reference on an application or resume. During your conversation with them, discuss your career goals and aspirations. Give them a copy of your resume and cover letter. Ask them to critique them for you and make any necessary changes. You should also ask the person to put your letter on his/her company letterhead and send your potential employer an original copy, not a photocopy.

Step 3:   Obtain all necessary contact information from them. You should know your references' professional name, job title, business address, e-mail address, phone number, and fax number so that your potential employer can contact them with ease.

Step 4:   Send thank-you letters to those who agree to serve as references for you. Stay in contact with them throughout your job search. Give them updates and a periodic thank-you in the form of a card, an e-mail, or a phone

SUCCESSFUL DECISIONS

Richard had never held a professional job. He had only held a series of odd jobs for friends and family members. When it came time for Richard to begin applying for a position, he was unsure who to ask to serve as his references.

He began to think about his past part-time job and decided that his old boss at the gas station, James Cartman, might help him. His boss was a friend of his father's and he only worked for him for two months during class break, but he knew that he had done a good job for Mr. Cartman.

Richard stopped by the gas station to ask if he could use Mr. Cartman's name on his applications. He told Richard that he would be happy to speak about his work ethic and reliability.

Now, Richard only needed two more people. He decided to ask his career advisor and his English teacher at the school. Both knew him from different situations and could speak to different things about his character, academic ability, and dedication. With their permission, Richard was ready to begin his job search.

Richard made a *successful decision*.

call. At the end of your job search, a small token of your appreciation may be appropriate, but a thank-you note is essential.

Step 5:   Develop a typed list of all references—including contact information—and take it with you to all interviews. It is now customary that you *do not* include the names of references on your resume. You simply state: "References available upon request" or do not mention references at all. Employers will ask if they need them.

In the space provided below, list three people whom you could ask to serve as references for you (or write you a reference letter). Once you have identified these three people, list the skills that each person could speak to on your behalf. Think about this carefully, as it is important to choose references who can speak to your many qualifications, not just one or two. Choose people who know you in different areas of success.

Example	
Person	**Qualifications He/She Can Write About**
JoAnna Thompson	My oral communication skills
	My attention to detail
	My ability to get along with others
Beau DeTiberious	My ability to form a team
	My ability to motivate team members
	My ability to meet deadlines
Person #1	Qualifications he/she can write about
	_____
	_____
	_____
Person #2	Qualifications he/she can write about
	_____
	_____
	_____
Person #3	Qualifications he/she can write about
	_____
	_____
	_____

DESIGN AND DISTRIBUTE ATTRACTIVE PERSONAL BUSINESS CARDS

Setting yourself apart from other job seekers is important, and designing/distributing attractive personal business cards can help with this endeavor. Business cards give you a professional edge, provide your potential employer another contact source, and help contacts stay in touch with you.

Business cards should be the standard size of 2 × 3.5 inches and should, if possible, be professionally designed and printed. If this is not possible, there are many computer programs and graphic packages to assist you. You can also purchase sheets of blank business cards for your home printer. You simply design, print, and separate them.

While including a simple graphic is fine (and can be very helpful), avoid flashy, unprofessional colors or "cutesy" graphics. Be certain to include your vital information:

Full name

Full address with ZIP code

Phone numbers (residence, business, cellular, and fax)

E-mail address

Web site

Study the examples of appropriate and inappropriate personal business cards.

Inappropriate personal card for business use.

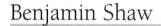

More appropriate personal card for business use.

BE PREPARED FOR THE INTERVIEW

You may have several interviews before you find the job you want, and you should prepare carefully for these interviews. In the beginning it is advisable for you to go to all interviews even if you're not sure you want the job. The more you interview, the more confident and comfortable you should become. The interview is the determining factor in getting a job and must be taken seriously. While an outstanding resume is important, it will not secure the job for you. The resume gets the interview; the interview gets the job!

Just as you prepared for exams, you will need to prepare for the interview. Please do not make the common mistake of thinking that your degree or work experience will get you the job. It may, but more often than you would believe it is the interview and the relationship that you establish that day that gets you the offer. Your experience and credentials are important, but nothing is more important than you and how well you are prepared for this day. As you prepare for your interview, consider the following sound advice:

DAYS BEFORE THE INTERVIEW

☐ Prepare extra copies of your resume to take to the interview. Though one person typically conducts interviews, some employers designate several people to sit in on the interview process.

☐ Place your extra resumes, references, and other job search information in a professional portfolio (leather binder) or nice folder. Avoid carrying loose papers, and never carry a backpack to an interview.

☐ Prepare a typed reference sheet and take several copies to the interview.

☐ If achievement portfolios are required, update your portfolio with any last-minute information.

☐ Using the research that you have done on the company, make a list of questions that you want to ask the interviewer. Never attend an interview without asking questions yourself. You are interviewing them just as they are interviewing you. Interviewers are much more impressed if they think you have researched the company and if you have questions.

☐ Have a friend or colleague sit with you and ask you questions that you might anticipate. Have them throw a few "surprise questions" your way, too.

☐ Ask someone whose opinion you trust to look at your interview outfit and give you advice and suggestions for improvement.

☐ Make sure you know how to get to the interview site. Make a dry run if you have to. Being late for your interview will be the "kiss of death" for that job.

☐ Check the night before to make certain that you have transportation and that all of your personal needs are met, such as child care and so on.

☐ Be sure you have enough gas to reach your destination if you are driving yourself. What is the availability for parking? Will you need to allow time for finding a parking place?

THE DAY OF—AND ON THE WAY TO—THE INTERVIEW

☐ Get up early and spend some time alone reviewing the job announcement, your resume, your portfolio, the company's profile, and other important information.

☐ Bring a pen, paper, and calendar with you to the interview. These can be kept in your portfolio, too.

☐ KNOW where your items are located so that you do not have to search for them during an interview. Fumbling around makes you look unorganized and unprepared.

☐ Prepare for the unknown: Take an umbrella, even if it is sunny; leave your home early, even though the interview site is only a few miles away.

☐ Be certain that your clothes are clean and pressed.

Arrive at your interview early, dressed, prepared, and ready to sell yourself.

☐ Be certain that your shoes are spotless and shined.

☐ Be certain that you are groomed and that your breath is fresh. Breath mints or sprays go a long way.

☐ Arrive at the interview at least 15 minutes early.

☐ If you are a smoker, DO NOT smoke in the car on the way to the interview, and try to avoid smoking in your interview clothes. Often, the smell of cigarette smoke lingers for hours on your clothing. For many, this is an immediate turn-off. Some employers will find a way not to hire a smoker.

☐ Do not carry any type of food or drink into the interview with you.

☐ Do not chew gum during the interview.

☐ Before you enter the building, TURN OFF your cell phone, pager, BlackBerry, iPod or any other electronic device except your hearing aid, pacemaker, or other life-assisting device. TURN THEM OFF. Period! There is NO excuse for your cell phone to ring during an interview. No one, **including you,** is that important.

☐ Do not take anyone with you to the interview unless the person remains in the car. Under no circumstances should you take anyone with you into the building!

DURING THE INTERVIEW

☐ Establish eye contact.

☐ Work to develop an immediate rapport.

☐ Offer a firm handshake to everyone in the room.

☐ Pay close attention to your posture (straight shoulders, positive stride, etc.).

☐ Speak with clarity and enunciate your words.

☐ Ask where to sit if you are not told upon entering the room.

☐ Enter with a positive and upbeat attitude.

☐ Jot down the names of everyone in the room as they are introduced to you. You may even draw an impromptu seating chart to remind you of who's who in the room.

☐ Refer to people by their names if you address them.

☐ Take notes during the interview.

☐ Answer every question asked as long as the question is legal.

☐ You don't have to be deadly serious or stodgy, but it is advisable to avoid jokes or off-color humor during the interview process.

☐ Consider your grammar and strive to use correct speech.

☐ If you need clarification on a question, ask for it before you begin your answer.

☐ NEVER downgrade or talk badly about a past job or employer. This will only come back to haunt you.

☐ If at all possible, do not discuss any aspect of your personal life such as children, marriage, or family.

☐ During the interview, jot down any questions that you did not already consider.

☐ If you are offered anything to eat or drink, accept only water just in case your mouth becomes dry during the interview.

☐ NEVER ask about money or company benefits during an interview, especially during the FIRST interview, unless the interviewer approaches the topic. Let them lead this discussion. If you are asked about salary requirements, respond with this question: "What is the range for this job?" In negotiations of any kind, you want the other person to offer information first. If you think you are highly qualified, respond with a salary amount close to the top of the range by saying, "Based on my qualifications and experience, I would consider a salary of $ _____.

☐ Strive to never appear desperate or "begging" for the job. There is a difference between excitement and desperation.

AFTER THE INTERVIEW

☐ Shake hands with everyone in the room and thank them for the opportunity to meet with them. Let them know that you were honored to have the opportunity. Humility goes a long way.

☐ Politely let them know that you enjoyed the interview and that you are very interested in the position.

☐ Ask each person in the room for a business card. This provides you with their correct name spelling, address, and e-mail address for use in future correspondence.

☐ Don't linger around the site unless you are told to wait. This makes you look desperate.

☐ Always follow up with a personalized thank-you note.

GENERAL TIPS

☐ Remember the cardinal rule of interviewing: Interviewers are not interested in what the company can do for you; they are interested in what you can do for the company. Therefore, you must present your case on why you want to work for the company and the contributions you are prepared to make.

☐ Be truthful in every aspect of the job search: the application, your resume, your cover letter, your portfolio, your references, your question responses, your salary history, and yes, your interest in the position.

☐ Be nice and gracious to everyone you meet. That may be the person with whom you interview in a few moments.

ANTICIPATE THE INTERVIEWER'S QUESTIONS

Richard Nelson Bolles, author of *What Color Is Your Parachute?* (2008), the most widely published job-hunting book in history (with over 10 million copies in print), makes an astounding assertion: "You don't have to spend hours memorizing a lot of 'good answers' to potential questions from the employer. There are only five questions that matter." Wow. Five questions!

DO NOT think that you will only be asked five questions. Rather, Mr. Bolles is suggesting that with every question asked of you, the interviewer is trying to get to the heart of the matter. The five basic questions are:

1. Why are you here?
2. What can you do for us?
3. What kind of person are you?
4. What distinguishes you from the nineteen other people who can do the same tasks that you can?
5. Can I afford you?

"These are the five principal questions that most employers are dying to know the answers to. ***This is the case, even if the interview begins and ends with these five questions never once being mentioned overtly by the employer***" (Bolles, 2008).

So, how do interviewers get to the heart of the matter? How do they pull the answers to these five questions from you? They do it by asking many, many other questions. This section will offer you insight into some common, and not so common, questions asked by employers.

It is usually customary for the interviewer to make small talk for a few minutes to give you time to relax. You should avoid answering questions with a simple "yes" or "no." Briefly elaborate on your answers without talking too much. For example, if the interviewer says, "I hope you had no trouble finding our building," you should not just

Interviewers will be asking a variety of questions about your background, preparation, experience, and goals. Be prepared.

answer "no." You might say something like, "Not at all. I live near here so I was familiar with the location. Actually, I had a part-time job when I was a sophomore and I brought materials to one of your managers from my department chair."

Interviewers will often say to you, "Tell me about yourself." They are not looking for your life history as much as they are gathering background information on you and observing how well you can present information. Provide highlights of your education, experience, and accomplishments. If you are just yourself and enjoy the process, this will show.

The interviewer might then ask, "What do you know about our company?" This is a good opportunity for you to show how prepared you are. You could open your portfolio and tell the interviewer, *"When I was researching the company, I found some interesting facts on your Web site. I know that you are an international company based in New York and that you have over 4,000 employees. I learned that you have several divisions, including food processing and distribution, restaurants, and contract food sales. In fact, this information is the reason I applied for a job with you through our Career Center. My minor in college is Restaurant Management, and I think this company will be a great place to put my knowledge and the skills to great use."*

You will, of course, have to adapt your answer to your own situation. There is no way to be completely prepared for questions an interviewer may ask. The key is to have anticipated the interviewer's questions and to be so comfortable with the message you want to convey about yourself that you sound confident and decisive. As you talk, remember to look at the interviewer and to lean forward slightly, which indicates that you are listening intently.

After a brief "let's get to know each other" session, you can anticipate more direct and important questions. Some of the more common questions that you might expect include:

- Why should we hire you?
- Why are you interested in this company and in the position?
- When did you decide on a career in _____?
- Tell me about your extracurricular activities.
- What are your strengths?
- What are your weaknesses?
- Why did you leave your last job?
- Do you have a geographic preference? Why?
- Are you willing to relocate?
- Are you willing to travel?
- Do you have job experience in _____?
- What can you do for the company?
- What other companies are you interviewing with?
- Tell me about a difficult problem you have had and how you solved it.
- Tell me about a time when you worked under stress.
- What kind of accomplishment gives you the greatest satisfaction?
- What are your long- and short-range goals?
- Where do you see yourself in five years?
- What one word best describes you?
- How do you deal with difficult people?
- Describe one goal you have set over the past six months and how you went about accomplishing it.
- What is the biggest mistake you ever made? What did you learn from it?
- What subject in school gave you the most challenges? Why?
- What experiences or courses have prepared you for this position?
- Would you prefer to work alone or with a group of people? Why?

Using ALL of the **ESSENTIAL CORNERSTONES**, consider how each one can help you (1) develop your job search materials, (2) interview well, and (3) land your perfect job. Address each of these three areas in your response.

Passion _____

_____

_____

_____

Motivation _____

_____

_____

_____

Knowledge _____

_____

_____

_____

Resourcefulness _____

_____

_____

_____

Creativity _____

_____

_____

_____

Adaptability _____

_____

_____

_____

Open-mindedness _____

_____

_____

_____

Communication _____

_____

_____

_____

Accountability _____

_____

_____

_____

Vision _____

_____

_____

_____

PREPARING FOR SUCCESS

Refer to page 269 of this chapter and answer the questions you developed from headings. You should also be able to answer the following questions if they were not on your list:

1. Why is a cover letter so important to your application package?

2. What are the three types of resumes?

3. Discuss at least four traits that employers seek in today's employees.

4. Why is it important to have business cards?

5. How can you best solicit people to serve as your references?

MY PERSONAL GOAL

Name _____

Goal Statement (with Action Verb and Target Date) _____
_____
_____

Action Steps (Concrete things you plan to do to reach your goal)

1. _____
2. _____
3. _____
4. _____

Narrative Statement (how your life will look when you reach your goal) _____
_____
_____
_____
_____
_____
_____
_____

I deserve this goal because:

1. _____
_____
2. _____
_____

I hereby make this commitment to myself.

_____   _____
MY Signature   Date

MY PERSONAL GOAL

Name _____

Goal Statement (with Action Verb and Target Date) _____

_____

_____

Action Steps (Concrete things you plan to do to reach your goal)

1. _____

2. _____

3. _____

4. _____

Narrative Statement (how your life will look when you reach your goal) _____

_____

_____

_____

_____

_____

_____

I deserve this goal because:

1. _____

_____

2. _____

_____

I hereby make this commitment to myself.

_____   _____

MY Signature   Date

MY PERSONAL GOAL

Name _____

Goal Statement (with Action Verb and Target Date) _____

_____

_____

Action Steps (Concrete things you plan to do to reach your goal)

1. _____

2. _____

3. _____

4. _____

Narrative Statement (how your life will look when you reach your goal) _____

_____

_____

_____

_____

_____

_____

I deserve this goal because:

1. _____

_____

2. _____

_____

I hereby make this commitment to myself.

_____   _____

MY Signature   Date

glossary

Academic freedom Professors in institutions of higher education are allowed to conduct research and to teach that research, regardless of controversial issues or subject matter. Academic freedom allows the professor the right to teach certain materials that might not have been allowed in high school.

Academic integrity You have read, fully understand, and adhere to the policies, codes, and moral values of your institution. It implies that you will not cheat, plagiarize, or be unfair in your academic, social, cultural, or civic work.

Accreditation Most high schools and colleges in the United States are accredited by a regional agency. This agency is responsible for ensuring that a minimum set of standards is held at all institutions that are members in the accreditation agency. The Southern Association of Colleges and Schools is one example of an accreditation agency.

Adding Adding a class during the registration period or during the first week of classes means that you will be taking an additional class in your schedule.

Administration The administration of a college is usually made up of nonteaching personnel who handle all of the administrative aspects of the college. The administration is headed by the president and vice presidents. The structure of the administration at each college varies.

Advising To make sure that you will know what classes to take and in which order, you will be assigned an academic advisor—most often a faculty member in your discipline or major—when you arrive on campus. This advisor will usually be with you during your entire degree. She is responsible for guiding you through your academic work at the college.

African American studies This curriculum deals with the major contributions by African Americans in art, literature, history, medicine, sciences, and architecture. Many colleges offer majors and minors in African American studies.

AIDS This acronym stands for acquired immune deficiency syndrome, a disease that is transmitted sexually, intravenously, or from mother to child. Currently, no cure for AIDS exists, but several medications, such as AZT and protease inhibitors, slow the deterioration of the immune system.

Alumna, Alumni, Alumnus These terms are used to describe students who hold degrees from a college. The term *alumna* refers to a woman, *alumnus* refers to a man, and *alumni* refers to woman or a man. The term *alumni* is used most often.

Anti-Semitism Discrimination against people of Jewish or Arabic descent.

Anxiety This term refers to the way your body reacts when you are afraid, nervous, or overly stressed about an issue. Many times you will hear the term *test anxiety,* indicating that a person is nervous or anxious about taking a test.

Articulation An articulation agreement is a signed document between two or more institutions guaranteeing that the courses taken at one college will transfer to another college. For example, if Oak College has an articulation agreement with Maple College, it means that the course work taken at Oak College will be accepted toward a degree at Maple College.

Associate degree The associate degree is a two-year degree that usually prepares the student to enter the workforce with a specific skill or trade. It is also offered to students as the first two years of their bachelor's, or four-year degree. Not all colleges offer the associate degree.

Attendance Each college has an attendance policy, such as "a student can miss no more than 10 percent of the total class hours or he will receive an F for the course." This policy is followed strictly by some professors and more leniently by others. You should always know the attendance policy of each professor with whom you are studying.

Auditing Most colleges offer the choice either to enroll in a course or to audit a course. If you enroll in a course, you pay the entire fee, attend classes, take exams, and receive credit. If you audit a course, the fee is usually lower, you do not take exams, and you do not receive credit. Course auditing is usually done by people who are having trouble in a subject or by those who want to gain more knowledge about a particular subject. Some colleges charge full price for auditing a course.

Baccalaureate The baccalaureate degree, more commonly called the bachelor's degree, is a four-year degree in a specific field. Although this degree can be completed in as few as three years or as many as six-plus years, traditionally the amount of academic work required is four years. This degree prepares students for such careers as teaching, social work, engineering, fine arts, and journalism, to name a few. Graduate work is also available in these fields.

Bankruptcy Bankruptcy occurs when a person files legal papers through a lawyer to declare that she cannot pay her bills. Filing for bankruptcy destroys one's credit history, and it takes 10 years for the bankruptcy to disappear from one's credit report.

Binge drinking Binge drinking is defined as having five or more alcoholic beverages at one sitting.

Blackboard Blackboard is a delivery platform for distance education courses taken over the Web. Several platforms exist, including WebCT and Course Compass.

Board of trustees The board of trustees is the governing body of the college. The board is appointed by government officials (usually the governor) of each state. The board hires the president and must approve any curriculum changes to degree programs. The board also sets policy for the college.

Campus   The campus is the physical plant of the university or college. The term refers to all buildings, fields, arenas, auditoriums, and other properties owned by the college.

Campus police   Each college and university has a campus police office or a security office. You will need to locate this office once you arrive on campus so that, in case of emergency, you will be able to find it quickly. Campus security can assist you with problems ranging from physical danger to car trouble.

Carrel   This is a booth or small room in the library. You can reserve a carrel for professional use throughout the semester or on a weekly basis. Many times, the carrel is large enough for only one person. Never leave any personal belongings or important academic materials in the carrel, because they may be stolen.

Case study   A case study is a story based on real-life events. Cases are written with open-ended conclusions and somewhat vague details to allow the reader to critically examine the story and develop logical solutions to resolve issues.

Catalog   The college catalog is a book issued to you at the beginning of your college career. This book is one of the most important tools that you will use in developing your schedule and completing your degree. The catalog is a legally binding document stating what your degree requirements are for the duration of your study. You will need to keep the catalog of the year in which you entered college.

CD-ROM   A compact disk (with read-only memory) containing information, images, and maybe video in an electronic format that must be used with a computer. Many texts now come with a CD-ROM that carries supplemental information to support the material in the text.

Certificate   A certificate program is a series of courses, usually one year in length, designed to educate and train an individual in a certain area, such as welding, automotive repair, medical transcription, tool and die, early childhood, physical therapy assistance, and fashion merchandising. While these programs are certified and detailed, they are not degrees. Often, associate and bachelor's degrees are offered in these areas as well.

CLEP   The College Level Examination Program, or CLEP, is designed to allow students to "test out" of a course. CLEP exams are nationally normalized and often are more extensive than a course in the same area. If you CLEP a course, it means that you do not have to take the course in which you passed the CLEP exam. Some colleges have limits on the number of hours that can be earned by CLEP.

Club drugs   Club drugs are drugs taken at raves, parties, or dance clubs. Some of the most common club drugs are GHB (gamma hydroxybutyrate), ecstasy, roofies, and meth.

Cognate   A cognate is a course (or set of courses) taken outside of your major. Some colleges call this a minor. For instance, if you are majoring in English, you may wish to take a cognate in history or drama. Cognates are usually chosen in a field close to the major. It would be unlikely for a student to major in English and take a cognate in pharmacy.

Commitment   A term that refers to a pledge or promise to do something that you have given your word that you will honor. It is also considered to be a personal contract to your own goals in life.

Communications   College curricula often state that a student must have nine hours of communications. This most commonly refers to English and speech (oral communication) courses. The mixture of these courses will usually be English 101 and 102 and Speech 101. This will vary from college to college.

Comprehensive exams   This term refers to exams that encompass materials from the entire course. If you are taking a history course and your instructor informs you that there will be a comprehensive exam, information from the first lecture through the last lecture will be included on the exam.

Continuing education   Almost every college in the nation offers courses in continuing education or community education. These courses are not offered for college credit, but continuing education units are awarded in many cases. These courses are usually designed to meet the needs of specific businesses and industries or to provide courses of interest to the community. Continuing education courses range from small engine repair to flower arranging, from stained glass making to small business management.

Co-op   This term is used to refer to a relationship between business/industry and the educational institution. During a co-op, the student spends a semester in college and the next semester on the job. Some co-ops may be structured differently, but the general idea behind a co-op is to gain on-the-job experience while in college.

Cooperative learning   In cooperative learning, learning, exploration, discovery, and results take place in a well-structured group. Cooperative learning teams are groups that work together on research, test preparation, project completion, and many other tasks.

Corequisite   A corequisite is a course that must be taken at the same time as another course. Many times, science courses carry a corequisite. If you are taking Biology 101, the lab course Biology 101L may be required as the corequisite.

Counseling   Most colleges have a counseling center on campus. Do not confuse counseling with advising. Trained counselors assist you with problems that might arise in your personal life, with your study skills, and with your career aspirations. Academic advisors are responsible for your academic progress. Some colleges do combine the two, but in many instances, the counselor and the advisor are different people with different job descriptions.

Course title   Every course offered at a college will have a course title. You may see something in your schedule of classes that reads: ENG 101, SPC 205, HIS 210, and so forth. Your college catalog will define what the abbreviations mean. ENG 101 usually stands for English 101, SPC could be the heading for speech, and HIS could mean history. Headings and course titles vary from college to college.

Credit   Credit is money or goods given to you on a reasonable amount of trust that you can and will repay the money or pay for the goods. Credit can come in several forms; credit cards and loans are the most common. Credit can be very dangerous to a person's future if he has too much credit or does not repay the credit on time.

Credit hour   A credit hour is the amount of credit offered for each class that you take. Usually, each class is worth three credit hours. Science courses, foreign languages, and some math courses are worth four credit hours because of required labs. If a class carries three credit hours, this usually means that the class meets for three hours per week. This formula may vary greatly in a summer session or midsession.

Credit score Your credit score is calculated by the amount of debt you have, your salary, your payment history, your length of residence in one place, and the number of inquires into your credit history, to name a few. Your credit score is used to determine if you will be extended future credit and the interest rate that you will be charged. A low score could mean that you cannot get credit or that you will pay a very high interest rate. Negative credit reports stay in your credit history for seven years.

Critical thinking Critical thinking is thinking that is purposeful, reasoned, and goal directed. It is a type of thinking used to solve problems, make associations, connect relationships, formulate inferences, make decisions, and detect faulty arguments and persuasion.

Curriculum The curriculum is the area of study in which you are engaged. It is a set of classes that you must take in order for a degree to be awarded.

Dean The word *dean* is not a name, but a title. A dean is usually the head of a division or area of study. Some colleges might have a dean of arts and sciences, a dean of business, and a dean of mathematics. The dean is the policy maker and usually the business manager and final decision maker of an area of study. Deans usually report to vice presidents or provosts.

Dean's list The dean's list is a listing of students who have achieved at least a 3.5 (B+) on a 4.0 scale (these numbers are defined under *GPA*). This achievement may vary from college to college, but generally speaking the dean's list is composed of students in the top 5 percent of students in that college.

Default A default is when a person fails to repay a loan according to the terms provided in the original loan papers. A default on a Guaranteed Student Loan will result in the garnishment of wages and the inability to acquire a position with the government. Also, you will receive no federal or state income tax refunds until the loan is repaid. Further, a Guaranteed Student Loan cannot be written off under bankruptcy laws.

Degree When a student completes an approved course of study, she is awarded a degree. The title of the degree depends on the college, the number of credit hours in the program, and the field of study. A two-year degree is called an associate degree, and a four-year degree is called a bachelor's degree. If a student attends graduate school, she may receive a master's degree (approximately two to three years) and sometimes a doctorate degree (anywhere from three to ten years). Some colleges even offer postdoctorate degrees.

Diploma A diploma is awarded when an approved course of study is completed. The diploma is not as detailed or comprehensive as an associate degree and usually consists of only eight to twelve courses specific to a certain field.

Distance learning Distance learning is learning that takes place away from the campus. Distance learning or distance education is usually offered by a computerized platform such as Blackboard, WebCT, or Course Compass. Chat sessions and Internet assignments are common in distance learning.

Dropping When a student decides that he does not enjoy a class or will not be able to pass the class because of grades or absenteeism, he may elect to drop that class section. This means that the class will no longer appear on his schedule or be calculated in his

GPA. Rules and regulations on dropping vary from college to college. All rules should be explained in the catalog.

Ecstasy Ecstasy, or "X," is a "club drug" that is very common at raves and dance parties. It produces a relaxed, euphoric state, which makes the user experience warmth, heightened emotions, and self-acceptance. It can cause severe depression and even death. Ecstasy is illegal to use or possess.

Elective An elective is a course that a student chooses to take outside of her major field of study. It could be in an area of interest or an area that complements the chosen major. For example, an English major might choose an elective in the field of theatre or history because these fields complement each other. However, a student majoring in English might also elect to take a course in medical terminology because she is interested in that area.

Emeriti This Latin term is assigned to retired personnel of the college who have performed exemplary duties during their professional careers. For example, a college president who obtained new buildings, added curriculum programs, and increased the endowment might be named president emeritus upon his or her retirement.

Ethnocentrism Ethnocentrism is the practice of thinking that one's ethnic group is superior to others.

Evening college The evening college program is designed to allow students who have full-time jobs to obtain a college degree by enrolling in classes that meet in the evening. Some colleges offer an entire degree program in the evening; others offer only some courses.

Faculty The faculty of a college is the body of professionals who teach, do research, and perform community service. Faculty members have prepared for many years to hold the responsibilities carried by this title. Many have been to school for 20 or more years to obtain the knowledge and skill necessary to train students in specific fields.

Fallacy A fallacy is a false notion. It is a statement based on false materials, invalid inferences, or incorrect reasoning.

Fees Fees refer to the amount of money charged by a college for specific items and services. Some fees are tuition, meal plans, books, and health and activity fees. Fees vary from college to college and are usually printed in the catalog.

Financial aid If a student is awarded money from the college, the state, the federal government, private sources, or places of employment, this is referred to as financial aid. Financial aid can be awarded on the basis of need or merit or both. Any grant, loan, or scholarship is formally called financial aid.

Fine arts Many people tend to think of fine arts as drawing or painting, but in actuality the fine arts encompass a variety of artistic forms. Theatre, dance, architecture, drawing, painting, sculpture, and music are among the fine arts. Some colleges include literature in this category.

Foreign language Almost every college offers at least one course in foreign languages. Many colleges offer degrees in this area. For schools in the United States, foreign languages consist of Spanish, French, Russian, Latin, German, Portuguese, Swahili, Arabic, Japanese, Chinese, and Korean, to name a few.

Formula A general rule of how something is done, usually expressed in mathematical symbols.

Fraternities A fraternity is an organization of the Greek system in which a male student is a member. Many fraternities have their own housing complexes on campus. Induction for each is different. Honorary fraternities, such as Phi Kappa Phi, also exist. These are academic in nature and are open to men and women.

Freshman This is a term used by high schools and colleges. The term *first-year student* is also used. This term refers to a student in his first year of college. Traditionally, a freshman is someone who has not yet completed 30 semester hours of college-level work.

Gay studies This curriculum deals with the major contributions by homosexuals and lesbians in art, literature, history, medicine, sciences, and architecture. Many colleges offer classes and/or minors in gay, lesbian, bisexual, or trans-gendered studies.

GHB, or gamma hydroxybutyrate GHB is a club drug that comes most often in an odorless, liquid form but that can also come as a powder. At lower doses, GHB has a euphoric effect and can make the user feel relaxed, happy, and sociable. Higher doses can lead to dizziness, sleepiness, vomiting, spasms, and loss of consciousness. GHB and alcohol used together can be deadly.

GPA, or grade point average The grade point average is the numerical grading system used by almost every college in the nation. GPAs determine if a student is eligible for continued enrollment, financial aid, or honors. Most colleges operate under a 4.0 system. This means that all As earned are worth 4 quality points; Bs, 3 points; Cs, 2 points; Ds, 1 point; and Fs, 0 points. To calculate a GPA, multiply the number of quality points by the number of credit hours carried by the course and then divide by the total number of hours carried. For example: English 101, Speech 101, History 201, and Psychology 101 usually carry 3 credit hours each. If a student taking these courses made all As, she would have a GPA of 4.0. If the student made all Bs, she would have a 3.0. However, if she had a variety of grades, the GPA would be calculated as follows:

	Grade	Credit	Q. Points	Total Points
ENG 101	A	3 hours	× 4 =	12 points
SPC 101	C	3 hours	× 2 =	6 points
HIS 201	B	3 hours	× 3 =	9 points
PSY 101	D	3 hours	× 1 =	3 points

30 points divided by 12 hours would equal a GPA of 2.5 (or C+ average).

Grace period A grace period is usually 10 days after the due date of a loan payment. For example: If your car payment is due on the first of the month, many companies will give you a 10 day grace period (until the 11th) to pay the bill before they report your delinquent payment to a credit scoring company.

Graduate teaching assistant You may encounter a "teaching assistant" as a freshman or sophomore. In some larger colleges and universities, students working toward master's and doctorate degrees teach undergraduate, lower-level classes under the direction of a major professor in the department.

Grant A grant is usually money that goes toward tuition and books that does not have to be repaid. Grants are most often awarded by state and federal governments.

Hate crime A hate crime is categorized as a violent act toward a certain group of people motivated by hatred of that group.

Hepatitis Hepatitis has three forms: A, B, and C. Hepatitis A comes from drinking contaminated water. Hepatitis B is more prevalent than HIV and can be transmitted sexually, through unsterile needles, and through unsterile tattoo equipment. Left untreated, hepatitis B can cause serious liver damage. Hepatitis C develops into a chronic condition in over 85 percent of the people who have it. Hepatitis C is the leading cause of liver transplants. Hepatitis B and C can be transmitted by sharing toothbrushes, nail clippers, or any item contaminated with blood. Hepatitis B and C have no recognizable signs or symptoms. Some people, however, do get flulike symptoms, loss of appetite, nausea, vomiting, or fever.

Higher education This term describes any level of education beyond high school. All colleges are called institutions of higher education.

Homophobia Homophobia is the fear of homosexuals or homosexuality.

Honor code Many colleges operate under an honor code. This system demands that students perform all work without cheating, plagiarism, or any other dishonest actions. In many cases, a student can be removed from the institution for breaking the honor code. In other cases, if students do not turn in fellow students who they know have broken the code, they, too, can be removed from the institution.

Honors Academic honors are based on the GPA of a student. Each college usually has many academic honors, including the dean's list, the president's list, and departmental honors. The three highest honors awarded are summa cum laude, magna cum laude, and cum laude. These are awarded at graduation for students who have maintained a GPA of 3.5 or better. The GPA requirement for these honors varies from college to college. Usually, they are awarded as follows:

>   3.5 to 3.7 cum laude
>   3.7 to 3.9 magna cum laude
>   4.0 summa cum laude

Honors college The honors college is usually a degree or a set of classes offered for students who performed exceptionally well in high school.

Humanities The humanities are sometimes as misunderstood as the fine arts. Courses in the humanities include history, philosophy, religion, and cultural studies; some colleges also include literature, government, and foreign languages. The college catalog will define what your college has designated as humanities.

Identification cards An identification card is essential for any college student. Some colleges issue them for free, while some charge a small fee. The ID card allows the student to use the college library, participate in activities, use physical fitness facilities, and many times attend college events for free. They also come in handy in the community. Movie theatres, museums, zoos, and other cultural events usually charge less or nothing if a student has an ID card. The card will also allow the student to use most area library facilities with special privileges. ID cards are usually validated each semester.

Identity theft Identity theft occurs when another person assumes your identity and uses your credit, your name, and your Social Security number. Identity theft can't always be prevented,

references

ACT. *National Dropout Rates, Freshman to Sophomore Years by Type of Institution.* Iowa City, IA: ACT, 2000.

Adler, R., Rosenfeld, L., and Towne, N. *Interplay. The Process of Interpersonal Communication,* 2nd ed. New York: Holt, Rinehart and Winston, 2006.

Advanced Public Speaking Institute. "Public speaking: Why use humor?" Virginia Beach, VA: Author, accessed at http://www.public-speaking.org/public-speaking-humor-article.htm. 2007.

American College Testing Program. *National Drop Out Rates.* ACT Institutional Data File, Iowa City, IA: ACT, 1995.

Amnesty International. Death penalty information, http://www.web.amnesty.org.

Anderson, D. *The Death Penalty—A Defence.* Sweden, 1998. Translated into English in 2001 at http://w1.155.telia.com/~u15509119/ny_sida_1.htm.

Anderson, L., and Bolt, S. (2008). *Professionalism: Real Skills for Workplace Success.* Upper Saddle River, NJ: Pearson Prentice Hall.

Armstrong, T. *Multiple Intelligences in the Classroom.* Alexandria, VA: Association for Supervision and Curriculum Development, 1994.

Astin, A. *Achieving Educational Excellence.* San Francisco: Jossey-Bass, 1985.

Bach, D. *The Finish Rich Notebook.* New York: Broadway Books, 2003.

Baldridge, L. *Letitia Baldridge's New Complete Guide to Executive Manners.* New York: Macmillan, 1985.

Barnes & Noble and the Anti-Defamation League. *Close the Book on Hate: 101 Ways to Combat Prejudice,* 2000. Available online at www.adl.org/prejudice/closethebook.pdf.

Beebe, S. A., and Beebe, S. J. *Interpersonal Communication: Relating to Others,* 3rd ed. Boston: Allyn & Bacon, 2002.

Benson, H. *The Relaxation Response.* New York: Caral Publishing Group, 1992.

Benson, H., and Stuart, E. *Wellness Encyclopedia.* Boston: Houghton Mifflin, 1991.

Benson, H., and Stuart, E. *The Wellness Book: The Comprehensive Guide to Maintaining Health and Treating Stress-Related Illness.* New York: Birch Lane Press, 1992.

Berenblatt, M., and Berenblatt, A. *Make an Appointment with Yourself: Simple Steps to Positive Self-Esteem.* Deerfield Beach, FL: Health Communication, 1994.

Beyer, B. *Developing a Thinking Skills Program.* Boston: Allyn & Bacon, 1998.

Boldt, L. *How to Be, Do, or Have Anything.* Berkeley, CA: Ten Speed Press, 2001.

Bolles, R. N. (2007). *What Color Is Your Parachute? A Practical Manual for Job-Hunters and Career-Changers, 2008 Edition.* Berkeley, CA: Ten Speed Press.

Bosak, J. *Fallacies.* Dubuque, IA: Educulture Publishers, 1976.

Boyle, M., and Zyla, G. *Personal Nutrition.* St. Paul, MN: West Publishing, 1992.

Bozzi, V. "A healthy dose of religion." *Psychology Today,* November 1988.

Brightman, H. Georgia State University Master Teacher Program: On Learning Styles, http://www.gsu.edu/~dschjb/wwwmbti.html.

Britton-Whitcomb, S. *Resume Magic: Trade Secrets of a Professional Resume Writer.* Indianapolis, IN: JIST Works Publishing, 2003.

Brodick, C. "Why Care About Your Credit Score?" InCharge Education Foundation, 2003.

Bucher, R. D. *Diversity Consciousness: Opening Our Minds to People, Cultures, and Opportunities.* Upper Saddle River, NJ: Prentice Hall, 2000.

Buscaglia, L. *Living, Loving, and Learning.* New York: Ballantine, 1982.

Business and Legal Reports. *Staying Safe on Campus.* Madison, CT: Author, 1995.

Cameron, J. *The Artist's Way: A Spiritual Path to Higher Creativity.* New York: Penguin Putnam, 1992.

Casperson, D. *Power Etiquette: What You Don't Know Can Kill Your Career.* New York: AMA Publications, 1999.

Cardinal, F. "Sleep is important when stress and anxiety increase." *The National Sleep Foundation,* April 10, 2003.

Cetron, F. "What students must know to succeed in the 21st century." *The Futurist, 30,* no. 4, July–August 1996, p. 7.

Character Counts! Coalition (2007). *The Six Pillars of Character.* The Josephson Institute of Ethics: Los Angeles. Downloaded from http://www.charactercounts.org.

Checkley, K. "The first seven . . . and the eighth." *Educational Leadership, 55,* no. 1, September 1997.

Chickering, A., and Schlossberg, N. *Getting the Most out of College.* Boston: Allyn & Bacon, 1995.

Chopra, D. *The Seven Spiritual Laws of Success.* San Rafael, CA: New World Library, 1994.

Christian, J., and Greger, J. *Nutrition for Living.* Redwood City, CA: Benjamin/Cummings Publishing, 1994.

Clegg, R. "The color of death." *National Review Online.* Accessed at June 11, 2001, at http://www. national review.com/contributors/clegg061101.shtml.

Cloud, J. "The pioneer Harvey Milk." Accessed at http://www.time.com.

CNN Money. "More credit late fees paid." May 12, 2002. Accessed at http://money.cnn.com/2002/05/21/ pf/banking/cardfees/.

Cohen, L. *Conducting Research on the Internet.* University of Albany Libraries, 1996a, http://www.albany.edu.

Cohen, L. *Evaluating Internet Resources.* University of Albany Libraries, 1996b, http://www.albany.edu.

City of Jacksonville, FL. "Consumer Affairs gets new tough law on car title businesses." Accessed at http://www.coj.net/Departments/Regulatory+and+ Environmental+Services/Consumer+Affairs/ TITLE+LOANS.htm, 2003.

Coldewey, J., and Streitberger, W. *Drama, Classical to Contemporary,* rev. ed. Upper Saddle River, NJ: Prentice Hall, 2001.

"College credit cards." September 15, 2006. Accessed at http://www.credit-card-articles.com.

"Commonly abused drugs." National Institute on Drug Abuse. Accessed at http://www.nida.nih.gov/ DrugsofAbuse.html.

Cooper, A. *Time Management for Unmanageable People.* New York: Bantam Books, 1993.

Cooper, M. "Alcohol use and risky sexual behavior among college students and youth." *Journal of Studies on Alcohol, 63*(2), 2002, p. S101.

Cooper-Arnold, Amy L. "Credit card debt: A survival guide for students." http://www.youngmoney.com/ credit_debt/credit_basics/o50804–02, 2006.

Daly, J., and Engleberg, I. *Presentations in Everyday Life: Strategies for Effective Speaking.* Upper Saddle River, NJ: Allyn & Bacon, 2006.

"Dan White." Accessed at http://www.findagrave.com/ php/famous.php?page=name&firstName=Dan& lastName=White.

Daniels, P., and Bright, W. *The World's Writing Systems.* England: Oxford University Press, 1996.

DebtSteps.com. "Learn about credit card debt." September 15, 2006. Accessed at http://www.debtsteps.com/ credit-card-debt-gacts.html.

DeVito, J. *Human Communication,* 10th ed. Upper Saddle River, NJ: Prentice Hall, 2006.

Donatelle, R., and Davis, L. *Health: The Basics.* Englewood Cliffs, NJ: Prentice Hall, 2002.

Dresang, J. "Liar! Liar! Won't get hired. In age of easy information, resume fibs can sabotage hunts for work." *Las Vegas Review Journal,* reprinted from *Milwaukee Journal Sentinel.* April 23, 2007.

Eddlem, T. "Ten anti-death penalty fallacies." *The New American, 18*(3), June 3, 2002.

Eisenberg, D. "The coming job boom." *Time Online Edition,* April 29, 2002, http://www.time.com/ time/business/article/0,8599,233967,00.html.

Ellis, D., Lankowitz, S., Stupka, D., and Toft, D. *Career Planning.* Rapid City, SD: College Survival, 1990.

Elrich, M. "The stereotype within." *Educational Leadership,* April 1994, p. 12.

Equifax.com. "Glossary of terms." Accessed at http:// www.econsumer.equifax.com/consumer/ forward.ehtml?forward=credu_glossaryterms.

Equifax.com. "Identity theft and fraud." Accessed at http://www.econsumer.equifax.com/consumer/ forward.ehtml?forward=idtheft_howitstrikes, 2003.

Equifax.com. "Teaching students about money and credit." Accessed at http://www.equifax.com/ CoolOnCredit/parent1.html.

Facione, P. *Critical Thinking: What It Is and Why It Counts, 2007 Updated Edition.* Santa Clara: California Academic Press, 2007.

Farr, M., and Kursmark, L. *15 Minute Cover Letter: Write an Effective Cover Letter Right Now.* Indianapolis, IN: JIST Works Publishing, 2005.

Finnigan, D., and Karasu, M. *From Learning to Earning: Success Strategies for New Grads.* New York: Sterling Publishing, 2006.

Freshman Survey Data Report. Cooperative Institutional Research Program sponsored by the Higher Education Research Institute (HERI). University of California, Los Angeles, 1999.

Fulghum, R. *All I Really Need to Know, I Learned in Kindergarten.* New York: Ivy Books, 1988.

Gardenswartz, L., and Rowe, A. *Managing Diversity: A Complete Desk Reference and Planning Guide.* New York: Irwin/Pfeiffer, 1993.

Gardner, H. *Frames of Mind: The Theory of Multiple Intelligences.* New York: Basic Books, 1983.

Gardner, H. "Reflections on multiple intelligences: Myths and messages." *Phi Delta Kappan, 77,* no. 3, November 1995, p. 200.

Gardner, J., and Jewler, J. *Your College Experience.* Belmont, CA: Wadsworth, 2000.

Gay, Lesbian and Straight Education Network. "Just the facts." New York: GLSE, 2000. Synopsis found at http://msn.planetout.com/people/teens/features/2000/08/facts.html.

Gonyea, J. C. "Discover the work you were born to do." MSN.com Careers, 2002, http://editorial.careers.msn.com/articles/born.

Gordon, E. *The 2010 Meltdown.* Westport, CT: Praeger, 2005.

Grilly, D. *Drugs and Human Behavior.* Boston: Allyn & Bacon, 1994.

Gunthrie, H., and Picciano, M. *Human Nutrition.* Salem, MA: Mosby, 1995.

Hales, D. *Your Health.* Redwood City, CA: Benjamin/Cummings Publishing, 1991.

Haney, D. "New AIDS drugs bring optimism." *Las Vegas Review Journal,* February 12, 2003.

Hanna, S. L. *Person to Person.* Upper Saddle River, NJ: Prentice Hall, 2003.

Hickman, R., and Quinley, J. *A Synthesis of Local, State, and National Studies in Workforce Education and Training.* Washington, DC: The American Association of Community Colleges, 1997.

"Hidden menace: Drowsy drivers." Accessed at http://www.sleepdisorders.about.com/library/weekly/aa062902a.htm.

Ireland, S. *The Complete Idiot's Guide to the Perfect Resume.* Indianapolis, IN: Alpha Publishing, 2003.

Jerome, R., and Grout, P. "Cheat wave." *People,* June 17, 2002, p. 84.

Kanar, C. *The Confident Reader.* New York: Houghton Mifflin, 2000.

Kiewra, K. A., and Fletcher, H. J. "The relationship between notetaking variables and achievement measures." *Human Learning, 3,* 1984, 273–280.

Kirby, D. "The worst is yet to come." *The Advocate,* January 19, 1999, p. 57.

Kleiman, C. *The 100 Best Jobs for the 90's and Beyond.* New York: Berkley Books, 1992.

Konowalow, S. *Planning Your Future: Keys to Financial Freedom.* Columbus, OH: Prentice Hall, 2003.

Lane, H. (1976). *The Wild Boy of Aveyron.* Harvard University Press: Cambridge, MA.

Lecky, P. *Self-Consistency: A Theory of Personality.* Garden City, NY: Anchor, 1951.

Leinwood, D. "Ecstasy–Viagra mix alarms doctors." *USA Today,* September 23, 2002.

Lieberman, B. "1 in 5 new HIV cases is a drug-resistant strain, study finds." *San Diego Tribune,* August 8, 2002.

Maker, J., and Lenier, M. *College Reading,* 5th ed. Belmont, CA: Thompson Learning, 2000.

"Managing and Resolving Conflict," http://hr2.hr.arizona.edu/06_jcl/jobdesc/groundrules.htm.

Manisses Communications Group. *Alcoholism & Drug Abuse Weekly, 13*(36), September 2001, p. 7.

McCornack, S. *Reflect and Relate: An Introduction to Interpersonal Communication.* Boston: Bedford–St. Martin's Press, 2007.

McGraw, P. C. *Life Strategies Workbook.* New York: Hyperion, 2000.

McKay, M., and Fanning, P. *Self-Esteem.* Oakland, CA: New Harbinger, 2000.

Moss, J. cited in Kates, W. "America is not getting enough sleep." *San Francisco Chronicle,* March 30, 1990, p. B3.

National Association of College Employers. "Top ten personal qualities employers seek." *Job Outlook,* NACE, 2000.

National Foundation for Credit Counseling. "National Foundation for Credit Counseling announces study results on the impact of credit counseling on consumer credit and debt payment behavior." Press release,

March 21, 2002. Accessed at http://www.nfcc.org/newsroom/shownews.Cfm?newsid=257.

Nellie Mae Study. *Credit Cards 101*, p. 1. 2005.

Nelson, D., and Low, G. *Emotional Intelligence: Achieving Academic and Career Excellence.* Upper Saddle River, NJ: Prentice Hall, 2003.

Newberry, Tommy. *Success Is Not an Accident.* Carol Stream, IL: Tyndale House Publishers, 2007.

Nevid, J., Fichner-Rathus, L., and Rathus, S. *Human Sexuality in a World of Diversity.* Boston: Allyn & Bacon, 1995.

Okula, S. "Protect yourself from identity theft." Accessed at http://moneycentral.msn.com/articles/banking/credit/1342.asp.

Ormondroyd, J., Engle, M., and Cosgrave, T. *How to Critically Analyze Information Sources.* Cornell University Libraries, 2001, http://www.library.cornell.edu.

Ormrod, J. E. *Educational Psychology: Developing Learners.* Upper Saddle River, NJ: Prentice Hall, 2003.

Pauk, W. *How to Study in College,* 8th ed. New York: Houghton Mifflin, 2007.

Paul, R. *What Every Person Needs to Survive in a Rapidly Changing World.* Santa Rosa, CA: The Foundation for Critical Thinking, 1992.

Popenoe, D. *Sociology,* 9th ed. Englewood Cliffs, NJ: Prentice Hall, 1993.

Powell, E. *Sex on Your Terms.* Boston: Allyn & Bacon, 1996.

Radelet, M. "Post-Furman botched executions." Accessed at http://www.deathpenaltyinfo.org/botched.html.

Rathus, S., and Fichner-Rathus, L. *Making the Most Out of College.* Englewood Cliffs, NJ: Prentice Hall, 1994.

Rathus, S., Nevid, J., and Fichner-Rathus, L. *Essentials of Human Sexuality.* Boston: Allyn & Bacon, 1998.

"Retention Rates by Institutional Type," Higher Education Research Institute, UCLA, Los Angeles, 1989.

Robbins, C., *The Job Searcher's Handbook,* 3rd ed. Upper Saddle River, NJ: Prentice Hall, 2006

Rogers, C. *On Becoming Partners: Marriage and Its Alternatives.* New York: Delacorte Press, 1972.

Romas, J., and Sharma, M. *Practical Stress Management.* Boston: Allyn & Bacon, 1995.

Rooney, M. "Freshmen show rising political awareness and changing social views." *The Chronicle of Higher Education,* January 31, 2003.

Salmela-Aro, K., and Nurmi, J. E. "Uncertainty and confidence in interpersonal projects: Consequences for

social relationships and well-being." *Journal of Social and Personal Relationships, 13*(1), 1996, pp. 109–122.

Schacter, D. *The Seven Sins of Memory: How the Mind Forgets and Remembers.* New York: Houghton Mifflin, 2001.

Sciolino, E. "World drug crop up sharply in 1989 despite U.S. effort." *New York Times,* March 2, 1990.

Seyler, D. *Steps to College Reading,* 2nd ed. Boston: Allyn & Bacon, 2003.

Shaffer, C., and Amundsen, K. *Creating Community Anywhere.* Los Angeles: Jeremy P. Tarcher Publishing, 1994.

Shattuck, R. (1980). *The Forbidden Experiment: The Story of the Wild Boy of Aveyron.* New York: Farrar, Straus, & Giroux.

Sherfield, R. *The Everything Self-Esteem Book.* Avon, MA: Adams Media, 2004.

Sherfield, R., Montgomery, R., and Moody, P. *Capstone: Succeeding Beyond College.* Upper Saddle River, NJ: Prentice Hall, 2001.

Sherfield, R., and Moody, P. *Solving the Professional Development Puzzle: 101 Solutions for Career and Life Planning.* Upper Saddle River, NJ: Prentice Hall, 2008.

Silver, H., Strong, R., and Perini, M. "Integrating learning styles and multiple intelligences." *Educational Leadership, 55,* no. 1, September 1997, p. 22.

Smith, B. *Breaking Through: College Reading,* 8th ed. Upper Saddle River, NJ: Pearson Education, 2007.

Southern Poverty Law Center. *Ten Ways to Fight Hate.* Montgomery, AL: Author, 2000.

Sternberg, Robert J. *Successful Intelligence.* New York: Plume, 1996.

Syemore, R., and O'Connell, D. "Did you know?" *Chatelaine, 73*(8), August 2000, p. 30.

"Ten credit card management tips." Accessed at http://www.aol1.bankrate.com/AOL/news/cc/20021218a.asp.

Texas A&M University. "Improve your memory." Accessed at http://www.scs.tamu.edu/selfhelp/elibrary/memory.asp.

The Chronicle of Higher Education, 54(1), August 30, 2007.

The Motley Fool. "How to get out of debt." Accessed at http://www.fool.com/seminars/sp/index.htm?sid=0001&lid=000&ref=.

The Student Guide: Financial Aid from the U.S. Department of Education. Washington, DC: U.S. Department of Education, 2008–2009.

The World Almanac and Book of Facts, 2002. New York: World Almanac Books, 2003.

Tieger, P., and Barron-Tieger, B. *Do What You Are: Discover the Perfect Career for You Through the Secrets of Personality Type*, revised and updated ed. Boston: Little, Brown and Company, 2007.

Uncle Donald's Castro Street. "Dan White: He got away with murder." Accessed at http://thecastro.net/milk/whitepage.html.

USA Today Snapshots (September 13, 2007). "Post-interview Thank-you notes influential." Accountemps, Money Section B, p. 1.

U.S. Bank. *Paying for College: A Guide to Financial Aid.* Minneapolis, MN: Author, 2002.

U.S. Department of Commerce. *2006 U.S. Census.* Washington, DC: U.S. Government Printing Office, 2006.

Velasquez, M., Andre, C., Shanks, T., and Meyer, M. (Fall 1987). "What is ethics?" *Issues in Ethics* IIE V1 N1.

Warner, J. "Celebratory drinking culture on campus: Dangerous drinking style popular among college students." *Parenting and Pregnancy,* November 5, 2002.

Warnick, B., and Inch, E. *Critical Thinking and Communication—The Use of Reason in Argument.* New York: Macmillan, 1994.

Watson, N. "Generation wrecked." *Fortune,* October 14, 2002, pp. 183–190.

Wechsler, H., and Wuethrich, B. *Dying to Drink: Confronting Binge Drinking on College Campuses.* New York: Rodale Press, 2002.

Werner, R. *Understanding.* Newport, RI: TED Conferences, 1999.

Whitfield, C. *Healing the Child Within.* Deerfield Beach, FL: Health Communication, 1987.

Wisegeek. "What is the difference between EQ and EI?" Retrieved February 13, 2008, from http://www.wisegeek.com/what-is-the-difference-between-eq-and-iq.htm.

Woolfolk, A. *Educational Psychology*, 9th ed. Boston: Allyn & Bacon, 2006.

Wurman, R. *Understanding.* New York: Donnelley & Sons, 1999.

Yale Study of Graduating Seniors. New Haven, CT: Yale University, 1953.

Young, J. "Homework? What homework?" *The Chronicle of Higher Education,* December 6, 2003.

Zarefsky, D. *Public Speaking: Strategies for Success,* 3rd ed. Boston: Pearson/Allyn & Bacon, 2001.

Zimring, F. *Capital Punishment and the American Agenda.* Cambridge, MA: Cambridge University Press, 1987.

index